Attachment Parenting

Attachment Parenting

Developing Connections and Healing Children

Edited by
Arthur Becker-Weidman, PhD,
and Deborah Shell, MA, LCMHC

JASON ARONSON
Lanham • Boulder • New York • Toronto • Plymouth, UK

Published by Jason Aronson
An imprint of Rowman & Littlefield Publishers, Inc.
A wholly owned subsidiary of The Rowman & Littlefield Publishing Group, Inc.
4501 Forbes Boulevard, Suite 200, Lanham, Maryland 20706
http://www.rowmanlittlefield.com

Estover Road, Plymouth PL6 7PY, United Kingdom

ATTACh. (2007). *White Paper on Coercion in Treatment.* (Available from the
Association for Treatment and Training in the Attachment of Children, www.
attach.org.) Used with permission.

British Library Cataloguing in Publication Information Available

Library of Congress Cataloging-in-Publication Data

Attachment parenting : developing connections and healing children / edited by
Arthur Becker-Weidman and Deborah Shell.
    p. cm.
Includes bibliographical references and index.
ISBN 978-0-7657-0754-3 (cloth : alk. paper) — ISBN 978-0-7657-0755-0 (pbk. :
alk. paper) — ISBN 978-0-7657-0756-7 (electronic)
1. Attachment disorder in children. 2. Child psychotherapy. 3. Parent and child.
I. Becker-Weidman, Arthur, 1953– II. Shell, Deborah, 1952–

RJ507.A77A876 2010
618.92'8588—dc22   2010005027

∞™ The paper used in this publication meets the minimum requirements of
American National Standard for Information Sciences—Permanence of Paper
for Printed Library Materials, ANSI/NISO Z39.48-1992.

Printed in the United States of America

Contents

Preface

Arthur Becker-Weidman and Deborah Shell

We began writing this book in response to the many parents who enjoyed our previous book, *Creating Capacity for Attachment,* and who wanted something specifically about parenting for parents. This book has grown out of our experiences working with families and developing an approach to parenting that is firmly grounded in Dyadic Developmental Psychotherapy, which is an evidence-based, effective, and empirically validated treatment (Becker-Weidman, 2006a, 2006b; Becker-Weidman & Hughes, 2008). Dyadic Developmental Psychotherapy is an approach to treating children who have trauma-attachment problems. It is a relationship-based approach (Dyadic), and it is grounded in attachment theory, which is a developmental theory (Developmental).

Within this model there is actually substantial overlap between what parents and therapists do. For this reason we will use the term "treatment" to broadly mean both, or either, what a parent does when using this model or what a therapist does when using this model. While parents and therapists have distinct roles and responsibilities, the emphasis on creating positive intersubjective experiences (shared emotion, intention, and attention), attunement, sensitive responsiveness to the developmental needs of the child, and the adult's reflective abilities are common themes in the parenting and therapy of children who have chronic histories of maltreatment and trauma. In this book you will learn about how to develop a therapeutic home that encourages the healing of your child. You will learn about the basic principles that heal children with trauma-attachment problems and you will read about specific methods and techniques that help you help your child.

Our approach to attachment-facilitating parenting is based on attachment-theory and is an attachment-facilitating and attachment-based treatment. Attachment-facilitating parenting was developed to heal children who are largely unresponsive to usual treatment or parenting approaches. Attachment-facilitating parenting focuses on maintaining a positive emotional connection with the child. Through an authentic emotional tie with the child and with empathy, the parent helps the child face and integrate the emotions, memories, and meanings of experiences that traumatized the child. In this manner, the parent helps the child develop a "secure base" in which the child can receive comfort and support, and feel safe, secure, loved, and lovable.

One of our central points is that it is your reflective, sensitive, and planful use of self that is essential to helping your child heal. What this means is that while technique suggestions can be helpful, it is much more important *how* you do things than the specific *what* that you do. That is why we focus so heavily on your creating a healing PLACE (Hughes, 2006) as the crucial approach to helping your child. PLACE stands for being Playful, Loving, Accepting, Curious, and Empathic; but more on that later.

Who is the book for? It is for you: for parents of children and teens who have experienced extensive and pervasive trauma during the first few years of life. These children come through the child welfare system, private adoptions, and international adoptions. Each child's story is unique, but a common thread is that these children have experienced profound disruptions in the primary caregiver-child relationship. Maltreatment has caused the primary attachment relationship to be disordered and disorganized to such an extent that these children are highly defended, difficult to reach, and have either no capacity or a limited capacity to form authentic, meaningful, affectional ties with caregivers. As a result, many usual forms of parenting are ineffective with these children.

Children with disorders of attachment have extensive histories of physical abuse, neglect, sexual trauma, or emotional abuse. Other children with these problems have had serious and painful medical conditions that interfered with the normal developmental process of forming attachment relationships with their primary caregivers. In these instances, the attachment-system was disrupted by experiences such as a premature birth that necessitated an extensive stay in a neonatal intensive care unit and painful medical interventions during the early years. Other children were raised in orphanages and, while having all their basic needs met, did not have responsive, sensitive, and reciprocal experiences with a primary caregiver. The effects of being raised in an institution in which the caregiver-infant ratio is 1:10 or higher are as devastating as physical abuse, maybe more so.

Reactive Attachment Disorder, Post-Traumatic Stress Disorder (Complex Type), and Developmental Trauma Disorder are the most common clinical diagnoses for these children. Many of these children, because of the previous neglect and lack of stimulation, may have other co-morbid conditions such as Sensory-Integration Disorders and a variety of Neuro-Psychological dysfunctions. We will discuss these issues, and what you can do, in later chapters in this book. In addition, a significant percentage of severely maltreated children who come through U.S. foster care also have a mood disorder such as Bipolar Disorder I. Approximately 2 percent of the population is adopted, and between 50 percent and 80 percent of such children have attachment disorder symptoms (Carlson, Cicchetti, Barnett & Braunwald, 1995; Cicchetti, Cummings, Greenberg & Marvin, 1990). Children with Complex Trauma and disorders of attachment also show significant delays in development in the areas of communication, daily living skills, socialization, and fine and gross motor skills (Becker-Weidman, 2009).

The cost to society of not treating such children is enormous. Many of the families that enter the child welfare system have extensive multigenerational histories of abuse and neglect. We know from research that a child's state of mind with respect to attachment is best predicted by the mother's state of mind with respect to attachment. If the primary caregiver has unresolved trauma or has been raised in an abusive or neglectful home, then the child is at grave risk of perpetuating this intergenerational cycle of violence. However, the good news is that this also means that therapeutic experiences with parents can have a substantial healing effect on children. Children who have experienced maltreatment are also at grave risk of developing severe personality disorders. Many of these children are violent (Robins, 1978) and aggressive (Prino & Pyrot, 1994) and as adults are at risk of developing a variety of psychological problems (Schreiber & Lyddon, 1998) and personality disorders, including antisocial personality disorder (Finzi, Cohen, Sapir & Weizman, 2000), narcissistic personality disorder, borderline personality disorder, and psychopathic personality disorder (Dozier, Stovall & Albus, 2008). Neglected children are at risk of social withdrawal, social rejection, and pervasive feelings of incompetence (Finzi et al., 2000). Children who have histories of abuse and neglect are at significant risk of developing Post-Traumatic Stress Disorder as adults (Allan, 2001; Andrews, Varewin, Rose & Kirk, 2000). Children who have been sexually abused are at significant risk of developing anxiety disorders (2.0 times the average), major depressive disorders (3.4 times average), alcohol abuse (2.5 times average), drug abuse (3.8 times average), and antisocial behavior (4.3 times average) (MacMillian, 2001).

These children present with a variety of symptoms and behavior patterns. Generally, these are children who do not trust because their experiences have taught them that adults are not reliable caregivers and that the world is chaotic, unpredictable, and nonresponsive. Most of the symptoms presented by these children can be seen as expressions of this working model of the world and relationships. The therapeutic environment that you will create in your home will be designed to address these issues directly and effectively. You will create a healing PLACE within which the child's distorted internal working models of self, caregivers, family, and relationships will be untwisted.

We begin this book with a description of the basic principles of attachment-facilitating parenting. This is important, since as we said before, what is vital is how you implement your role as parent. Effective parenting involves sensitive attunement and a deep emotional investment. All the parents we work with, as do we, wish that it were as simple as giving you a list of the ten things to do and all will be well . . . wouldn't that be grand? But, as you know, that just doesn't work. You've probably tried many different approaches, some of which may have even worked for a time or a little bit, but nothing seems to make real change in your family or long-lasting change. This book will help you move beyond that to develop effective ways of parenting your child to health.

In later chapters we move on to describe how to select a good therapist, the basic logistics of attachment-facilitating parenting such as how to organize the household, school issues, and what a typical day might look like. You will then find chapters that address common problems encountered when parenting children with trauma-attachment problems, adjustments to make when parenting teens, and the role of therapy and therapists, including a brief description of adjunctive treatments.

Next are chapters about your use of self in parenting and some reflections on how your family of origin may be affecting your ability to parent. There are chapters by parents about their experiences parenting.

We end the book with chapters about therapy after therapy ends and parenting after treatment ends. At the back of the book you will find several chapters with a variety of helpful resources.

We would like to acknowledge the families we've worked with who shared their journeys with us and taught us so much about love, perseverance, connections, and commitment. We would also like to thank and acknowledge the contributors to this volume, whose dedication to this work helped create a book that parents and professionals will find valuable and useful.

Acknowledgments

I would like to dedicate this book to my son, David Becker-Weidman, who has taught me about being a father by being my son. His glorious, ever-present smile as a baby, his warm loving heart, his sense of humor, and his hardworking spirit are an inspiration to me. I could not be more proud of him.

Arthur Becker-Weidman

I dedicate this book to my amazing family: my spouse, Fred; our children, Mae, Scarlet, Emi, and Eva; my stepchildren, Greg and Julie; and grandson, Seaney. From our deeply shared experience, the constant learning and re-learning about the special ways each of you experiences the world, knowing you again and again, loving you as infants, children, teens, and now adults, I have been both witness and participant to the power of commitment, the blessings of emotional safety, and the rewards of enduring relationship. Thank you.

Deborah Shell

1

Theory Basis for Attachment-Facilitating Parenting

Arthur Becker-Weidman and Deborah Shell

This brief chapter will give you a basic understanding of Attachment Theory, how attachment develops, and the effects of your child's very difficult and painful history on development and relationships. As you will see, it is important that you understand the principles of attachment-facilitating parenting. By gaining insights into how the attachment relationship normally develops, you will be able to develop specific ways of helping your child that account for your child's unique history and experiences.

A few short definitions are in order. *Parent* is used in this chapter to be a biological, foster, or adoptive parent or any other significant primary caregiver. *Attachment* is a general term that describes the state and quality of an individual's emotional ties to another. *Attachment behavior* is any type of behavior that causes a person to attain or to retain proximity to a preferred individual and that results in an increased sense of safety and security. It is initiated by a perceived separation or a perceived threat of separation from the attachment figure. The attachment system is an internal working model or blueprint of the world in which the self, significant others, and their relationships are represented and are then acted upon.

John Bowlby developed Attachment Theory in the 1950s. Unlike other theorists at the time, Bowlby believed that his clients suffered from real loss and trauma. Bowlby broke with psychoanalytic theories that viewed patients' disorders as being based on fantasy. Unlike many other theories of child development, which are based on the study of adult psychopathology, Attachment Theory relies on the study of how children normally develop and on the effects of loss and trauma on children to understand adult development and psychopathology. Attachment behavior is activated by fear, pain, or fatigue. The behavior activated is directed toward achieving closeness with the mother so that the fear, pain, or fatigue is eliminated and a sense of safety, security, and comfort achieved. A primary goal of the attachment system is the creation of a secure base from which the child can explore the outside world and to which the child can return to refuel and be nourished physically and emotionally.

An essential marker of a healthy and secure attachment is the ability to tell a coherent story about one's life, regardless of how difficult that life may have been. Those with an insecure attachment (ambivalent or avoidant) and those with a disorganized attachment have difficulty forming and maintaining authentically meaningful emotional relationships. Their narratives are either dismissing of their past and lacking in details, or are overly detailed and stuck in the past, or lack coherence and consistency and contain verbal oddities such as talking about a deceased person as if that person were still living.

The importance of early experiences on later development can be seen in the work of Tizard (1977), who confirmed Bowlby's theories that between six months and four years of age is critical for the capacity to form stable relationships. She found that children adopted after the age of four years remained antisocial in school behavior despite their having formed close and loving bonds with their adoptive parents. Furthermore, ample evidence for the intergenerational transmission of attachment problems can be found in the work of Mary Main (1990) and Erik Hesse (2009) and others. The best predictor of a child's state of mind with respect to attachment is that of the parent(s) (Main, 1991). Parents' early childhood experiences critically influence their capacity to respond to their child in an attuned and sensitive manner. Children whose mothers respond sensitively to the child's signals and who provide responsive comfort are children who respond most appropriately to others' distress. These children grow up to become parents who respond sensitively to their children. For example Wolkind, Hall, and Pawlby (1977) found that mothers who had a disrupted family of origin (had a history of separation from one or both parents before the age of eleven) spent nearly twice as long, on average, out of sight of their babies. In addition, these mothers spent significantly less time holding, looking at, and talking to their infants.

Once established, patterns of attachment tend to persist and be self-perpetuating by creating an internal mind-set or internal working model of the self, the other, the world, and relationships. These internal working models are the lenses through which relationships and behavior are viewed. The raw data of sensory input is filtered through these internal working models so that meaning is developed. The person responds to their perceived meaning of the behavior experienced, not to the raw experience. It is in this manner that internal working models perpetuate the established pattern of attachment that develops in the first few years of life. So, while initially the pattern of attachment is a property of the relationship, by the end of the first two or three years of life the pattern becomes a property of the child. There are substantial research findings that support this. For example, Main and Cassidy (1988) found that the pattern of attachment assessed at twelve months of age is highly predictive of the pattern at six years of age.

These internal working models are created by repeated experiences of relationship with the primary caregiver during these early years. The model of self evolves from the experiences the child has with the parent and reflects the parent's image of the child as expressed in behavior. These models then govern how the child feels about himself, each parent, and how the child expects others to treat him.

The central therapeutic process of attachment-facilitating parenting is intersubjectivity, which refers to shared emotion (attunement), shared attention, and shared intention. Concordant shared intersubjective experiences are a major basis for healing. Parents who can create positive shared concordant intersubjective experiences with their child help create a relationship within which the child can heal. Attunement is an emotional experience in which two people are in emotional sync, communicating verbally and nonverbally in a responsive and emotionally sensitive manner. The model of a healthy attuned relationship is the connection between a responsive and sensitive mother and her infant. This is not to discount other relationships. There is a hierarchy of attachment figures, the maternal figure being the most important. Using attachment terms, the parent creates a secure base so that the child experiences safety and security. From this secure base the child can explore the world, learn, and develop new relationships and experiences. Therapeutically, the parent creates a secure base so that the child can experience enough safety to allow the child to reexperience dissociated, disturbing, shameful, and feared emotions with the parent.

The parent provides the safe conditions within which healing can occur. The parent does this primarily by accepting the child's emotions and the meanings that the child has developed. Only after accepting the child's emotional world and view can the parent begin to challenge misperceptions and misunderstandings. First the child has to experience acceptance, then the child can explore alternative meanings and perceptions. The basis of attachment-facilitating parenting is to create a healing PLACE; being playful, loving, accepting, curious, and empathic.

THE DEVELOPMENT OF ATTACHMENT

The attachment system is a biologically driven system that evolved to ensure survival. Attachment behavior functions to maintain proximity with the mother so that the child survives. In times of stress or threat, the attachment system is activated and proximity-seeking behaviors emerge. One's basic pattern of attachment and the working models encoded are developed within the first few years of life. The human infant is born in a markedly helpless state. Unlike other mammals, the human infant cannot walk or feed itself at birth and requires continual care if the infant is to survive. Sunderland, in *The Science of Parenting* (2006), posits that this is due to the pelvis narrowing as humans evolved into traveling bipeds—a fully developed body, head, and brain could no longer be birthed.

Why is attachment so important? Healthy and secure attachment is necessary for the implementation of full intellectual potential. Children raised in a maltreating (meaning neglect, abuse of various kinds, or institutional care such as found in an orphanage) environment, which is nonresponsive or only marginally responsive to the child's needs, develop a working model of the world that is random, chaotic, and not attuned to their needs. Such children often come to develop a working model of the world in which their efforts make no difference. As a result, they often do not put effort into academic activities. Such children often test poorly because they give up before they actually try. Healthy and secure attachment is also necessary for the development of the ability to think logically. Cause-effect thinking develops when a child has a relationship with the parent in which the parent is responsive to the child's needs, and the child's actions produce consistently reliable responses from the world (parent). Other positive outcomes of a healthy and secure attachment include the ability to cope with frustration, a broad range of emotional regulation, the development of emotionally meaningful relationships, the capacity to effectively manage fear, anxiety, and stress without becoming dysregulated.

First Year

Initially the child requires continual care for the child's needs to be met. Food, temperature regulation, and stimulation all come from the parent. Infants communicate their needs by crying. The responsive parent notices the infant's cries and responds by meeting the need for food, stimulation, comfort, or by alleviating other discomforts. In fact, this is the beginning of language. Gradually over time, the infant learns that if the infant cries in one way food will be provided, while if the infant cries in a different way other discomforts will be removed. The parent and child in their contingent and interactive, responsive, relationship will learn to recognize and respond to each other in a sensitive manner. The cycle begins with the infant expressing a need, the caregiver responding to this need, the infant experiencing relief or gratification, and then the cycle beginning again. This normally happens hundreds of times each week and thousands of times in the first year. As a result of this interaction, sometime during or by the end of the first year, the infant develops a sense of basic trust:

1. Trust that the world is safe
2. Trust that the infant's needs will be met
3. Trust that the infant can effectively influence the world
4. Trust that the parent is reliable and good
5. Trust that the child is good

Second and Third Years

The theme of the child's toddler years is "wants." During the toddler years, a primary task of the caring and responsive parent is to set appropriate limits for the child as the child begins to explore the world. In this manner the parent keeps the child safe, while facilitating the child's exploration of the environment. During the toddler years, parents frequently use the word "no" as limits are set. In order for the child to progress from experiencing shame to experiencing guilt, a pro-social shift, there must be repeated repair of the relationship disruptions that the parent's limit setting normally causes. The "shame cycle" begins with the child and caregiver being in sync or in a state of emotional attunement. At this point the child experiences the parent's approval. The child then engages in some activity that the parents disapprove of. Usually, the child may be doing something that the child thinks the parent may approve of or is unaware of doing something bad. The parent sets a limit and the child experiences shame. One can see this in toddlers who respond to a "no" or a scolding by covering their eyes, turning away, or hiding. The child is experiencing shame and emotion that is painful and causes the child to want to hide or disappear. The attuned parent then repairs the relationship by reengaging the child and demonstrating, through the parent's behavior, that the child is lovable and cared about even if the behavior is not acceptable. The child makes amends, feels good, and the cycle renews. As this occurs, hundreds of times, these experiences enable the child to move from feeling a sense of shame to being able to experience guilt, in other words from feeling that the child is bad to feeling that the child is good, although the child's actions may at times be unacceptable to the parent. Once this occurs, the child is able to experience guilt. One way to think about the distinction between shame and guilt is that shame is about who you are, while guilt is about what you do. Shame is an isolating emotion, which leads to wanting to be alone or hiding. Guilt, while it may create a variety of other problems, is a very pro-social emotion, resulting in the person feeling engaged and connected. When an individual feels guilt that person wants to fix what it is he has done wrong, and make amends to others—he is now distressed by lack of connection.

Perhaps an example may serve to illustrate these points. You and your toddler are in the living room. As you drink your coffee and read the newspaper your child gleefully shows you the pictures she is drawing. You smile and say, "What a great dog," as you go back to your paper. You and your child are in sync, each taking joy in the other. Now your child goes on to do another "good thing" that will make you smile and make you happy. Your child goes to grab that pretty thing on the table with the smoke coming out if it; your cup of hot coffee! You scream, "Don't touch that!" as you lunge for your child, who bursts into tears, sits down on the floor, and looks down. At this point your child is feeling shame. Your child is surprised by your actions, which are not what your child expected. No, your child had thought that this next thing was also going to get you to smile and laugh. Shame causes your child to look away. Most likely what you now do is say, "Oh, honey, I'm not mad at you. This is hot coffee and I was scared you'd get burned. I don't want you to get hurt." Your child now looks at you, you smile, brush away the tears, and say, "Come here, let's draw together," or something like that. What you are doing is repairing the relationship. You are demonstrating that you love your child; that your child is loved and lovable. This type of interaction occurs many times a day; hundreds of times a week, and eventually the child comes to feel that while you may not always like what the child does and may be angry, you always love the child. Now the child experiences guilt when doing something wrong, feeling that what was done was bad, although still feeling good and lovable as a person.

ORIGINS

Disorders of attachment have many causes. Maltreatment, including emotional and physical neglect and emotional, physical, and sexual abuse are the most obvious and common causes of attachment difficulties. Chronic maltreatment, or its equivalent, is, by definition, inconsistent with responsive attuned childcare. It is the chronic nature of the maltreatment that creates the distorted internal working models of self, other, and relationships that become a pervasive and enduring trait of the person. The chronic nature of the maltreatment results in the child having repeated and significant experiences that confirm a worldview that is chaotic, untrustworthy, unpredictable, and unresponsive. There can be other causes of attachment difficulties. For example, if the birth mother is under extreme stress and is ambivalent about the pregnancy, then her stress hormones will affect the developing fetus. The brain is a delicate organ, and chronic stress can cause actual changes in brain structure and function. Prenatal stresses can result in a child that may be a "difficult" baby. Add to this, parents, maybe a single parent, under stress, and one has a potential recipe for early attachment difficulties. Other "red flags" to consider when assessing for attachment problems include sudden separations from the caregiver, maternal depression, frequent moves into and out of foster care, multiple and inconsistent caregivers, institutional and orphanage care, and premature birth coupled with extended neonatal intensive care or early chronic painful conditions, such as repeated surgeries to correct birth defects.

Institutional care of infants and children, while providing for the physical needs for shelter and calories, can be quite emotionally neglectful. According to studies done in Canada in the 1990s (Ames, 1990, 1997; Chisholm, 1998; Groze & Ileana, 1996; Nelson, Zeanah, Fox, Marshall, Smyke & Guthrie, 2007) the mean birth weight of 252 consecutive referrals from Russia was 2,509 grams while 48 percent had low birth weight (under 2,500 grams); 27 percent of the children were premature. The average alcohol consumption in Russia is 38 liters of 100-proof vodka per adult per year or about three shots per day. Prenatal alcohol exposure was present in 91 percent of the referrals. In my experience, a large number of older children brought from Russia for "summer camp" experiences with pre-adoptive families in the United States have significant neurological difficulties and attachment disorders. They exhibit controlling behavior with peers and caregivers, difficulties with affect regulation and impulse control, disturbed problem-solving abilities, impaired ability to defer gratification, difficulties with transitions, and other difficulties with higher cognitive functions commonly described as "executive functions."

Signs and Symptoms

There are many "symptoms" of attachment disorders. You can find numerous lists and checklists on the Internet and in various books, such as the list below. Many of the symptoms tend to group themselves in clusters that define different subtypes. There are a number of ways to describe attachment. Mary Ainsworth (1978) described the following categories: secure attachment and two types of insecure attachment, anxious and avoidant. Mary Main and Erik Hesse (1990) added a fourth subtype, the disorganized subtype. The three subtypes described by Mary Ainsworth are organized responses to maternal behavior. The disorganized subtype is seen when the parent, who is supposed to be the secure base, is also the source of threat. In these instances, the child does not develop an organized attachment strategy. It is the disorganized subtype that is most likely to develop into Reactive Attachment Disorder. The most significant problem with listing of behaviors and making checklists is that these are merely lists of symptoms. It is the cause of the behavior that is more important, since that is what you treat. In addition, attachment resides in a relationship and exhibits itself in relation to a significant caregiver; so it is best measured using interactional methodologies or process measures.

Many psychiatric disorders have overlapping symptoms. Differential diagnosis requires the consideration of cause and looking at the symptoms in the context of the child's past history and current social environment. For a child to have an attachment disorder, the child does not need to have all the following symptoms. Similarly, a child who exhibits one or two symptoms does not necessarily have an attachment disorder. Assessment can only be made by a licensed, experienced, and properly trained mental health professional. The professional should have had specific training and related experience in the diagnosis and treatment of children in the child welfare system and of those with disorders of attachment. Such a professional should at least meet the minimum standards to be a registered clinician with the Association for the Treatment and Training in the Attachment of Children (ATTACh). The following list is merely a listing of behaviors that a child with a disorder of attachment may exhibit. It should not be used as a diagnostic tool and it should be recognized that children with other disorders may exhibit some of these behaviors. Therefore, it is vital that a thorough assessment be secured to determine the cause of the problem behaviors.

SYMPTOMS OF PROBLEMS

1. My child teases, hurts, or is cruel to other children.
2. My child can't keep friends for an age-appropriate length of time.
3. My child doesn't do as well in school as my child could do even with a little more effort.
4. My child pushes me away or becomes stiff when I try to hug, unless my child wants something from me, in which case my child can be affectionate and engaging.
5. My child argues for long periods of time, often about meaningless or silly things.
6. My child has a large need to control everything.
7. My child is hypervigilant.
8. My child acts amazingly innocent, or pretends that things aren't really bad or a problem when caught doing something wrong.
9. My child does dangerous things such as runs away, jumps out of windows, or other potentially harmful actions. My child seems oblivious to the fact that my child may be hurt.
10. My child deliberately breaks or ruins his things or other's things.
11. My child doesn't seem to feel age-appropriate guilt when my child does something wrong.

12. My child is impulsive. My child seems unable or unwilling to stop doing something my child wants to do.
13. My child teases, hurts, or is cruel to animals.
14. My child steals, or shows up with things that belong to others with unbelievable, unusual, or suspicious reasons for how my child got these things.
15. My child likes to sneak things without permission, even though my child could have had these things if my child had asked.
16. My child doesn't seem to learn from mistakes, consequences, or punishments (my child continues the behavior despite the consequences).
17. My child makes false reports of abuse or neglect. My child tries to get sympathy from others, or tries to get us in trouble, by telling others that I abuse, don't feed, or don't provide the basic necessities.
18. My child seems not to experience pain when hurt, refusing to let anyone provide comfort.
19. My child does not usually ask for things. My child demands things.
20. My child lies, often about obvious or ridiculous things, or when it would have been easier to tell the truth.
21. My child is quite bossy with other children and adults.
22. My child hoards, sneaks food, or has other unusual eating habits (eats paper, straight sugar, nonfood items, package mixes, baking chocolate, etc.)
23. My child often does not make eye contact when adults want to make eye contact with my child.
24. My child has extended temper tantrums.
25. My child chatters nonstop, asks repeated questions about things that make no sense, mutters, or is hard to understand when talking.
26. My child is accident-prone (gets hurt a lot), or complains a lot about every little ache and pain (needs constant attention).
27. My child acts cute or charming to get others to do what my child wants.
28. My child is overly friendly with strangers.
29. My child has set fires, or is preoccupied with fire.
30. My child prefers to watch violent cartoons and/or TV shows or horror movies (regardless of whether you allow your child to do this).
31. My child was abused/neglected during the first year of life, or had several changes of primary caretaker during the first several years of life.
32. My child was in an orphanage for more than the first year of life.
33. My child was adopted after the age of twelve months.

Infancy

In infants there are several red flags that suggest further assessment and the possibility of attachment difficulties.

- Weak crying response or rageful and/or constant whining
- Tactile defensiveness
- Poor clinging and extreme resistance to cuddling: seems "stiff as a board"
- Poor sucking response
- Poor eye contact, lack of tracking
- No reciprocal smile response
- Indifference to others
- Failure to respond with recognition to mother or father
- Delayed physical motor skill development milestones (creeping, crawling, sitting, etc.)
- Flaccid or physically limp

Psychiatric diagnoses, such as Reactive Attachment Disorder, Bipolar I, Oppositional Defiant Disorder, Attention Deficit/Hyperactivity Disorder, Post-Traumatic Stress Disorder, and others can be useful and have their place in assessing a child. However, psychiatric diagnoses are largely based on behavior and not underlying causes. The symptoms of these and other disorders often substantially overlap, yet there are different treatments for different conditions, and the treatments are directed at the causes not the surface behavior. A much more useful concept is the clinical construct of Complex Trauma (ATTACh, 2009; Cook, Blaustein, Spinazolla & van der Kolk, 2003; Cook, Spinazzola, Ford, Lanktree, Blaustein, Cloitre, et al., 2005; Courtois & Ford, 2009). This construct captures the pervasive effects of chronic early maltreatment within a caregiving relationship. Such maltreatment can cause impairments in several domains including: attachment, behavioral regulation, emotional regulation, biology, dissociation and defensive functions, cognition, and self-concept. Such an integrating concept enables parents and therapists to take a more holistic approach to helping a child heal.

Children often present with a constellation of symptoms that largely reflect the pattern of maltreatment. For example, many, but not all, children who have spent considerable time in an institution are often superficially engaging and present as "as-if" children, with little authenticity. These children often respond with whatever answers they think are correct at the moment. Of course, this behavior was adaptive in the institution. This pattern of response is more likely to get the approval of the institutional caregivers and result in more attention and other scarce resources. Children with significant experiences of emotional neglect often appear devoid of affect. In many instances, they are unable to identify feelings beyond simply "good" or "bad," much as an infant experiences the world. Other children may be more angry, violent, and aggressive. In all instances there are several commonalities among all "subtypes." First, all these children experienced significant and chronic maltreatment. Second, these children exhibit difficulties with emotional regulation, frustration tolerance, and impulse control. Third, these children lack a sense of basic trust. Fourth, they have internal working models in which they experience themselves as defective, unloved, and unlovable. It is not unusual for these children to act out actively or passively when living in homes in which intimacy and closeness are an intrinsic part of daily life.

When untreated, children with severe trauma-attachment disorders, such as Reactive Attachment Disorder, are at high risk of becoming adults with severe personality disorders such as: Antisocial Personality Disorder, Borderline Personality Disorder, Avoidant Personality Disorder, and Dependent Personality Disorder, among others.

THE BRAIN AND ATTACHMENT

While this is not a text on neurology, it may be helpful to understand the effects of chronic maltreatment on child development and the attachment relationship. It is the effects of maltreatment on brain development that provide the linkage between these early negative experiences and later difficulties. The intersection of neurobiology and attachment theory has opened up some exciting areas of research and theory that have profound implications for parenting children with disorders of attachment. Brain development is largely experience-dependent. How stimuli are perceived, interpreted, and acted upon depends, to a large extent, on prior experience. Internal working models of the world develop from patterns of interactions and early attachment experiences and are encoded within the brain. This section will briefly describe some of the key elements of the neurobiology of interpersonal experience and implications for parenting.

The brain is divided into two hemispheres that function differently. The right hemisphere ("right brain") operates primarily in a holistic manner and is largely responsible for social "thinking," psychosocial development, emotional memory and experience, and the perception and storage of interpersonally related information. The left hemisphere ("left brain") is largely language based and "linear or logical" in its functioning. The right hemisphere is dominant during the first three years of life. As language functions develop, the left hemisphere becomes the more dominant hemisphere.

Early interpersonal experiences have a profound impact on the brain because the brain pathways responsible for social perception are the same as those that integrate such functions as creating meaning, regulating body states, regulating emotion, organizing memory, and the capacity for interpersonal communication and empathy (Siegel, 2001). Stressful experiences that are overtly traumatizing or chronic cause persistent elevated levels of neuroendocrine hormones (Siegel, 2001). High levels of these hormones can cause permanent damage to the hippocampus, which is critical for memory (McEwen, 1999). Based on this, we can assume that psychological trauma can impair a person's ability to manage memory and resolve trauma.

Internal working models that develop during the early years of life are stored primarily in the right hemisphere and operate outside of conscious awareness. Working models are internal representations of the world, relationships, self, and others that act as schemas or lenses, filtering and interpreting experience and sensations. These internal working models are the lenses through which we filter new experiences and relationships. They color how we perceive others and our world.

These internal working models are largely stored in the right hemisphere. Explicit memories are located in the left hemisphere and are memories that are experienced as remembering, such as when you recall your high school prom or last Thanksgiving. Implicit-procedural memories often operate outside of conscious awareness, such as occurs when driving a car or one's basic orientation to strangers. Internal working models (from the right brain, and largely unconscious) guide ones orientation to the world and ones approach to experience. These are the schemas that operate outside of awareness and guide behavior so that conscious thought is not required for each interaction.

Two of the essential components of mental health are a coherent autobiographical narrative and the ability to regulate one's level of arousal, including emotional regulation. Autobiographical narratives represent the integration of left hemispheric explicit memories with right hemispheric affect and implicit memories. Trauma interferes with this integration. Without a normal left/right integration our sense of self with a past, present, and future can become vague and hazy.

Early experiences create brain pathways that, depending on the quality of the experiences, either facilitate healthy, functional, and integrated mental states or result in rigid response patterns and dissociated and nonintegrated mental states. It is the effect of early experiences on brain development and later functioning that provides the link between these early experiences and later behavior. The effect of maltreatment on the brain is the reason that these early experiences have such a profound and lasting impact on socialemotional functioning.

How the Brain May View Life as One Long Emergency

Maltreatment (abuse, neglect, or institutional care) causes poor emotional regulation because the various neurological systems involved in emotional regulation are not properly integrated. The way the brain is wired, impulses from the eyes and ears reach the amygdala (the part of the brain that is responsible for the stress responses of flight, fight, freeze) before these stimuli are processed by the neocortex. In other words, we react before we "know" what we are reacting to. If past experience has chronically excited these pathways, then the brain will be chronically exposed to various stress hormones and neurotransmitters. The more the fight-flight-freeze-appeasement pathways in the limbic system (which is the part of the brain responsible for emotional management) and amygdala are used, the easier it becomes to trigger those pathways. Over time chronic maltreatment causes a stressful response trait to become an enduring state of emergency without end. The child remains in perpetual high alert, hyperaroused, and hypervigilant. Furthermore, there is evidence that these stress-related hormones and neurotransmitters interfere with memory and new learning. This may explain some of the learning problems that maltreated children experience. In addition, chronic trauma can cause an over-pruning of connections between the amygdala and the orbitofrontal cortex (which is the part of the brain responsible for integrating emotional responses in the limbic system with the higher cognitive functions of the neocortex, such as planning, judgment, and the evaluating of alternatives), so that amygdala-driven states ("emergencies") are expressed without cortical inhibition or involvement. In this case, responses will tend to be rigid and lacking the flexibility that is characteristic of cortex-mediated responses involving planning and judgment and other higher functions. It can now be perhaps more easily seen how in addition, this disconnect between the limbic system and higher cortical functions may be a basis for dissociation (such as "spacing out") and other pathological responses such as those found in Post-Traumatic Stress Disorder. In this case the higher corticolimbic areas become inefficient and ineffective in regulating emotions and in providing responses that are more functional. They essentially fail to respond.

Chronic neglect in institutions may create the opposite effect, where the child is in an under-aroused state. The chronic lack of stimulation may create such deficits that the child does not develop a discrete sense of danger. This may be the reason such children appear to have no "fear" of strangers and willingly go to anyone around. These effects of trauma and dissociation can be viewed as a lack of integration among key brain functions.

Other effects of maltreatment include difficulties with perceiving social cues, problems with motivation, and other symptoms associated with attachment disorders.

The Bad News

Children who have experienced early physical and sexual abuse show EEG abnormalities in frontotemporal and anterior brain regions (Teicher,

Ito & Glod, 1996). Chronic exposure to a hyperactive stress system alters the development of the prefrontal and orbitofrontal cortex, causing fewer synapses and fewer neurons to develop.

Chronic maltreatment creates a profound regulatory failure in various brain regions. It is the dysregulation in these systems that is expressed as the emotional dysregulation that is at the core of trauma-attachment disorders. The child experiences a profound inability to process and regulate stress, emotions, and relationships. One sees hypersensitivity of key sympathetic and parasympathetic pathways so that it is as if the child's emotional accelerator and brake are both being applied at the same time. As discussed earlier, the basis for this dysregulation is that the chronic stress of chronic maltreatment causes structural changes in the brain, fewer synapses and neurons in key brain regions required for emotional regulation.

The attachment relationship is one of the major influences on the limbic system, orbitofrontal cortex, and right hemisphere development. Chronic maltreatment in infancy leads to failure of various regulatory functions. Chronic maltreatment by a caregiver with a disorganized state of mind with respect to attachment is the best predictor of disorganized attachment in the child (Main & Hesse, 1990).

A misattuned caregiver can create a dysregulated and dysregulating environment, which over time will result in the child developing a disorganized attachment (Main & Hesse, 1990). Such caregivers induce extreme levels of arousal in their children by providing too much unregulated stress and arousal (abuse) or too low a level of stress and arousal (neglect). Without interactive repair, the child's negative emotional states last for long periods of time and become internalized as part of the working model of self. A child with such an internal working model of self will experience himself or herself as an unwanted, unworthy, unlovable, bad, and defective person.

Positive Findings

A birth mother's attachment classification before the birth of her child can predict with 80 percent accuracy her child's attachment classification at six years of age (Main & Cassidy, 1988). Encouragingly, recent research by Dozier (2001) found that the attachment classification of a foster mother has a profound effect on the attachment classification of the child. Dozier found that the child's attachment classification becomes similar to that of the foster mother after three months in placement. These findings show that there is a nongenetic mechanism for the transmission of attachment patterns across generations and for the beneficial impact of a healing and healthy relationship.

DYADIC DEVELOPMENTAL PSYCHOTHERAPY

Dyadic Developmental Psychotherapy and the parenting approaches that derive from this approach are based on these findings from the neurobiology of interpersonal experience. Since the best predictor of a child's state of mind with respect to attachment is that of the parent, work with the parent is a crucial element of Dyadic Developmental Psychotherapy. Furthermore, since the attachment system is a mutually co-regulated system, treatment has to involve the whole system: parent and child. These neurobiological findings have other implications for treatment:

1. Concordant intersubjective experiences are a key healing component of treatment and parenting. Maintaining attunement with the child is essential for successful parenting-treatment to occur. However, when parents have their own unresolved trauma that may interfere with their attunement with their child, it becomes imperative for the therapist to actively demonstrate and model attunement with the parent for the child to eventually develop empathy and reflective capabilities.
2. Repeated cycles of attunement-intense affect-disengagement-reattunement-interactive repair, are essential for healing to occur. Through this process children and parents learn, experientially, that relationships can be disrupted and then reintegrated. This "teaches" that the individual, at the core, is valuable and lovable, worthy of reconnection efforts.
3. Another essential dimension of treatment is the co-regulation of affect. Since children with trauma-attachment disorders exhibit chronic and severe difficulty regulating affect (both positive and negative affect), the parent and therapist regulate the child's affect until the child has internalized this skill. This is a process that usually occurs as part of normal development during infancy. When infancy is characterized by chronic maltreatment, co-regulation of affect does not occur and the child is easily dysregulated.
4. Trauma often causes various memories and emotions to be split off and dissociated. One result of successful treatment is the development of a more coherent autobiographical narrative with appropriate affect. The presence of a coherent autobiographical narrative may be evidence of a healthy integration of right and left hemispheric functions and processes.
5. Parenting interventions, while often verbal, are primarily initiated to create experiences—experiences that provide attunement, co-regulated affect, and demonstrate a deep respect, empathy, and caring. The therapy is primarily experiential.

6. Trauma can be revisited in order to integrate the cognitive and affective components. What was overwhelming when experienced as a young child and without support can be tolerated and integrated within a supportive therapeutic relationship.

FACTORS THAT RESOLVE TRAUMA

There are five factors (from Siegel, 2001) that are important for the development of a healthy and secure attachment and that are also critical for the resolution of trauma. These factors are the following:

1. Contingent collaborative communication
2. Reflective dialogue
3. Interactive repair
4. Coherent autobiographical narrative
5. Affective communication

Contingent collaborative communication refers to responsive dyadic communication. Each response is guided by and in reference to the proceeding communication. Contingent collaborative communication involves eye contact, facial expressions, tone of voice, body gestures, and the timing and intensity of response. Contingent collaborative communication is synchronized interaction. It is the coupling of emotional communication between parent and child and the development of a system of co-regulation. This communication helps create a coherent core self. This type of reciprocal communication facilitates healing trauma by providing a supportive context within which a sense of safety and security can develop. Contingent collaborative communication creates an environment within which the individual feels supported, understood, and, on an affective level, joined with another. One element of trauma that is particularly dysregulating is the sense of isolation and aloneness that occurs. Contingent collaborative communication is one element that diminishes this sense of aloneness.

Reflective dialogue, generally referred to as the reflective function, involves a sense of self and other as discrete independent objects. Reflective dialogue involves communication about one's own internal state of mind, and comments and observation about the other. In one sense, reflective dialogue is a stream of consciousness communication in which the individual shares with another one's own internal thoughts, experiences, and emotions. It is through this sharing that a child comes to learn how to make sense of his or her own internal experiences. Reflective dialogues create meaning for the child so that the child can make sense of experience.

Children learn about their own emotions, and their own value, by seeing themselves reflected in their parents' eyes.

The healing dimension of interactive repair is that it reduces shame. Furthermore, it helps a child progress developmentally from a shame-based identity to the experience of healthy and appropriate guilt. Interactive repair refers to the parents' actions to repair the relationship and to emotionally reconnect with and reestablish an attuned relationship with the child after there has been a breach in the relationship. Typically, the breach in the relationship is caused by some action on the part of the child. The parent setting a limit may cause the breach. The disruption in the relationship that occurs typically leads young children and toddlers to experience a sense of shame. The cycle of experiencing positive affect following negative experiences teaches the child that negative emotions can be tolerated and resolved. Over time as the healthy parent reestablishes attunement, the child begins to experience himself or herself as intrinsically good, although as one who occasionally does "bad" things. It is this movement from feeling that one is bad to feeling that one is good, but does bad things, that is at the core of the developmental step from shame to guilt.

People with a healthy and secure state of mind with respect to attachment have personal narratives that are coherent, consistent, and integrated, reflecting an integration of right and left hemispheric functions and an integration of emotional and linear memories or episodic and procedural memories. Children who have experienced chronic trauma frequently have disjointed, split, and dissociated autobiographical narratives. Elements of the trauma are split off and dissociated. While the emotional sequelae of the trauma are clearly active in the child's behavior, the child is not aware of its impact. Revisiting the trauma in detail so that the emotions are experienced in the safe and secure setting of the therapy session and in the home allows for the integration of affective and episodic memories and the conscious awareness of how these events and feelings are operating in the present. It is this awareness that provides an important healing dimension to treatment. Once dissociated elements are integrated into a coherent autobiographical narrative the child is able to manage the underlying affect and engage the reflective function to select an appropriate and self-advancing response.

Finally, it is emotional communication, which is largely nonverbal, that is at the core of the healing experience and at the core of all experiences that facilitate the development of a healthy and secure state of mind with respect to attachment. Emotional communication is the verbal and nonverbal interchange between two persons. There is always an implicit, or nonverbal, dimension. In addition, there may be a verbal and explicit dimension. Without this attuned emotional communication, there can be no healing. It is the sharing of affective experiences on both the verbal and nonverbal levels that creates attunement and helps the child to feel safely held, understood, and accepted. Communication that does not have this emotional dimension to it, while useful for sharing information, is not healing since at the core of the difficulties experienced by these children are distortions of interpersonal relationships, affect regulation, and the integration of affect. Emotional communication facilitates the integration of affect since communicated affect is shared and will not be as overwhelming as it may be when experienced alone. In addition, emotional communication facilitates the development of a more coherent autobiographical narrative by making explicit what may have been dissociated or implicit.

RESEARCH ON DYADIC DEVELOPMENTAL PSYCHOTHERAPY

Successful treatment requires both parenting and therapy. In our experience when a child heals, 80 percent of the credit goes to the parents while 20 percent to therapy. Therapy addresses the underlying trauma and supports and coaches the parents in their work.

Dyadic Developmental Psychotherapy has been found to be an evidence-based, effective, and empirically validated treatment (Becker-Weidman & Hughes, 2008). The Center For Family Development completed a follow-up study of sixty-four closed cases of children who meet the DSM IV criteria for Reactive Attachment Disorder (Becker-Weidman, 2006a, 2006b). Of these sixty-four cases, thirty-four had been treated with Dyadic Developmental Psychotherapy and thirty received "usual care," such as family therapy, play therapies, residential treatment, and so forth, from other providers at other treatment centers.

All children were between the ages of five and sixteen when the study began. Seven hypotheses were explored. It was hypothesized that Dyadic Developmental Psychotherapy would reduce the symptoms of attachment disorder, aggressive and delinquent behaviors, social problems and withdrawal, anxiety and depressive problems, thought problems, and attention problems as measured with the Child Behavior Checklist or Ackenbach.

Significant reductions were achieved in all measures studied for the treatment group. The results were achieved in an average of twenty-three sessions over eleven months. These findings continued for an average of 1.1 years after treatment ended for children between the ages of six and sixteen years. There were no changes in the "usual-care" group subjects, who were retested an average of 1.3 years after the evaluation was completed. The results are particularly significant since 82 percent of the treatment-group subjects and 83 percent of the usual care-group subjects had previously received treatment with an average of 3.2 prior treatment episodes. (An episode of treatment is defined as several treatment sessions directed at treating a specific diagnosis.) This past history of unsuccessful treatment further underscores the effectiveness of Dyadic Developmental Psychotherapy as a treatment for children with trauma-attachment problems. In addition, 53 percent of the usual care-group subjects received "usual care" but without any measurable change in the outcome variables measured. Children with trauma-attachment problems are at significant risk of developing severe disorders in adulthood such as Post-Traumatic Stress Disorder, Borderline Personality Disorder, Narcissistic Personality Disorder, and other personality disorders.

In an extension of that study (Becker-Weidman, 2006b), the families were recontacted and again completed the Child Behavior Checklist. All of the control group families had sought and continued in treatment, with an average of fifty sessions. Despite receiving extensive treatment, the control group actually exhibited an increase in symptoms over the 3.3 years since the original study was completed. We found a clinically and statistically significant increase in anxious and depressive symptoms, attention problems, rule breaking behavior, and aggressive behavior, as measured by the Child Behavior Checklist.

Forty-two percent of the treatment group received treatment after completing Dyadic Developmental Psychotherapy. Most of this continued treatment was for co-morbid conditions, such as Bipolar Disorder and Attention Deficit/Hyperactivity Disorder. The majority received medication management treatment. For this group we found continued clinically and statistically significant improvements nearly four years after treatment ended, as measured by the Child Behavior Checklist; in fact all six measures remained in the "normal" range.

These empirical studies support several of O'Connor & Zeanah's (2003) conclusions and recommendations concerning treatment. They state, "Treatments for children with attachment disorders should be promoted only when they are evidence-based" (p. 241). The results of this study are a beginning toward that end. While this study has limitations, it indicates that Dyadic Developmental Psychotherapy shows significant promise and suggests that further study is worthwhile.

These studies demonstrate that Dyadic Developmental Psychotherapy is an effective intervention for children with trauma-attachment problems (Becker-Weidman & Hughes, 2008).

2

Beginnings

Arthur Becker-Weidman and Deborah Shell

The old sayings abound:

The hand that rocks the cradle rules the world.

Give me a child until the age of seven and I will show you the man.

Train up a child in the way he should go; and when he is old, he will not depart from it.

Mothers and fathers in every culture know that the relationship they have with their child will affect the way their child thinks, feels, and acts. Science supports the meaning of the old sayings, and due to developments in brain research we know more than ever about how relationships actually influence brain structure growth and development. We also know that relationships continue to affect the way we make meaning, think, feel, and act throughout the life span. The experience of attuned, contingent relationships in the first year of life ensures the development of social skills and sets the stage for successful future relationships. And it is through this very experience of relating that children deprived of these opportunities (due to maltreatment or loss) can be helped to heal and grow. Integration of various brain functions occurs through the actual experiencing of attuned relationships. Relationships are somehow like water on seeds; something is awakened and brought to life.

Most likely you probably already have the fertile field in which your child can grow and learn: a safe environment, predictable routines, clean clothes, nutritious meals, toys, books, and games. And you've already begun your quest for more information by reading this book. We hope to help you consider how the actual quality of relationship you cultivate with your child can bring to life the dormant seeds of love and connection your child requires. In this chapter we will describe how to select a therapist to guide you, what to expect from an evaluation, and what to expect from therapy. For children over the age of three or four it is usually necessary to use both attachment-facilitating parenting and an attachment-based therapy, such as Dyadic Developmental Psychotherapy. Younger children, and those less disturbed, will respond quite favorably to attachment-facilitating parenting alone. Combinations of treatment modalities, such as Dyadic Developmental Psychotherapy and Theraplay, as well as other adjunct therapies described in this book, may be quite effective with these children.

GETTING A THOROUGH EVALUATION

The place to begin is with a thorough assessment (ATTACh, 2009). While you may have gotten reams of paper about your child, or nothing at all, many of these past evaluations and assessments may not have been provided by a therapist specifically trained and experienced in evaluating and treating children with disorders of attachment or children who have been adopted or are in foster homes. Unfortunately, most clinical mental health diagnoses and treatment are made based on symptoms but not causes. When you think about it, this is rather odd. This is like going to your doctor with a cough and your doctor treating the cough without bothering to consider the cause: TB, allergies, the flu, cancer, and so on. Differential diagnosis is very important because there are different treatments for different conditions and these treatments, while effective for one condition, may be ineffective for other conditions. We know from previous research (Becker-Weidman, 2006a) that more than 80 percent of families seeking treatment for disorders of attachment had more than three prior episodes of treatment before getting effective treatment for their child's difficulties. We believe just about all of those other providers are competent and that the care they provided was good treatment. We can only conclude that the diagnosis was incorrect so that the wrong treatment was provided, or else, the provider did not know how to provide the proper treatment. A child with a disorder of attachment may have the following symptoms: argumentative, defiant, difficulty paying attention, easily distractible, difficulty sitting still, problems concentrating, difficulty playing quietly, not completing homework or other tasks, frequently losing or breaking things, temper tantrums, chronically irritable, mood swings, difficulty with friends or no close friends, aggressive, hitting others with objects, stealing, lying, and so on. Such a constellation of symptoms would meet the diagnostic criteria for Attention Deficit/Hyperactivity Disorder, Oppositional Defiant Disorder, Post-Traumatic Stress Disorder, Conduct Disorder, Sensory-Integration Disorders, or Bipolar I Disorder, to name just a few. Since one would treat each of these disorders differently, a differential diagnosis is vital if you are to get helpful care for your child. One of the critical issues to consider is cause. In this book we will talk a lot about the cause of behavior; what is motivating the behavior; what is driving the behavior, because that determines how you effectively treat or parent. Further complicating the diagnostic picture is the fact that some of these diagnoses should really be included under the diagnosis of Reactive Attachment Disorder. Many children diagnosed with Reactive Attachment Disorder also meet the criteria for Oppositional Defiant Disorder or Post-Traumatic Stress Disorder. The diagnosis of Reactive Attachment Disorder subsumes those other diagnoses, and treatment would focus on the disorder of attachment in order to remedy the oppositional symptoms or the PTSD issues. Sensory-Integration Disorders can look just like ADHD. Fetal Alcohol Spectrum Disorders can look like ADHD or other neuropsychological issues. So, a thorough assessment by a therapist who is trained and experienced in these areas is vital to your getting good treatment, good advice, and to access other needed services such as special education program, wraparound programs, or early childhood intervention services, to name just a few. Clinically, the concept of Complex Trauma (Cook, Blaustein, Spinazolla & van der Kolk, 2003; Cook, Spinazzola, Ford, Lanktree, Blaustein, Cloitre, et al., 2005) is much more useful than the psychiatric diagnosis of Reactive Attachment Disorder. So, what constitutes a thorough assessment?

First of all, a thorough assessment must include an evaluation of the child's mental status, consideration of other mental health conditions, a screening for sensory-integration and neuropsychological difficulties, a detailed social history, a detailed evaluation of the child's state of mind with respect to attachment, the child's developmental, social, medical, and educational histories, the current family dynamics, and the primary caregiver's attachment history (ATTACh, 2009).

While each practitioner may have a particular approach to assessment, a reasonably thorough assessment might include the following elements:

1. Meet with parents.
2. Gather history of child and relationships within the family.
3. Prepare a chronological history of the child's placements and reasons for changes.
4. Assess the caregiver's reflective capacities, capacity to provide sensitive, responsive, and attuned care as well as providing a safe, secure, and structured home, and caregiver's attachment history. It is very important that the parent view experiences through the child's eyes and have theories of mind about the child that consider the child's past experiences and how these may be impacting on present relationships.

5. Review past records including the following:
   i. Protective service reports. These reports provide you with some understanding of the extent of the maltreatment.
   ii. Police reports. Police tend to be excellent reporters. Police reports can provide detailed and accurate descriptions of conditions in the home. This information can be very useful in formulating theories about the child's experience and for the development of role-plays and psychodramatic reenactments.
   iii. Previous evaluations: social history, psychological, occupational therapy, speech therapy, medical, genetic, neurological, and developmental
   iv. School records
   v. Court documents
6. Psychological tests and questionnaires
   i. Primary
      1. Child Behavior Checklist: parent, child, and teacher versions (Achenbach, 1991)
      2. Vineland Adaptive Behavior Scales (Becker-Weidman, 2009; Sparrow, Cicchetti & Balla, 2005). Many children who have experienced a chronic history of maltreatment are developmentally delayed. This instrument can provide results that are useful with schools and parents. Parents often find it very helpful to have an instrument that shows the developmental delay of their child. It often helps the parent appreciate that, while the child may be physically one age, the child is functioning at a much younger age.
      3. Caregiver's autobiography. This information can be useful in understanding the caregiver and what aspects of parenting may be easier and more difficult for the caregiver.
      4. Behavior Rating Inventory of Executive Function (Gioia, Isquith, Guy & Kenworthy, 2000)
      5. Sensory-Integration screener (Becker-Weidman, 2008)
      6. Attachment Story Completion Test (Bretherton, Ridgeway & Cassidy, 1990; Emde, Wolf & Oppenheim, 2003)
      7. House-Tree-Person projective test, both achromatic and color (Buck & Warren, 1992)
      8. Child Apperception Test
      9. Parent Stress Index (Abidin, 1995)
   ii. Secondary. These assessments may be added, depending on the purpose of the evaluation, age of the child, and the parents' issues.
      1. Millon Adolescent Personality Inventory

2. MCMI-III
3. Ainsworth Strange Situation
4. Structured observation and play session
5. Trauma Symptom Checklist for Young Children
6. Adult Attachment Interview (Hesse, 2009; Steele & Steele, 2008)
7. Connors Rating Scales

SESSION WITH CHILD

The main purpose of meeting with the child is to evaluate how the child relates to others, the child's capacity for reflective engagement, and to begin to assess internal working models. A semi-structured interview may be used in which the process of what occurs is the primary focus. The following elements may be incorporated into this session:

House-Tree-Person Projective test (both achromatic and chromatic). We find this a good way to begin as many children are quite "therapy savvy." How the child manages this semi-structured situation is as important as what drawings are produced.
Attachment Story Completion Test provides a window into the child's state of mind with respect to attachment.
Review of history and the child's understanding of and meaning ascribed to the child's past history.
Child's understanding of the child's behavior.

We like to ask four questions:

1. What is the thing you've done that you are most proud of?
2. What is the worst thing you've done?
3. What is the best thing that ever happened to you?
4. What is the worst thing that ever happened to you?

We often ask the child to pick colors, from a set of primary colors plus black, gray, and orange, for mad, sad, glad, and scared and to write these at the bottom of a page. The child is then asked to draw a big heart and to fill in the heart with the proportion of each feeling that the child usually has most of the time. We often get accurate responses to this question, and the information is useful in determining how the child approaches relationships and feelings.

SESSION WITH THE CAREGIVERS

When meeting with the caregivers, the main purpose is to review the assessment, diagnosis, make treatment recommendations, and referrals (such as to an SIPT certified occupational therapist for sensory-integration issues or to a neuropsychologist for neuropsychological evaluation).

In this session we also discuss the treatment recommendations and how treatment may proceed.

    iii. During this session, if the family wants to engage in treatment, we will provide several resources about attachment-facilitating parenting.

    iv. In this session Dyadic Developmental Psychotherapy is briefly described, and then we set a time to meet to begin parent training.

Based on the assessment, further evaluations may be necessary. For example, if there are concerns that the learning difficulties, neuropsychological issues raised by the Behavior Rating Inventory of Executive Function, or other screening instrument, or behavioral rigidity are related to prenatal exposure to alcohol, then an evaluation by a developmental pediatrician for Alcohol Related Neurological Dysfunction (ARND) or Fetal Alcohol Syndrome (FAS) may be necessary. You can find such a professional at your regional children's hospital or at your regional university hospital. It is important that you find a professional who has experience evaluating internationally or domestically adopted children with ARND/FAS. In addition, you may need to get a complete neuropsychological evaluation.

Evaluation by an Occupational Therapist who is SIPT certified is appropriate if the assessment reveals indications of sensory-integration difficulties. Since many adopted and foster children with histories of chronic maltreatment have sensory-integration difficulties and since these difficulties are often misdiagnosed as ADHD, we suggest considering sensory-integration difficulties before ADHD. In other words, secure an evaluation by an SIPT certified OT, and treatment if indicated, before looking at ADHD as the cause of attention problems.

When the neuropsychological screening (usually from the Behavior Rating Inventory of Executive Function, our clinical interview, and a review of records) suggests difficulties in this area, a good educational assessment and neuropsychological assessment are indicated.

SELECTING A THERAPIST

If it is determined that your child has a disorder of attachment, Complex Trauma, or a related condition and would benefit from an attachment-based treatment, such as Dyadic Developmental Psychotherapy, then your next task is to select a therapist. The therapist should be a licensed mental health professional. In addition to being licensed in your state, the therapist should have had substantial training and experience in evaluating and treating adopted and foster children and those with disorders of attachment. One place to find such a person is to look at the list of registered clinicians or registered agencies on the website for the Association For the Treatment and Training in the Attachment of Children (www.attach.org). Your therapist should either be on that list or at least meet the criteria to be on the list. Specifically we recommend that the therapist have had at least eighty hours of relevant postgraduate training in the evaluation and treatment of children with trauma-attachment disorders. The therapist should devote at least 50 percent of the person's time to evaluating and treating adopted and foster children. In addition, the therapist should have a regular consultation or supervision relationship with an experienced therapist. The therapist should be able to show you a detailed description of the treatment to be provided, treatment philosophy, safety procedures, and a detailed informed consent document.

Some specific questions you might want to ask a prospective therapist are:

- What specific training have you had in evaluating and treating adopted and foster children and disorders of attachment in the last five years? In the previous year?
- What percentage of your practice is with adopted and foster children?
- What professional organizations do you belong to?
- Do you meet the criteria to be a registered clinician with the Association for the Treatment and Training in the Attachment of Children?
- How do you evaluate outcome or progress?
- How many years have you specialized in treating disorders of attachment?
- What is the approach you use and is it supported by empirical data?
- Can I see your informed consent document and treatment descriptions?

Obviously, an important factor in selecting a professional is that you should feel comfortable with the person. The therapist should be attending specifically to you and your unique situation. If you don't feel comfortable with the person or approach, then you might want to consider getting a second opinion. The therapist should show you the same degree of empathy, support, and understanding that is shown to your child and that is expected you show to your child. If you feel blamed, criticized, or shamed, then this is a red flag that should be discussed with the therapist. You did not create the difficulties your child is experiencing. While you have the obligation to help your child heal and to take the necessary steps to help achieve this, your child's symptoms and difficulties are not your fault. A professional who causes you to feel blame and shame probably does not have a good understanding of how traumatized children can affect a family. A good therapist will provide you with the support and tools necessary to help heal your child.

A good rule of thumb is that if you don't see some movement in ninety days to four months, then you should reconsider the diagnosis and clinical assessment or increase the intensity of therapy. If you've not had the child out of school, maybe the child does need to be home on a full-time basis. If you are meeting once a week, perhaps twice a week is necessary. And, of course, you should consider whether the diagnosis and treatment are correct.

DYADIC DEVELOPMENTAL PSYCHOTHERAPY

Our experience is that it works best when sessions can be two hours in length, typically once a week. Following the assessment, the first several sessions are usually just with the parents during which we discuss attachment-parenting principles and methods. Often it will work best for the family and child if the child is removed from school and at home with the primary caregiver. This allows for a safe, secure, and contained environment within which the attachment-facilitating parenting can be enacted. Many of these children often function at the developmental level of a toddler, and thus, keeping the child home to focus on building the attachment relationship is often most effective. The therapist will have to provide a letter to the school indicating that it is an essential and necessary part of treatment for the child to be home with the parent. However, since children with relationship challenges will often "try" to make schooling and schoolwork a battle, we want to remove as many obstacles to the parent-child relationship as possible. What is often actually going on is that the child may be comfortable with a degree of emotional distance in relationships with adults and so will act in a way to create an emotional tone in the relationship that the child is familiar with. Therefore, we do not want the parent to homeschool the child; rather, and to avoid power struggles between the child and parent, we recommend a tutor to work with the child on schoolwork. Upon receipt of the letter from the therapist, the school district will then provide a tutor. In New York, a tutor is provided two hours a day, five days a week. Although parents do worry about a child having to repeat a grade, we have found that in the last ten years only two or three children actually had to repeat the grade.

Our experience is that parents can be enormously creative in finding ways to stay home with their child. The federal Family Medical Leave Act allows a parent to take off up to twelve weeks a year to care for an ill family member. This is one helpful resource. The therapist can complete the necessary paperwork for the working parent, which the parent can get from his or her company's human resources department. Changing working hours, job-sharing, and switching shifts are just some of the creative ways families have made it work so that the primary caregiver could be at home with the child. Finally, many children have an adoption subsidy. The evaluation we provide is frequently used as the basis for changing the subsidy to either a special or extraordinary rate, which can also help a family allow the primary caregiver to stay home with the child.

Once parents are comfortably introduced to attachment-facilitating principles and expectations, typical sessions allow time to meet with the parents for twenty to thirty minutes alone, while the child is in an adjacent office connected by closed-circuit TV so that the child may be monitored for safety. During this part of the session we discuss the week and how the parents are doing. If a parent is experiencing difficulty, this time is extended. During the next sixty to ninety minutes the parents and therapist meet with the child. At the end, we may "debrief" with the parents, discussing the session and what was observed and the parents' experience of the session.

Many insurance companies will provide coverage for this treatment. Your therapist will probably have made arrangements with the company for this service, or the therapist may need to talk with a case manager to arrange coverage for this treatment.

This treatment approach can even be used in therapeutic foster homes, group homes, or residential treatment centers. You can find detailed descriptions of how this can be done in our other book, *Creating Capacity for Attachment* (Becker-Weidman & Shell, 2005).

DYADIC DEVELOPMENTAL PSYCHOTHERAPY

This section briefly describes Dyadic Developmental Psychotherapy, which is the basis for attachment-facilitating parenting. Most often children require both attachment-facilitating parenting and Dyadic Developmental Psychotherapy in order to heal. Dyadic Developmental Psychotherapy addresses the underlying trauma that continues to activate the child's negative internal working model. In addition, the therapy provides support and guidance for the parents so that they are able to effectively implement attachment-facilitating parenting interventions. When a parent's own history gets activated by the child and the results are not what the parent wants to occur, the therapist can assist the parent in managing those issues so that the parent is more effective and successful.

The findings on neurobiology and factors that resolve trauma strongly suggest that effective treatment requires an affectively attuned relationship. Siegel stated, "As parents reflect with their securely attached children on the mental states that create their shared subjective experience, they are joining with them in an important co-constructive process of understanding how the mind functions. The inherent feature of secure attachment—contingent, collaborative communication—is also a fundamental component in how interpersonal relationships facilitate internal integration in a child" (1999, p. 333). This has implications for the effective treatment of maltreated children. For example, when in a therapeutic relationship the child is able to reflect upon aspects of traumatic memories, and experience the affect associated with those memories without becoming dysregulated, the child develops an expanded capacity to tolerate increasing amounts of affect. The child learns to self-regulate. The attuned resonant relationship between child and therapist and child and caregiver enables the child to make sense (a left hemispheric function) out of memories, autobiographical representations, and affect (right hemispheric functions).

Dysregulation

When a child is dysregulated, the child is unable to accurately interpret the meaning of the current event or the intentions of the therapist and parent. A dysregulated child often acts as if he is being hurt, even though he is not. Maintaining emotion regulation is a goal of therapy, so that even while talking about and revisiting challenging interpersonal moments, the child is able to maintain a secure emotional balance. Dysregulation is the result of unresolved traumatizing experiences. Purposely dysregulating a child is to be avoided. Dysregulation does not help a child to integrate past traumas because the child experiences again, in the present time, feelings of rejection, abandonment, and hurt without the healing benefits of being within a secure, safe, nurturing relationship. It is the goal of therapy to encourage a child to experience his feelings without shame or fear. Sadness, anger, frustration, and grief are healthy expressions of past experience, yet many children confuse past treatment of themselves with current experience.

What distinguishes Dyadic Developmental Psychotherapy from other clinical work with children is the strong emphasis on maintaining an affectively attuned relationship with the child, a deep acceptance of the child's affect and experience, and greater emphasis on experience and process rather than on verbalization and content. The practice of Dyadic

Beginnings

31

Developmental Psychotherapy requires the therapist to become affectively attuned with the child, and to develop and maintain a meaningful emotional connection with the child, often at a nontraditional verbal and experiential level. Dyadic Developmental Psychotherapy is highly interactive, and therapists will demonstrate a greater use of self than, for example, Cognitive Behavioral Psychotherapy, behavioral approaches, or strategic or structural family therapy interventions. Closed doors and sessions in which the parent is not included are not productive; you can expect to participate in every session.

As you have read already, Dyadic Developmental Psychotherapy is an approach to treating trauma-attachment disordered children that is based on attachment theory (Bowlby, 1980, 1988) and the previously mentioned processes. This treatment seeks to repair the negative working model of such children, using experiential methods that have several important and overlapping dimensions: modeling the healthy attachment cycle, reducing shame, safe and nurturing physical contact that is containing, reexperiencing the affect associated with the trauma in order to integrate the experience and not dissociate, and the interpersonal regulation of affect. Maintaining an affectively attuned relationship with the child enacts these dimensions. Accepting the child's affect and more importantly the motivation behind the behavior or affect, which is the deeper affective meaning for the child, which is based on early experiences of trauma that created the child's current working model expressed in the present, is central to effective treatment and resolution of attachment difficulties. The use of curiosity and acceptance to uncover that deeper meaning is an important element of Dyadic Developmental Psychotherapy and the creation of a new meaning for the child in the present. These dimensions are also addressed through the use of eye contact, touch, tone of voice, cognitive restructuring, psychodramatic reenactments, and repeated implementations of the first year (needs) and second year (shame) attachment cycles. Goals of treatment include a capacity to affectively internalize their adoptive or foster parent's love, structuring, and nurturing, resulting in increased ability to tolerate affect without becoming dysregulated or dissociated and develop a more coherent sense of autobiographical memory, increased trust, and increased self-esteem.

Overall, successfully treated children will use their caregivers as a secure base for comfort from which they can explore their world. Behaviorally, such children exhibit lower levels of aggression, delinquent behaviors, thought disorders, depression, anxiety, and withdrawn behaviors. It is through the healthy internalization of the caregiver that the child comes to trust the caregiver and experience a desire to please the caregiver. This is the beginning of conscience and morality.

Dyadic Developmental Psychotherapy is a treatment developed by Daniel Hughes, PhD (Hughes, 2004, 2005, 2006, 2007). Its basic principles are described by Hughes (2005) and summarized as follows:

- A focus on both the caregivers' and therapists' own attachment strategies. Previous research (Dozier, 2001; Tyrell, 1999) has shown the importance of the caregivers' and therapists' state of mind for the success of interventions.
- Therapist and caregiver are attuned to the child's subjective experience and reflect this back to the child. In the process of maintaining an intersubjective attuned connection with the child, the therapist and caregiver help the child regulate affect and construct a coherent autobiographical narrative.
- Sharing of subjective experiences.
- Use of PACE and PLACE are essential to healing.
- Directly address the inevitable misattunements and conflicts that arise in interpersonal relationships.
- Caregivers use attachment-facilitating interventions.
- Use of a variety of interventions, including cognitive-behavioral strategies.

Dyadic Developmental Psychotherapy interventions flow from several theoretical and empirical lines. Attachment theory (Bowlby, 1980, 1988) provides the theoretical foundation for Dyadic Developmental Psychotherapy. Early trauma disrupts the normally developing attachment system by creating distorted internal working models of self, others, and caregivers. This is one rationale for treatment in addition to the necessity for sensitive caregiving. As O'Connor and Zeanah have stated, "A more puzzling case is that of an adoptive/foster caregiver who is 'adequately' sensitive but the child exhibits attachment disorder behavior; it would seem unlikely that improving parental sensitive responsiveness (in already sensitive parent) would yield positive changes in the parent-child relationship" (2003, p. 235). Treatment is necessary to directly address the rigid and dysfunctional internalized working models that traumatized children with attachment disorders have developed.

Current thinking and research on the neurobiology of interpersonal behavior (Siegel, 1999, 2001; Schore, 2001) is another part of the foundation on which Dyadic Developmental Psychotherapy rests.

The primary approach is to create a secure base in treatment (using techniques that fit with maintaining a healing PACE (Playful, Accepting, Curious, and Empathic) and at home using principles that provide safe structure and a healing PLACE (Playful, Loving, Acceptance, Curious, and Empathic). Developing and sustaining an attuned relationship within which contingent collaborative communication occurs helps the child heal. Coercive interventions such as rib-stimulation, holding-restraining a child in anger or to provoke an emotional response, shaming a child, using fear to elicit compliance, and interventions based on power/control and submission, and so on, are never used and are inconsistent with a treatment rooted in attachment theory and current knowledge about the neurobiology of interpersonal behavior (see ATTACh, 2006).

Frequently, the caregiver's autobiographical narrative is a focus of discussion. Effective parenting methods for children with trauma-attachment disorders require a high degree of structure and consistency, along with an affective milieu that demonstrates playfulness, love, acceptance, curiosity, and empathy (PLACE). During treatment caregivers receive support and are given the same level of attuned responsiveness that we wish the child to experience. Quite often caregivers feel blamed, devalued, incompetent, depleted, and angry. Parent support is an important dimension of treatment to help caregivers be more able to maintain an attuned connecting relationship with their child. Broadly speaking, the treatment with the child uses three categories of interventions: affective attunement, cognitive restructuring, and psychodramatic reenactments. Treatment with the caregivers also uses three categories of interventions: first, teaching effective parenting methods and helping the caregivers avoid power struggles; second, address-

---

Engagement

Two-year-old Billy is happily building a tower with blocks; he looks at you and smiles, you smile back, maybe make a positive comment about how tall the tower is. Billy experiences your approval and continues to build.

Disruption: Baby sister Debbie crawls too close and knocks the tower down. Billy throws a block at her. You pick up and soothe the baby while reprimanding Billy not to throw blocks. Billy starts to cry and kicks the blocks.

Interactive repair: You recognize that Billy was acting on his appropriate feelings, but with poor judgment on how to make it right again for himself. You comfort and soothe Billy, by validating his feelings (anger at Debbie for not being careful, or if it was intentional, validate that he felt it wasn't fair of her to knock down his tower). You tell him he can build another tower, and this time you'll help keep Debbie from crawling too close while he is building. You tell Billy that babies are tender and not to hurt her ever, no matter what, and then you help him to say he's sorry to his sister. Billy says he is sorry to Debbie, and you hug him and he hugs you and then he begins to build once again.

ing the parent's autobiographical narrative as this influences the parent's interactions with the child; and, third, maintaining the proper PLACE or attitude. Parents are encouraged to maintain a high degree of structure within the household, which provides physical and emotional safety for the child. Within this lovingly structured environment, the caregiver maintains a high degree of affective attunement that is nurturing and that repeatedly enacts the healthy attachment-cycle of engagement, disruption, and interactive-repair (Siegel, 2001; Schore, 2001).

Dyadic Developmental Psychotherapy focuses extensively on the nonverbal experiential level of interaction as a way of addressing negative internal working models and as a way of creating a safe and secure base from which the child can explore past trauma. While many treatments rely on empathy, attunement, acceptance, developing a coherent autobiographical narrative, psychodramatic reenactments and role-playing, and nonverbal processes, Dyadic Developmental Psychotherapy is unique in its use of these elements together as an integrated strategy to revise negative internal working models, develop a coherent autobiographical narrative, and foster the development of a secure and healthy attachment (Becker-Weidman & Hughes, 2008). The therapy is an affect-modulating therapy that combines elements of several recognized approaches into a unique reconfigured mix to address the severely dysregulating effects of traumatic, chronic maltreatment.

Coherent Autobiographical Narrative

Coherent Biographical Narrative is the unique story of one's life that is described in understandable and accurate terms. A healthy person is able to describe her life experiences in fairly accurate chronological order and includes both happy and sad aspects communicated in a coherent fashion. Many traumatized children do not have significant representation of their experiences, because no one was capable of reflecting with them about when, where, how, with whom, and what effect the circumstances of their lives had on their development. Healthy families use reflective stories to develop cohesion and bring meaning to the events of a child's life. These stories eventually help form a child's accurate sense of self.

Since much of the trauma took place at a preverbal stage of development, the child's reactions to unforeseen triggers require attention. Therapy involves careful noting of the emotions, behaviors, and cognitions associated with currently challenging situations, thereby creating an understanding that is shared between the therapist, the child, and the parents. For example, noting a child's expressed reluctance to bathe may "make sense" when understood from the child's perspective as being associated with pain. Helping the parent and child to engage deeper meanings, with acceptance and empathy, helps the child integrate the past experience. Movement from a negative association (fear-based) to one of sadness and grief results in an integration of past experience as discrete from current experience. Treatment interventions are designed to create experiences of safety and affective attunement so that the child is affectively engaged and can explore and resolve past trauma. This affective attunement is the same process used for nonverbal communication between a caregiver and child during attachment-facilitating interactions (Hughes, 2002; Siegel, 2001). The therapist's and caregivers' attunement results in co-regulation of the child's affect so that is it manageable. Cognitive restructuring interventions are designed to help the child develop secondary mental representations of traumatic events, which allow the child to integrate these events and develop a coherent autobiographical narrative. Treatment involves multiple repetitions of the fundamental caregiver-child attachment cycle. The cycle begins with shared affective experiences, is followed by a breach in the relationship (a separation or discontinuity), and ends with a reattunement of affective states. Nonverbal communication, involving eye contact, tone of voice, touch, and movement, are essential elements to creating affective attunement.

Affective (or Emotional) Attunement

Think of the quintessential picture of mutual love you see when a father cradles his infant on his knees. With eyes focused only on each other, this mutual gaze of adoration captures a timeless moment of unfettered love, depicting an emotional connection felt by both father and child. Think of your partner's emotional understanding of you at times when you are tired and worn down. Being emotionally in sync doesn't mean you have to feel the same way. It is the expressed support and understanding that is felt between us, communicated by supportive words and body language, affectionate hugs and supportive gestures (such as being given a cup of tea), or just an expressive look that lets you know you are understood and validated.

The treatment provided adhered to a structure with several dimensions. It is pictured in figure 2.1. First, behavior is identified and explored. The behavior may have occurred in the immediate interaction or have occurred at some time in the past. Second, using curiosity and acceptance the behavior is explored, and the meaning to the child begins to emerge. Third, empathy is used to reduce the child's sense of shame and increase the child's sense

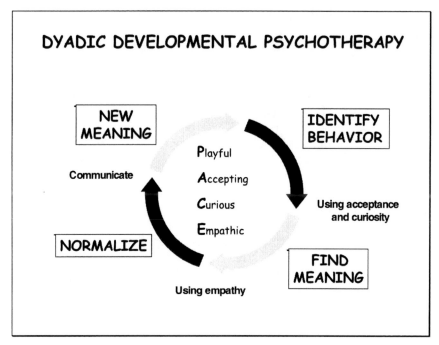

Figure 2.1.   Dyadic Developmental Psychotherapy

of being accepted and understood. Fourth, the child's behavior is normalized. In other words, once the meaning of the behavior and its basis in past trauma are identified, it becomes understandable that the symptom is present. Fifth, the child communicates this understanding to the caregiver. Sixth, finally, a new meaning for the behavior is found, and the child's actions are integrated into a coherent autobiographical narrative by communicating the new experience and meaning to the caregiver.

An example of such an interaction is the following:

Child: I kicked a hole in the door last night.

Therapist: What happened?

Mom: I told him he couldn't go out and ride his bike until he emptied the dishwasher.

C: It wasn't even raining anymore! She never lets me go out!

T: Wow. I see you got so angry when your mom asked you to empty the dishwasher. What made you so angry about that?

C: She's always mean to me and never lets me play. I hate her.

M: Do you really feel that way, sweetie?

C: (Looks at mom and mumbles) Yes.

T: Oh, I see . . . you thought mom was being mean and didn't want you to have fun or love you. Maybe it felt like when you were with your first family and you had to take care of yourself and your brother and baby sister almost all the time. You really didn't get to play much at all!

C: Yeah. I didn't think mom would let me go out. She'd just find more work for me to do, like she always does.

T: Wow. You were really worried. I can understand how hard that must have been for you when she'd give you so much work. Mom said to empty the dishwasher and you thought that you'd never get to ride your bike before it began to rain again.

C: Yeah. I hate work.

T: Mom, did you know he was so worried?

M: No, I didn't. Oh, honey, I just wanted you to take care of the dishes and then go out and spend the rest of the afternoon riding your bike! I promise I won't ever give you so much work that I forget to let you play.

C: (Looks at mom and nods head as she says this to him.)

T: I can see that you were worried your mom might forget you're a kid and need to ride your bike. In your first family you were so little and you had to do things for yourself and you didn't get to play, so maybe now you worry sometimes that will happen again . . .

Child: I hit my mom last night (looks down and away).

Therapist: What happened?

Mom: I just told her it was time to stop playing and to put her toys away.

T to Child: What happened?

C: She took my favorite doll and put it on the bookshelf and told me to stop playing . . . she never lets me play.

T: Wow, I see how you got so angry when your mom asked you to pick up your toys. What made you angry about that?

C: She's always mean to me and never lets me play. I hate her.

M: Do you really feel that way, sweetie?

C: (Looks at mom with a sad face and mumbles) Yes.

T: You thought she was being mean and didn't want you to have fun or love you. Maybe you thought she was going to take everything away and leave you like your first mom did, like when your first mom took your toys and then left you alone in the apartment that time.

C: She took my bestest doll and was going to keep it or get rid of it and I was so scared I'd never get it back and I got mad and I hit her and then bit her leg and now she's going to get rid of me, I heard her talking with the social worker this morning.

T: Oh, wow! You were really scared! Oh, I can really understand now how hard that must be for you when Mom said to clean up. You really felt mad and very scared. That must be so hard for you.

C: Yes, I get scared a lot.

T: Mom, did you know she was so scared?

M: No, I didn't. Oh, honey, I just put your doll on the bookshelf so it wouldn't get stepped on while we cleaned up.

C: Really?

M: Yes. I just called the social worker this morning to reschedule our appointment. You're my little girl. I love you . . .

Consequences

Right about now you might be wondering: Who fixes the hole in the door? Shouldn't he be punished for kicking the door? More on consequences later ,but for now, keep in mind the following: One can make a child do almost anything, if enough force is used. The point of parenting and creating a healing PLACE is to help a child feel safe by creating a safe base from which the child can explore and internalize a sense of right and wrong.

Past traumas are revisited by reading documents and through psychodramatic reenactments. These interventions, which occur within a safe attuned relationship, allow the child to integrate the past traumas and to understand the past and present experiences that create the feelings and thoughts associated with the child's behavioral disturbances. The child develops secondary representations of these events, feelings, and thoughts that result in greater affect regulation and a more integrated autobiographical narrative.

As described by Hughes (2006, 2002), the therapy is an active, affect modulated experience that involves acceptance, curiosity, empathy, and playfulness. By co-regulating the child's emerging affective states and developing secondary representations of thoughts and feelings, the child's capacity to affectively engage in a trusting relationship is enhanced. The expectation is that the parents will enact these same principles. If parents have difficulty engaging with their child in this manner, then sessions with just parents are indicated.

ATTACHMENT STYLES

Attachment behaviors are actually the strategies a child has developed (based on prior experience) to receive help and safety and to modulate the child's interpersonal relationships to secure comfort and security. These are biologically primed behaviors meant to protect the child from perceived harm. Infants and little children may be afraid of many things, some of which warrant concern and caution. Some of what may elicit fear in a child is not actually harmful, and by watching your reaction, your child will learn what is and isn't dangerous. Little children perceive and feel the parent's response to situations without words. Parents regulate children's emotions in a physiological dance that is biologically protective by teaching what to fear and how to respond accordingly through the nonverbal sharing of emotion.

You have probably noted how difficult it can be to persuade a frightened child to overcome a particular fear. A child frightened by the need for an injection may cry and cling to you for protection. Even though your calm, reassuring words may not remove the immediate fear, over time the dread will be reduced to dislike, a response much less upsetting and much more tolerable. Now picture a child who does not cry or cling to you for support because past experience with parents has proven that going to a parent doesn't reduce discomfort and fear. In fact for an abused child, using the biologically primed response (moving closer to the parent for safety) is negated, and the child has no reliable way to reduce the fear. Without understanding the underlying reasons causing this child to resort to name-calling, running wildly, throwing things around the doctor's office, a very unhelpful response might be elicited from the adults in charge, furthering the child's belief that adults don't help.

It may help you to think about your child's personal attachment style/ habit of responding to fearful situations. Remember that *to your child*, things like waking up to an empty house, being hungry for days without relief, wearing a dirty diaper until an infection has set in, being hit, isolated, be-rated, and so forth, have changed even the most potentially benign daily occurrences into a fear of potential maltreatment. Your child is always ready for trouble. Scanning the environment for signs of impending abuse is now a habitual way of life.

So, what if you've provided your child with an abuse-free environment, routines, suggestions for success, friendly reminders, stickers, incentives, and she or he has not stopped looking for trouble, inciting arguments, fights, bullying, "pushing buttons." What else is there to do?

Okay, let's understand how your child responds to experiences. When a baby has an experience, whether it be a physical experience (gas pain, teething, tired, hungry, cold, wet) or an emotional one (lonely, frightened, happy, excited), ideally the attuned caregiver responds accordingly, thereby regulating the baby's physical and emotional experience. Actually, these processes are so connected that it's not really accurate to separate the physical from the emotional experiences! When happiness is regulated (picture your corresponding smile, making baby sounds, picking the baby way up in the air), the baby experiences releases of hormones that contribute to a sense of well-being and joy *with* you. Similarly, the baby's experience of discomfort requires your attuned response to prevent escalation and terror. You actually co-regulate the baby's emotions by the way you respond and tend to the baby's experience. You cocreate meaning of these experiences, thereby developing an authentic narrative for the baby to use to develop a sense of self, self with other (you), and self in the world. The baby's brain responds with neuron activity, growing a brain that will be appropriately endowed with responses to situations encountered in the course of living each day. Dysregulation occurs when there is not an attuned response from a caregiver, and so the baby tries to mitigate these physical and emotional experiences, alone.

Attachment styles are descriptions of organized behavioral strategies, usually recognized as patterns of responses to a perceived threat, be it the result of inaccurate/inappropriate response to the baby's subjective experience, or fear requiring an attuned caregiver's response (to reclaim safety). These strategies do not indicate mental illness. All of us have strategies to help ourselves cope with stress, or threats such as fear and illness, or loss. If your child has experienced appendicitis and surgery, for example, the next few stomachaches in the same abdominal vicinity will most likely result in your worried child coming to you for comfort and resolution. It makes "sense" that your child would become anxious and seek you out for help. Methods for "seeking you out" depend largely on your child's past experiences getting help. A child with a preoccupied attachment style may not initially go directly to you for help, instead becoming whiny, clingy, or irritable without verbalizing the actual problem. An avoidant attachment style is characterized as a child using distraction such as wanting to stay up longer, play longer, or refusing to be with you even though you invite the same routines as usual. These strategies developed from previous experience with a caregiver during times of discomfort; their origins are thought to be the result of the ways in which the child coped with the caregiver's response during times of distress. The goal of the strategy was to reduce the discomfort. If no caregiver was available (either physically or emotionally), the child developed coping strategies that may still be applied by the child during times of stress.

In similar fashion to the child who had endured an appendectomy, your child's prior experience with maltreatment can be triggered by anything that reminds or is similar to experiences that resulted in pain (physical or emotional). As you may know firsthand, these responses can seemingly come "out of nowhere," they may be way out of proportion to what you recognize as a rather benign situation, and they can endure for hours to days at a time. A baby who did not have an attuned caregiver to help regulate his emotions can become a child who does not know how to "use" you to get relief. The child's brain may quickly respond as if an emergency has occurred. In fact, such a child may be afraid of you if his prior experience was that his caregiver was frightening or frightened and unable to respond to him.

Knowing your child's typical style of coping will help you to "read" what's going on so that you can respond appropriately to the underlying need—not necessarily to the expressed behavior. Resolution of past traumatic or habitually inappropriate responses to the child's dependency needs requires you to respond to your child's distress, as your child perceives it. By helping your child identify and validate the emotional experience motivating the response, you help reduce fear, anxiety, and isolation. Bruce Perry (Perry, Pollard, Blakely, Baker & Vigilante, 1995) describes how states (environmental and relational) become traits (internalized expectations) without our explicit memories remembering what happened, or how, over time, a pattern of experience and coping developed. A child's brain develops in a "use dependent" fashion (Perry, Pollard, Blakely, Baker & Vigilante, 1995). Thus, a child's anxious attachment style may be describing how, over time, the ways in which the child was responded to have become evident in the child's tendency to isolate, or to use methods of distraction (counting, ordering objects), or complain about headaches or tummy aches. Such tendencies describe how your child has adapted.

BEHAVIORS REPRESENT ADAPTIVE TENDENCIES

Once useful, now problematic because they are no longer adaptive to this relationship, behaviors that wreak havoc can be understood in terms of a child's inability to reconfigure his internal working model of the world, especially the value and safety of parents. Your child has not yet changed his view of parents as hurtful, and that is why he mistrusts your good intentions. This is a visceral, emotional understanding, not a cognitive one that can be taught like the multiplication tables can be taught. He hears your requests very differently than you intended. This can catch a parent off guard, and can trigger one's own emotional response. How your own self-worth developed out of your own life experiences created the belief that you could be a good parent in the first place. Or maybe, like so many parents who have inadvertently adopted hurt children, you hadn't given much thought to how parenting such a child would be different than one who had appropriate beginnings. Can you still remember when you used to pride yourself on your ability to interact with children and how much they liked you? Hadn't you thought of yourself as a collaborative, competent adult? Your angry reaction to the child who wreaks havoc when misinterpreting your intentions is likely based on your sense of self as failing with this child. Herein lies the danger; your child will attempt to elicit the emotions that replicate past abuse. You are in a sense a pawn in his daily routine, because he does not see or know otherwise. One minute you are giving him a new toy and nice things to eat, and the next you are demanding that he clean up a mess. He can't trust you. You make him uncomfortable, "just like" that other parent. Because he doesn't know what is appropriate and what isn't, what is safe and what isn't, and he doesn't have any basis for recognizing someone who cares for him more than anything in the world, he lashes out with the same intensity whether you ask him to brush his teeth (appropriate request) or go sleep outside with the dog while mommy goes away for the night (inappropriate).

Your child's attachment styles will tell a story about how he was cared for as an infant. Even if you aren't able to learn about your child's history of neglect and abuse, his current behavior will represent past experience. Behavior represents the child's emotional beliefs and expectations about the world and his place in it. This can be enormously helpful when living with a child whose misattuned responses to ordinary daily living is so out of sync with what is actually occurring. Any time there is an emotional response out of sync with what is actually occurring or intended, you can bet there is something going on for your child that his mind is recalling from past experience. Remembering that it isn't you who is requesting something inappropriate but that your child is hearing something different than you intended can help you to pause, get a hold of the underlying emotion and what it represents, and respond in a supportive manner.

So, what if asking your child to empty the dishwasher before dinner is responded to with swears, refusal, kicking the door, and threats to break every glass? And, to make things more confusing, yesterday he did it without any complaining. You've been busy all afternoon helping your child with an art project you specially organized because you know how much your child likes to do it, and then you skipped your tea to clean up, get dinner, and arrange tomorrow's snacks for your youngest child's school trip. All you ask of your child is to empty the dishwasher, and that's the thanks you get!

Now, it wasn't a mistake to ask your child to do his task. The mistake is in assuming that he will want to thank you for your efforts today by doing something for you, and do it without a fuss. The mistake is in connecting his current refusal (and inappropriate behavior) to him not appreciating what you did for him all day long. You have an understanding of relationships that implies reciprocity. Your child has no such experience, because such an understanding is only developed from having had many, many, many experiences of loving responses to his early dependency needs; his love for his parent would have naturally flowed from him to her as she lovingly cared for his bodily needs. Her coos as she diapered him, kisses, smiles, and tickles would have made him feel so special to her. When he was a few months old he would have begun to respond by smiling back, showing her how much he enjoyed her playful attention and careful ministrations. So, without any overt expectation of reciprocity he would have naturally begun to "give back," and the beautiful mother/baby dance would have developed into a collaborative, safe, dependable relationship so that years later, asking him to do his task would not be met with such vehement objections or disconnection from your experiences and feelings about having spent so much energy on doing something nice for him. When your child acts inappropriately to your requests, don't make the mistake of assuming he doesn't appreciate what you did all day for him. He might very much, or he might not if he was not emotionally available to experience what you thought he would enjoy. Either way, you will only feel worse if you attribute his misbehavior as a sign of you not having pleased him and him not appreciating what a good mom, or dad, you are. The problem is that feeling worse about yourself, or giving negative attribution to his actions, impedes your ability to respond in a helpful manner.

A helpful concept to connect to current interactions might be to think about a healthy mother caring for her infant: even though yesterday he enjoyed being naked on the blanket after his bath, for some reason, today he is screaming and it is clear to her that he isn't enjoying any part of it. Getting angry with him, telling him she set it all up for him because she thought he would like it and he doesn't appreciate all that she does for him isn't the response that's needed.

Figuring out how to comfort your child and restore his sense of safety and feeling cared for is the primary helpful response. Being perplexed is fine, but obviously anger has no place in the development of trust, communication (the baby is telling you something), or current need. Giving negative attributions to your child's actions is more about what you might be feeling at the moment, not about your child's actual experience.

The following is an abusive supermarket scenario depicting inaccurate attributions placed onto a child by a tired, needy caregiver. A little girl, about four years old, was sitting in the metal shopping cart chewing on a plastic toy as her mother hastily grabbed items. It was getting late, and the girl was tired and hungry. As the cart swung around the aisle, she reached for a bag of cookies. She upset the display, dropped her toy, and began to cry loudly. Her mother, tired, hungry, and overwhelmed herself, lashed out at the little girl. "You never take care of anything I get you! If you don't want that I'll just give it to someone who will. Now look what you did! Sit still if you know what's good for you. I got to finish shopping you (ungrateful, troublemaking) little b——."

Clearly this parent missed many cues her child gave. With accurate expectations of her child's developmental needs and appropriate proactive responses, she could have avoided the negative scene and made shopping together a reasonably enjoyable experience. This mother also attributed inaccurate motivation to her child's actions, most likely based on her own unresolved needs and issues, as well as emotional vulnerability due to her own hunger and fatigue.

When parenting a child with relationship deficits, it is imperative to plan for the "worst" all the time. Much like parenting a two-year-old, it is proactive to build in lots of extra time between activities. If you try to squeeze in too much to suit your schedule and if it backfires when your little one (and he's still your little one even if he is eleven!) poops his pants, has a tantrum, spills the juice, breaks the plant, then it is better to remind yourself that your expectations didn't match his capabilities, rather than to blame him, tell him he knows better, or that he didn't take your needs into account.

You've got to become your own fan club; don't expect your child to praise your efforts to please him, or to notice when you could really use a break because you've bent over backwards doing for him all day long. He's really still very little, and he will not be capable of connecting what you've done earlier in the day with how he feels right now. He doesn't know when his feelings will erupt, or why yesterday he was able to accept your requests without a fight and today he isn't. He doesn't even remember how he felt this morning, let alone yesterday. His emotional experiences aren't connected the way yours are; much of the time the way he feels is out of his awareness. This is his protective adaptation still in activation, even though it is no longer useful (no maltreating environment), and it prevents him from interacting in an appropriate manner and according to current living circumstances.

It will take a long time, perhaps longer than you think, to change a hurt child's mind (by literally growing new neural pathways) and to mend and rebuild your child's trust. It isn't crazy to want a reciprocal relationship with your child; all parents want and expect this once their child is mature. From science we know the way to build empathic relationships is by showing your child (by the way you treat him), every day and as often as you can, that you accept his needs as valid and real.

It isn't only this relationship with your child that can benefit from a new attitude about others' motivation. Giving others the best possible attributions for their behavior reduces the chance of compounding a conflict with meanings that don't apply. This frees you to feel your feelings, for example, feeling disappointment that your husband forgot the ice cream, without adding to the mess by attributing his forgetfulness as proof he no longer cares for you.

For therapy to be helpful and effective, problematic affect is not avoided. It is brought into awareness, and then set within a new context of meaning. Parental cradling, touch, and playful interventions can help create a sense of safety. Many children who have experienced chronic and severe maltreatment have a disorganized attachment and Reactive Attachment Disorder. Such children experience ambivalence and exhibit disorganized behavior in the presence of their parents, the secure base. The reasons for this have been previously cited in the work of Main and Hesse (1990); the source of safety is also the source of threat. This simultaneous activation of the fight-flight system and the attachment system results in disorganized behavior. Now that you have a framework for continuing to help your child, you can move on to the next chapter about logistics. That chapter describes specific activities and actions you may find helpful, all within the framework this chapter presented. We've described why a thorough evaluation is important and what are its elements. You've read about selecting a therapist and what Dyadic Developmental Psychotherapy has to offer as an evidence-based, effective, and empirically validated treatment. Now, let's move on to describing more of what you and your family can do at home.

3

The Details

Arthur Becker-Weidman and Deborah Shell

This chapter will describe some of the details and practical aspects of providing attachment-facilitating parenting in the home. We will describe how to set up your home, how to manage being with your child 24/7 while the child is out of school, and a model day with activities and suggestions. We don't expect you to follow this outline in a rigid sort of way. It is provided so that you get some idea of what your day might look like and activities to do and avoid doing.

BEGINNINGS

Reading, Getting Support, Taking Care of Yourself

Reading, getting support, and finding ways to nourish yourself are important first steps. Have a plan in place to keep yourself rested, recharged, and nourished. Therapeutic parenting and maintaining a healing PLACE is very demanding work, physically, emotionally, and intellectually. You cannot give what you do not have. If you are depleted, burned out, and feeling defeated, you will not be able to provide the kind of nurturing, attuned, positive emotionally healthy home that your child needs.

Reading

You've already started on your journey and have brought along one very important provision: this book! You can also look in the resource section for a variety of useful materials. But to begin with, we recommend that you read the chapter about parenting in *Creating Capacity for Attachment*, edited by Arthur Becker-Weidman and Deborah Shell (2005/2009), and the chapters written by parents in that book. Reading about other parents' experiences will help you recognize that you are not alone and that others have successfully gone down the path you are embarking upon.

A second book to read is *Building the Bonds of Attachment*, second edition, by Daniel Hughes (2006). This book tells the story of a child who is born into a maltreating home and her journey from a healthy newborn to a child with a severe disorder of attachment to a healed child. The book aptly describes how a child comes to have a disorder of attachment because of severe and chronic maltreatment. The book then goes on to describe how a child heals in a home and how important is the parenting and healing PLACE. The book underscores the importance of the parent being able to reflect on his or her own use of self, on the parent's own family of origin and how this can be both a source of strength and difficulty for the parent.

A third book is the Association for the Treatment and Training in the Attachment of Children's *Therapeutic Parenting Manual* (2008). It has some very specific and helpful suggestions.

These three books, in addition to this book, will give you a very good foundation for the work you are beginning, helping your child heal.

Getting Support

Therapeutic parenting is very demanding, both physically and emotionally. One vital aspect of being prepared for this work is making sure you have support in place. Supports can include your partner and relatives. You might want your relatives and friends to take a look at some of the materials in this book or suggest that they read *Building the Bonds of Attachment*. It is reasonable to expect that your friends and family, who want to help, get a basic foundation in how they can help effectively. Your child's difficulties, how these developed, and what is necessary to help heal your child are important for them to understand if they are to be real supports. Family members and friends who criticize you, second guess you, and are not with you should be avoided for now. You can let them know what you need, and if they are not able to do that, let them know that, for now at least, it is best if they don't have contact with you or your child. You love them, they love you, everyone loves everyone else, but for now, they need to not be a part of your family's life because they will be a drain on you and undercut your work. In this regard you and your partner need to be one solid united front.

The Internet can be a good source of support. There are many websites that have information for parents of children with trauma-attachment disorders. Some are excellent, others terrible. Good sites do not denigrate children. They do not refer to children as "RADishes," which implies that the child is the diagnosis; rather, the child's behavior is a reflection of a deeply painful set of experiences that cause the child to act "as if" the child is still living in a chaotic, dangerous, and neglectful home. Sites that advocate control and submission solely for the sake of compliance should also be avoided. One can make a child do almost anything, if enough force is used. The point of parenting and creating a healing PLACE is to help a child feel safe by creating a secure base from which the child can explore and internalize a sense of right and wrong.

Taking Care of Yourself

Taking care of yourself is vital if you are to be successful in this endeavor. When children heal, we'd guess that 80 percent of the credit goes to the parents' efforts. That means you have to find a way to stay rested, recharged, and in balance. You must find a way to recharge your emotional batteries when you begin to feel depleted. Reading helps, Internet chat sites help, family supports are vital. You may find support among friends, members of local support groups, and from your priest, rabbi, imam, or minister and among the members of your congregation, church, or mosque.

What is it that you used to do for fun that you've given up? Was it taking a thirty-minute walk each day? Knitting, quilting, going to the gym, gardening, woodworking, what? Bring that back into your life. Think about what nourishes you and helps you to feel whole and be sure to make that a part of your day, week, and life on a regular basis. Taking fifteen minutes each day to have a cup of tea, a soak in the tub, watch the news . . . you need to find a space and time each day to help you recharge. This is where a partner can be so important by providing you the emotional, physical, and time support you need.

Another way to take care of yourself is having your child go to the child's room between seven and eight each night. Obviously, you cannot make the child go to sleep . . . that tends to be self-correcting anyway since if there is a regular wake-up time, the child will gradually fall into a healthier pattern. The early bedtime is for you, so that you have some time at the end of the day to relax, pay bills, reconnect with your partner, or do whatever. After a full day of therapeutic parenting in which you are mindful of each interaction, considering the feelings that are driving the behavior of your child and yourself, you will be pretty tired and worn out. The child can read in her bedroom, draw, play with a toy, or just lie in bed. The idea is that this is the child's quiet time, and your recharge time.

Okay, so what if the child is noisy or repeatedly wants to leave the room? First off, one of the tools that we've found helpful for parents and children is to have an alarm on the child's bedroom door, one that operates with a key and magnetic contacts. This will let you know when your child leaves the room; you can relax and not worry or wonder whether the child is wandering or waking up in the middle of the night getting into trouble. As you may know, many children who have been molested and who experience Post-Traumatic Stress Disorder symptoms often have difficulty sleeping. They have difficulty falling asleep, they may frequently wake up in the middle of the night, and they may be restless light sleepers. We find that many such children actually sleep better when there is an alarm on their door. They seem to feel safer knowing that no one can sneak in without their (and your) knowledge. So, if the alarm goes off because the child is scared, threatened, or overly anxious, you would naturally soothe the child. But, what if the child is purposely setting off the alarm for some reason? Well, first you need to understand the feelings driving the behavior. By now you should know that our approach focuses on uncovering the emotions driving or motivating the behavior and not focusing only on the surface behavior. So, your response will be driven by what is causing the child's behavior. If the child is angry because the child does not want to be in the room, you will still need to uncover what is making the child angry. Is it that the child thinks you are mean? That you don't care about the child? That this reminds the child of times the birth parent abandoned the child? In each instance you may respond in a different manner. The scared child needs comfort and security. The angry child who perceives you as mean and not caring needs reassurance and empathy. The child who is reminded of being abandoned needs empathy and help seeing the difference between the there and then experiences of abandonment and the here and now experiences in this family . . . you did come and respond. The child who is fearful of intimacy or threatened by it and who opens the door to "make you mad" needs a calm parent who is not pushed away and who can maintain the healing place. In all instances, a calm reassuring presence can help. You might then involve the child in an activity that you were going to have to do anyway, so that you are not feeling annoyed about the "intrusion" into "your time." For example, you might enlist the child who cannot sleep and who comes out of the room to help you clean the bathroom or kitchen, fold laundry, put away dishes, and so on; whatever chore you'd have to do and for which you'd appreciate the help can work well to calm an anxious child. We will talk more about repairing relationships and natural consequences in later sections of this book.

LET'S GET GOING

So, let's now assume that you have a therapist and you've been coached in attachment-facilitating parenting. You've read this and other books and are ready to begin. The first step is to organize and set up your home and your child's room. The basic principle is to protect the child from being hurt or hurting others, just like you would protect any child. However, the home should be managed and arranged around the child's developmental age, not the child's chronological age. This is one reason a good assessment is important. Many children are significantly younger developmentally than their chronological age; this is one of the effects of Complex Trauma (Becker-Weidman, 2009).

We often hear the question, should we parent this child differently than the others? Is that fair? Or should we parent all our kids the same? The answer is yes! Our experience is that you can use attachment-facilitating parenting principles to parent all your children or just use what we will be describing here for the child you have in treatment. Whatever is more comfortable for you. We find that if you parent all the children the same way, your children who do not have attachment disorders will understand that your parenting determinations regarding each child's ability to handle privileges are based on each child's capacity, not necessarily chronological age, and when capacity is assessed accurately, they will handle the expectations and responsibilities that come with the preferred activity as you hoped. If not, helping them along by using natural consequences generally promotes skill-building no differently than the way they learned all the other skills they now possess; they'll want to contribute and comply not out of fear of punishment, but because it feels good to do what is good for oneself, for family members, friends, and community. It feels good to belong to a healthy society.

Let's summarize the basic parenting principles that promote healing:

1. Create a healing PLACE.
2. Parent the child based on the child's developmental age.
3. Avoid power struggles by controlling the relationship without being controlling (no threats, bribes, force).
4. You set the rhythm, tone, and PACE of the relationship.
5. The positive concordant intersubjective sharing of experience is your key to success. Maintaining a positive emotional relationship with your child despite the child's fear of intimacy is essential.

PLACE

Now you know what to consider when creating a healing PLACE. PLACE is also the essential relational ingredient and describes the overall therapeutic, interactional theme present in attachment-facilitating parenting. Being playful, loving, accepting (of the underlying feelings and of what is driving the behavior), curious, and empathic are your keys to success. Being playful is one way to maintain a positive loving emotional tone in your family.

Being playful *shows* that you love and enjoy your child. Sarcastic, mocking, derisive, or snide communication does not maintain a positive emotional tone or demonstrate that the child is loved and lovable, even if the behavior is not. Being loving is essential to healing a hurt child. The child has been damaged by abuse, neglect, and a variety of experiences that have taught the child to believe that the child is not loved, lovable, valued, or valuable. Accepting the child and what is driving the behavior is a major element of being a therapeutic parent. If you only try to address and control the surface behavior you may end up in a battle to secure compliance. While you may win that battle and get the child to capitulate, you will lose the more important "war" of healing a hurt child and helping that child experience a close intimate loving relationship. By going deeper and addressing what is driving the behavior you will be more effective in the end. Addressing only the surface behavior is a lot like playing that arcade game "Wack-a-Mole" in which more moles keep popping up . . . the only way to make the moles stop is to shut down the underlying mechanism. Curiosity refers to asking questions in order to develop empathy. The idea is to ask questions so that you come to understand what is really underlying the child's behavior. While your child may look angry, often what is driving the behavior is fear. While lying may look sneaky and deceitful, it is often driven by overwhelming shame. Shame causes one to want to hide. Lying is just another way of hiding. The point is that when you understand (have empathy for) what is causing the child's behavior, when you are able to identify the underlying emotion driving the behavior, then how you feel about the child will reflect this understanding. Then, your behavior is much more likely to be therapeutic because you are addressing the motivating feelings the child needs help to manage. The meaning we ascribe to behaviors influences our reactions; we feel differently toward a "liar" than toward a person who is feeling bad, defective, unlovable, and full of shame. We feel differently toward a child who is "angry and violent" than toward a child who is terrified.

Developmental Age

A child's chronological age is easy to determine. A child's developmental age is more difficult. No responsible parent would expect a four- or five-year-old to function like a fifth grader. What an eleven-year-old is capable of is far beyond what any four- or five-year-old can reasonably be expected to manage. But how often have you thought that your eleven-year-old is acting like a four-year-old? Perhaps you became annoyed and wanted your child to just "grow up and act his or her age." Many children who have experienced chronic maltreatment, neglect, and abuse are developmentally stunted and are functioning like a toddler or young child and not like their chronological age (Becker-Weidman, 2009). Tests like the Vineland Adaptive Behavior Scales–II can demonstrate that. Most of the children we see have developmental ages that are substantially lower than their chronological ages. A pattern we frequently see is that not only is the child's ability to communicate delayed, but in addition, the child's receptive developmental age is often notably lower than the child's expressive developmental age. This is a very important issue since one usually speaks with another at the same "level" that the other speaks to you. What this means is that it may often be the case that your explanations or requests are "over the head" of your child and so what looks like oppositional and defiant behavior may, at times, actually be caused by the child's just not understanding. (Another reason to respond to what is driving the behavior and not merely respond to the surface behavior.)

Responding to the child and treating the child at the child's developmental level will often eliminate many sources of argument, fights, and bad feelings. You will find that the child is more successful, less stressed, and that you feel more competent and loving. Treating the child at the child's developmental age, regardless of the child's chronological age, is protective and will help avoid putting the child into situations in which the child gets into trouble. Asking a three-year-old to do the laundry alone is just asking for trouble, regardless of the fact that the child might be chronologically eleven years old. Keeping a developmentally young child nearby will eliminate many typical problems such as "stealing," "lying," and "sneaking." Toddlers left with a plate of cookies or candy will take one, but we generally don't call that stealing. A five-year-old may not see you looking and deny that they spilled juice out of fear and shame. A four-year-old may touch a pretty object that he has been told not to because the child was left alone with the tempting object; we generally don't define that as sneaky, but as typical four-year-old behavior. Seeing the child at the child's developmental age can dramatically change how you define behavior, which will have a profound effect on how you feel and then on how you act. Sippy cups, brushing the child's teeth, washing the child, dressing the child, playing "momma bird and baby bird" and feeding the child cut up grilled cheese, rocking, snuggling on the couch while reading a story, playing a variety of "young child" games, and other such activities are all appropriate for developmentally young children. The essential point is to treat the child at the child's developmental age and to not shame or force the child to succeed in activities he isn't ready to do alone.

Control without Being Controlling

One of the biggest challenges facing a parent of a child with a disorder of attachment is how to maintain a positive emotional connection with the child and not let the child's fear of intimacy control the relationship. Controlling the relationship without being controlling is one of your keys to success. In other words, you set the rhythm, tone, and pace of the relationship by having the child respond to you. This is also an effective way of avoiding power struggles, arguments, and nonproductive interactions. So, how do you do this? First, it is necessary to begin thinking about the process, rhythm, and tone of each interaction as more important than the content. Think about the process of interaction. Who is responding to whom? Who is leading and who is following? Who is setting the emotional tone? Who is asking the questions and who is answering? Once you begin to be able to view the process, then you will be better able to effectively intervene. One effective way to do that is to be the one to ask questions. Another is to avoid being "pinned down" when it is unnecessary to be pinned down. Finally, not all questions need immediate answers; often a reflective stance will be most beneficial and helpful to your child

Let's consider the following example. Your ten-year-old has just said he wants to go to a friend's home. You feel this is not a good idea at this point for several reasons. What do you do?

Child: I want to go to Jimmy's house now.

Parent: You really want to see him, don't you? What do you like about Jimmy?

Child: Well, can I?

Parent: Wow, you really want to go. What do you like about going to Jimmy's house?

Child: His mom lets us play video games and she's hardly around to bother us like you do.

Parent: You don't like it when I watch what you and your friends do? Why do you think I do that?

Child: Because you are mean.

Parent: That must be really hard for you to feel I am mean to you. Hmmm . . . what's that like?

Child: I don't like it . . . why do you have to be so mean anyway?

Parent: What makes you feel I am mean?

Child: You never let me do what I want. You don't want me to have fun. You hate me.

Parent: This must be so hard for you to feel I hate you. It must be really, really sad and probably makes you angry.

Child: Yes, it does.

Parent: What would make me want to make you miserable?

Child: I don't know, why?

Parent: I have some ideas about what may make you feel this way; do you want to know what they are?

Child: Yes.

Parent: I think you spent so many years living in homes where no one paid attention to you and where you did whatever you wanted to do, where no one watched over you and helped keep you safe, that it must get confusing for you to have a parent who does watch over you.

Child: But why can't I go to Jimmy's house.

Parent: That's a good question, what do you think?

Child: I don't know, because his mom doesn't watch us?

Parent: What happened last time you were there?

Child: You mean when we got in trouble for breaking the neighbor's windows?

Parent: Yes, I feel badly for you when you get in trouble. I don't want you getting into trouble and feeling bad. You sure felt bad that day, remember?

Child: Yes, I was scared when the cops came.

Parent: I just want to be sure you have fun and are safe: both.

You can see a number of processes going on here. First, the parent accepts the child's view and with curiosity, comes to understand it better and help the child go deeper. By asking questions to try to understand the child, the parent avoids being pinned down and made to be "mean" or to say no. In the end both parent and child have a better understanding of each other; a fight is avoided and they have come to know the other's thinking and feelings more deeply.

Positive Intersubjective Experiences and Attunement

Attunement is merely another word for being emotionally sensitive and in tune with your child. This is the main vehicle for healing. By being attuned to your child's inner emotional life you will be better able to respond to the emotions driving the behavior. This will allow you to reframe words, feelings, and actions in a more positive way. In the above example, the parent was attuned to the child's past experiences and how these may still be affecting the child. The parent used that understanding to stay connected to the child and reframe the attacks as fear based and therefore could respond in a sensitive rather than defensive manner. Instead of arguing with the child that the parent is not mean . . . the parent explored the child's perception and came to a better understanding. Instead of just saying "no" to the child's initial request, the attuned parent knew that there was something deeper going on and began to explore that in a sensitive and responsive manner.

A broader and even more useful concept is intersubjectivity. This refers to shared emotions (attunement), shared intentions, and shared attention. Maintaining positive intersubjectivity that is concordant will be most therapeutic. When an interaction isn't going well, it is helpful to figure out where the mismatch is occurring. Consider the following three dimensions of an intersubjectve experience: Let's say you're playing a game with your child. All seems well, and then all of a sudden your child throws over the board and storms out screaming, "It's not fair!" What went wrong? You both seemed to be having fun (shared emotions), both were focused on the game (shared attention), but maybe your intentions were not concordant or congruent. You may have wanted to play the game to have fun with your child, not caring who wins or loses, just enjoying time with your child. Your child may be playing to win. For your child, winning or losing may influence your child's self-esteem and self-concept. Losing may cause the child to feel bad and that you are mean. Knowing this, you now can create positive concordant intersubjective experiences by playing games that don't have a win/lose element. In this instance, your choice of activities can be thoughtfully made to enhance positive interactions between you and your child; for the time being, win/lose games would be eliminated until your child can associate winning or losing as discrete events not representative of self-worth. Many young children aren't able to "see" their behavior as something separate from self-worth; remember, you can help structure your child's day with activities that match the child's developmental capacities. When you do that, you are creating, with your child, opportunities to experience the three healing elements of intersubjectivity.

Repair of Relationship

There will inevitably be ruptures in any relationship. Misunderstandings can lead to hurtful words and hurtful actions. It is *after* the deeper meaning is uncovered that the attuned parent helps the child repair the damage to the relationship that the child's words or actions caused. This is an important component of healing. It helps the child move from a pervasive sense of shame (I am a bad, unlovable child . . . I must lie about this, or hide . . .) to being able to experience healthy guilt (I am a good child, I am loved, I made a mistake, help me fix this). Taking the time to teach your child how healthy parents help their children repair the relationship after emotional distancing behaviors have been expressed (a product of shame) goes a long way toward creating healing opportunities in which your child can experience feeling deeply understood and cherished . . . even the bad feelings. An important part of therapeutic parenting is the creation of opportunities for relationship repair to occur over and over again; this demonstrates your unconditional regard for the child. It is not connected to performance. Positive regard becomes a product of the relationship between you and your child; eventually, it will become internalized by the child as a representation of your love, affecting the child's concept of self as lovable. Repair of the relationship means helping the child do something to fix the damage. It is more than just saying "sorry." In fact, saying sorry may not even be necessary and may be counterproductive. Actions speak louder than words. Repairing the relationship means doing something that makes the "victim" feel better. It is not about punishment, retribution, compliance, or control. This means that if the child likes and even enjoys the repair action, so much the better; the child is more likely to do it. Remember, repairing the relationship is about making you feel better so that the past damage is in the past, and you get over it and can reconnect with your child. A few examples may serve to clarify this concept:

A six-year-old girl kicks her mother and leaves a bruise. After the incident is explored and the underlying emotions and meaning are uncovered, then repair of the relationship and "consequences" can occur. In this instance, maybe having the child give the mom a foot massage would help the mom feel better and allow the child to repair the hurt.

One mom I know will often ask her child to clean the bathroom. The mom really doesn't like to clean the bathroom, but her child loves to! The child is more than happy to clean the bathroom for the mom as a way of repairing the relationship when the girl does something hurtful or mean. The mother feels good once the task is done, and she's able to put the incident in the past, feeling the relationship has been repaired. This has greatly reduced the conflict between the parent and child and markedly reduced the child's shame. The child is now much more able to tell her parents when she does something wrong and is much quicker to make amends.

Another child in residential treatment lied about an incident that took his social worker several hours to sort out. In order to make up for the time he wasted and repair the relationship so that the social worker did not feel abused, she had the boy clean the snow off her car at the end of the day for a couple of days. He enjoyed the time in the snow, and she enjoyed having a car ready to go at the end of the day.

Natural Consequences versus Punishment

Punishment is about retribution, getting even, and inflicting hurt. This is not therapeutic for either party. A child who experiences overwhelming shame feels like a bad person, defective, unlovable, and unloved. As a protection, it is best to be as proactive as possible so that the child cannot get into trouble; that is the idea behind keeping the child near you at all times, time-in and not time-out, and keeping the child at home and out of school. However, inevitably your child will misbehave or act in a way to damage the relationship. This is the idea behind natural consequences; by engineering situations and interactions, you can arrange things so that it is the child's actions that directly cause an effect for the child. This helps the child learn about cause and effect and strengthens the child's ability to think, plan, and anticipate. What are natural consequences? These are actions that flow directly from and are caused by the child's actions. Not wearing a coat in winter leads to being cold. Throwing a toy leads to its being broken. Studying leads to good grades. Helping out leads to praise and feelings of belonging.

Because of the early maltreatment, children with disorders of attachment often don't connect their actions with outcomes. Cause and effect are disconnected. It is important to help the child develop these connections. Natural consequences are one way of achieving this connection. Let's go through a few examples summarizing how what we have discussed so far might lead a child to begin making cause and effect connections.

Let's say Sarah, age twelve, is misbehaving at the table. She is chewing loudly and food is falling out of her mouth while she talks nonstop, interrupting everyone who tries to speak. Sending her away from the table might seem like the obvious solution, but this may only serve to further isolate her and reinforce beliefs that she is unloved and unwanted. Instead, what might happen if you said, "Wow, Sarah, you really have a lot to say, don't you? Let's just put that food away for now so we can chat." And then you stop eating and have a conversation with her.

Does this seem counterintuitive? The idea here is that Sarah will receive undivided attention from you and then you may both resume eating. Sarah learns that what she has to say is important to you. So are manners. The issue of poor manners is treated within the context of her desire to be heard. Once her need for attention is satiated, at least temporarily, she may resume eating and no more food will fall out of her mouth. Pointing out to her that you noticed how her actions communicated a stronger need for talking rather than eating, coupled with your understanding of her underlying emotions, you understood why her manners were compromised.

Another example concerns nine-year-old David who is pinching his eleven-year-old sister in the car while you are taking them to school in the morning. Well, maybe the simplest thing is to separate them and have them sit in distant locations in the car. Or maybe you can use this as an opportunity to see that what may be driving David's behavior is jealousy and his need for attention. Maybe a solution is to have each child brought to school by a different parent so that each gets some special time. Or maybe the sister would really like to ride the bus, and if not, maybe she would ride the bus and then get a special treat each day or at week's end for helping out.

The principle to consider is that in order to protect your child from getting into trouble (and then feeling more shame) you will need to treat your child at the child's developmental age. This often means keeping the child within a three- or four-foot radius of you so that you can easily monitor physical and emotional safety. Simply doing this will often eliminate 80 percent of the problem behaviors such as lying, stealing, and hitting. And as you would with a young child, it's best to put away valuable, precious, and easily breakable items. Help your child avoid creating distance between you; distancing tactics represent fear-based intimacy. Distance may be more comfortable to a child unused to safety in close relationship with a loving caregiver. In fact, a general principle here is to remove all obstacles to an intimate, close, loving, responsive relationship. This is one reason that television, video games, radios, and other distractions are strongly discouraged. Most children don't have trouble watching TV or listening to an MP3 player. Children with disorders of attachment do have difficulty with family and relationships. To our thinking, this means that they need more practice in relationships and family life and less practice watching TV, being alone, and being isolated from people. The point here is to develop an emotionally positive attuned relationship with your child. The more time spent together, the easier it will be to "read" your child and for your child to experience a positive relationship, which makes the disparity between what "was" and what "is" much more evident. To begin to feel safe and comfortable with intimacy and to trust others takes time in addition to quality of the relationship.

In a similar vein, simplifying the child's room will eliminate potential problems and obstacles to your relationship and reinforce that family time is important. The child's bedroom is, ideally, just for sleeping. This means that the room does not need toys, books, or other such items. These items should be in a space in which you can interact with your child. At bedtime, if your child settles better with a book or a special toy or stuffed animal, it should be given to the child by you. The bedroom is for rest and sleeping only, not time-out. However, it may be used for safety at times. If an older child is becoming dangerous and the choice seems to be for that child to escalate into a violent rage or be in the bedroom to quiet down, being in the bedroom is preferable. However, short of that, best is to practice time-in. Staying with or very near your upset child helps the child regulate escalating negative emotions and reduces shame.

The bedtime environment works best within a calm, quiet atmosphere. The therapeutic parent organizes this time so that there is a felt sense of safety, security, and comfort. Bedtime rituals are very important and should be followed regardless of whether the child had a "good" or "bad" day. Such rituals may involve reading a story to the child, telling a story, just sitting quietly on the child's bed, tucking the child in, whatever seems natural and comforting to the child. This is another way that you create experiences that demonstrate the child is loved and lovable, even if the child's behavior has been difficult earlier in the day. Some parents use this time to deepen that experience by placing a little note or sticker in the child's bed ahead of time, and making a little game of "finding" the item which would typically state "I love you." Sometimes using a "transfer object" helps a child feel your loving presence even when you have left the room. This might be a special stuffed animal you give to the child each night, or a bean-filled pillow that your child "finds" under the covers all warmed up from the microwave.

Finally, doing things for the child is another way you demonstrate your caring and affection, in addition to meeting the child where the child is developmentally. Since so many of the children we see are operating developmentally and emotionally as toddlers or young children, activities such as laying out the child's clothes each day, helping the child dress, washing up the child, making a game of occasionally feeding the child, are all activities that can be comforting and developmentally appropriate. Many children with disorders of attachment have poor hygiene. Sometimes that can be because the child never had anyone help them brush teeth, wash up, bathe, and so forth, or these habits were not lovingly applied. Sometimes poor hygiene results from sexual molestation or abuse. Obviously, one has to be sensitive to the underlying cause of the behavior and respond in a manner that takes negative associations into account. Quite often these basic routine activities become times of stress and discord between parent and child. The child doesn't brush teeth well or lies about it, the child pretends to shower or wash hair or use soap. These activities then become battlegrounds in which the child is setting the rhythm and tone of the relationship. By doing these things for and with the child you remove a big obstacle to your relationship, you demonstrate that you care about the child (meeting physical needs), and you demonstrate that you enjoy the child (spending time together). So, brushing the child's teeth, washing, drying, and brushing hair, helping with bathing or making bath time playtime are all ways to therapeutically manage the relationship. The natural development of healthful habits is typically the result of attuned interactions between the infant/child and the parent/s through mutually enjoyable interactions. Enjoyment/joy (Schore 2001) are reciprocal experiences that build relationship; it's easier and fun to do these activities with your child when the value of these interactions is fully appreciated.

AN EXAMPLE OF A DAY IN THE LIFE OF YOUR CHILD

Here is a description of a typical day in the life of a family with a child who has a disorder of attachment. The general principles are:

1. Interact with your child in a way that reduces shame.
   a. Keeping the child near you at all times helps!
2. Interact with your child in a way that is responsive and respectful of the child's social and emotional developmental age.
3. Avoid power struggles and efforts by the child to create emotional distance between the two of you.
4. Control the rhythm, tone, and emotional quality of the relationship without being controlling.
5. Keep a sense of humor, have a decent support system, and find ways to keep your emotional batteries fully charged.
   a. A good night's sleep will do wonders for you.
   b. Having a hobby or some nourishing activity that you enjoy will help.
   c. Having a support network of friends and family who understand what you are trying to do and why will be very helpful.
6. Create opportunities for your child to rely on you and discover a new type of parent-child relationship.
   a. Having the child rely on you by asking for almost everything can create situations that allow the child to experience you as responsive, supportive, and as able to meet the child's needs in a consistent and reliable manner.

Okay, so now your child is at home with you. The child's room is set up for bedtimes, and the rest of the house is childproofed, based on your child's developmental capacity. Generally the child's room only needs a bed and some storage for a few items of clothing. Toys and related items can be kept elsewhere as you will be giving your child these items during the day. When you arrange the environment so that your child asks you for things, you have created many opportunities to demonstrate your responsiveness and attunement. When you anticipate that your child may want a snack, a drink, to play a quiet activity or a large-muscle activity, you demonstrate your attunement with your child and demonstrate your love.

You and your child will go through each day together. Your child will be with you and can help you with various activities to the extent the child is able to do so. You and your child will have time to play, eat, and engage in other activities.

Being out of school and at home with you on a full-time basis is important and can really make a huge difference in how fast the child heals . . .

sometimes it is the difference between healing and not. You will need a mental health professional to write a letter to the school explaining that this is a medically necessary and essential part of the child's treatment, no different than if the child where home in traction. The school district is then obligated to provide a tutor. Many districts will provide a tutor two hours a day five days a week. We find that most school districts are quite willing to be helpful. On occasion a district may place obstacles in your way, and we've found the quickest way around those is to just have your pediatrician write a note concurring with your therapist and the recommendations.

Why is having the child at home on a full-time basis so important? Well, to help a child with a disorder of attachment heal takes certain qualities in the relationship and it also takes time. A typical schedule for a child may only allow for two to four or five hours a day with the family and with you. The child is spending more time in school than with you. This time away can undo or undermine much of what you may accomplish at home. In addition, in order to create a healing environment, you need the time to be able to reflect on each interaction and experience without feeling pressured or rushed. While it may not be possible in all instances, for financial or other logistical reasons, to have a child at home in this manner, our experience is that it makes a tremendous difference to have this as a part of treatment. It is not unusual for us to begin working with a family that cannot keep the child home, only to find after two or three months that little if any progress has been made. Frequently such families then opt to keep their child home, and then the progress they make is quite gratifying for the parents. Flexible schedules can help make this possible. The federal Family Medical Leave Act allows a parent to take time off to care for an ill family member. We frequently complete the FMLA forms for parents so that they can do this. Your employer's human resources or personnel department will have the forms necessary.

Wake Up

At the appropriate time you can poke your head in the door and wake up your child. You may want to lay out the clothing for the day or help your child dress. You will want to help your child dress if this has been a problem in the past, and you'll interact in the same manner you would help a toddler dress; being helpful, supporting, encouraging, and taking pleasure in the child's accomplishments and advances. The morning cleanup routine will depend on your child's needs. Many children have difficulty with personal hygiene; they may never have had anyone take enjoyment in helping them wash, to notice the goodness of being fresh and clean, helping to brush little teeth, go potty, and so on. They may have never had anyone who cared what the child looked like or smelled like; no one who valued them in ways that demonstrated such deep caring. If that is the case for your child, then you can help him by washing him, making brushing teeth a fun game to do together, and in other ways showing how you care. Other children may be able to do all this without any difficulty if you are just physically present. And for some children this is not an issue.

Once the child is up and washed, then moving on to breakfast is probably the next step. If you can organize things so that the other children are off to school before you begin with the child who is at home with you, you will probably find that the day moves along more smoothly. It can be therapeutic if you get your child's breakfast rather than having the child make or get the child's own breakfast. As we've discussed before, this allows you to meet the child's need and for the child to experience you as attuned with the child and as a caring parent; obviously you will be choosing items you believe your child might like. During this time you can make feeding the child a game. After breakfast, you can both clean up and move on with the day.

During the morning you might do chores together, such as sorting laundry, doing the wash, dishes, cleaning, yard work, or other activities. If your child needs sensory-integration exercises, you can intersperse those throughout the day as breaks in the routine. Including fun activities is also essential; read a story, make a snack, build a tower, walk outdoors, notice the birds, flowers, sky. These activities should be interactive and engaging. You will learn to assess your child's capacity for "fun." Some children have difficulty with high positive emotions as well as negative emotions. If your child's excitement becomes too much, you can redirect the activity to something less stimulating or completely different. You are in emotional control so you can redirect using a calm, sure tone that lets your child know he can count on you to help him regulate uncomfortable or unfamiliar emotions. You want to be setting the rhythm and tone to keep the interactions and relationships on an even keel.

Need some ideas for interactive games and activities to keep in your back pocket? Planning ahead goes a long way toward maintaining the calm, attuned relationship that is so healing.

Building Constructs: Legos, Lincoln Logs, Soft Blocks, Dominoes
Art Supplies: Paper, Finger Paints, Crayons, Coloring Books
Manipulatives: Play Dough, Sculpey, Puzzles, Macrame
Interactive Pretend Play: Paper Dolls, Plastic or Flocked Animal Families, Playmobil Sets
For large-muscle activities there are walks outdoors (even in the rain!), swimming, going to the park, basketball, building a snowman, digging in the garden.

Story time at the local library, choosing books, reading together, making collages, dress up with pictures (to show the rest of the family later) are just some of the activities that can be worked into your days together. No TV, PC, CD, VCR, etc. . . . only interactive activities or activities that require the parent and child's active involvement. However, that is not to say that watching a DVD together isn't okay. A family activity might be to pop some popcorn and all watch a movie on Friday night. It is not the "screens" themselves that are the problem, it is the lack of interaction that is unhelpful.

As some point during the day, the tutor will arrive. This will provide you with a break to make phone calls or do other things that may require privacy. It is important that the tutor be educated about your child's special needs, understanding the issues and dynamics. It is okay to let what occurs in tutoring be between the tutor and your child. While you do need to know what happened and what is expected, it is up to the tutor to respond to the child. For example, if the child does not do an assignment, the child should get an appropriate grade, based on what the child actually hands in on the date due; the same for homework. Your role in all this is to provide an opportunity and forum for the child, if the child needs help. You may want to designate the time before dinner as the hour when you will be available to help the child with homework or projects. Then, each day at 5:00, you can ask the child if the child needs your help or any materials. If the child wants help, you should provide it. If the child says no or that the child has no assignments, you can let it go. The tutor will address this if it is not true. Then, later, depending on the outcome you can address the deeper issue with the child: "I wonder why you hadn't let me know you had homework. Sounds like maybe you weren't comfortable telling me . . . maybe you were worried that I'd 'make' you do it when you didn't want to? What do you think?" Then, you can discuss the outcome with the child:

Parent: So, what happened?

Child: The tutor gave me a zero.

Parent: How do you think I feel about that?

Child: Mad?

Parent: What makes you think that?

Child: Because you always used to yell at me about school.

Parent: I am sorry about that. But, no, I'm not mad, I'm sad that you got a zero when you'd shown me the day before that you knew the work. What do you think will happen?

Child: I don't care!

Parent: It sounds like you are getting mad . . . are you?

Child: Yes, this is stupid!

Parent: That must be hard for you. Maybe you don't believe me and think I am mad?

Child: Aren't you?

Parent: No, I'm just sad that you're having such a hard time. You need a hug; let's get a snack.

As you become more attuned with your child, you will be able to recognize when your child has "had enough" and needs a break from talking with some quiet time to calm down. Quiet time might involve having the child play quietly in the same room with you while you read, pay bills, or are engaged in some other activity. If the child asks for a snack, that's fine. Better yet is when you can anticipate that your child may be hungry or thirsty and meet that need. It is quite similar to the way one responds to an infant. A responsive parent tries to anticipate the needs of the infant, but in any event, the parent will respond when the infant cries and indicates that something is amiss.

Dinner can be good time for the whole family to get together. However, it often becomes a battleground for parents and child. If your child turns family dinnertime into a grim and gruesome activity, then you may want to consider ways to break the cycle of mealtime negativity. An option may be for you to eat at a separate time with your child. This way, child-initiated emotional distancing is avoided; the child will not then control the environment by setting a negative tone and rhythm during family meal time. Avoiding problems by removing obstacles is the key here. It may be helpful to picture the dinner scene with an infant. As you and your partner take turns bouncing a colicky baby, you keep in mind (and remind each other) that eventually the baby will grow to enjoy participating in family mealtimes. But for now, you plan ahead, maybe feed the baby early (they always seem to fuss when dinner is being prepared!) or make other accommodations to keep peace. For different reasons, your child may have underlying issues resulting in distress and discomfort having to do with a previously maltreating experience involving food, family togetherness, domestic violence, and so forth. If some activity is not fun for the child, then you can find another activity to engage in with the child so that both the child and other family members have an enjoyable time. If you have a partner, then you and the partner can take turns eating at this other time with the child . . . it can become your "special" time together. Until your child has healed enough to associate family dinnertime as a positive experience, it is best to avoid power struggles. Your attitude of acceptance toward your child's underlying distress will go a long way toward achieving the goals of healing: emotional safety, feeling deeply cherished and understood.

Once dinner is finished, then the evening begins to wind down. Cleaning up the table and beginning to get ready for bed is the primary focus here.

Since children with trauma-attachment problems often have great difficulty regulating their emotions, you'll want to keep this time somewhat quiet and calm. After cleaning up from dinner, a quiet game or reading activity may be best. This can be followed by getting washed, into pajamas, and then the bedtime rituals. If your child does not wash well, perhaps because no one ever spent the time with the child teaching/helping the child, then you can avoid a lot of problems by doing this with your child. If your child had bad experiences (or no experiences with parents) getting washed up, then asking the child to do this alone will often result in problems (lies about teeth brushing, using soap, clean underwear, etc.). Remove all these barriers by doing these activities for the child or with the child, always based on the child's demonstrated developmental age. Many children, even older ones, enjoy having mom or dad help wash their face and brush their teeth. Getting the bedtime clothing ready and laying out the next day's clothing for the child is another way you show your love and caring. Finally, a bedtime ritual that stays the same each night can be a wonderful reassurance for the child. Reading a story, telling a story, or just lying there talking together can be a very special time.

Some children will wander at night. We have found that putting a magnetic alarm on the door can help you get a good night's sleep. You won't have to wonder if your child is wandering. In addition, it protects the child from leaving the room and getting into trouble. For children who have been sexually molested or abused, knowing no one can get into their room without your knowledge can help reduce anxiety that prevents restful sleep. As we discussed earlier, if the child comes out of the room, you can use that time to do some chores together. Calm interactions, doing routine activities can help an anxious child relax. Expecting that your child may have difficulty with bedtime due to past history can help you prepare for the event and avoid expressing irritability toward the child for needing help at this time of day or night.

As time goes by, with many opportunities to reexperience negatively associated activities within a positive, supportive, and loving environment, your child will make progress. Small steps forward, little by little and with many, many repetitions, your child will come to feel the security and safety so rightly deserved. Therapeutic parenting is not easy, nor is it a quick fix; the satisfaction comes from knowing you are providing the healthy environment in which relational skills can grow. These skills have the potential to increase your child's capacity to enjoy life, to partake of opportunities awaiting in the future, and to feel a sense of rightness, goodness, belonging, security, and boundless love.

4

Reasons for Misbehavior

Daniel Hughes

There is a certain simplicity in the idea that if we give our child a consequence or punishment for the behavior we are able to exert control over the behavior. Thus, if we provide a favorable consequence, the behavior will increase; and if we provide an unfavorable consequence or punishment, it will decrease. While this may be true in certain species of animals some of the time, it is often not true when we apply it to our children. It is especially not likely to be true when we attempt to apply it to children whose behavior is influenced by prior experiences of abuse, neglect, abandonment, and loss. While we may achieve compliance in the moment, the compliance is not likely to be evident later. What we actually are hoping for is that the child will internalize emotional and behavioral control and our values and act accordingly whether or not we are present. These children make us aware that it is better to first understand the reasons for the behaviors before deciding upon what, if any, consequence is appropriate.

When a parent is able to understand the motives and reasons for the child's behaviors, the parent is much more likely to be able to respond to the child in a manner that will be the most helpful for the situation, the child, and the relationship. When the child is also able to understand why the child is engaged in those actions, the child is more likely to be able to modify the action. Understanding "whats it's all about" can truly be the key for modifying quite entrenched behavioral problems.

Making the effort to understand the reasons and motives for a child's behaviors is very important. The following reasons come to mind:

WE OFTEN INCORRECTLY ASSUME THAT WE KNOW "WHY"

Too often parents see or hear about their child's behaviors and jump to the conclusion as to "why" their child did what the child did. The parents may then react in a manner that not only tries to "deal with" the behavior but also with the *assumed* motive. When a parent thinks that the child teased the dog because "he just wanted to make me mad" that parent is likely to react with greater anger or harshness in response to both the behavior and the assumed motive than if the parent were reacting to just the behavior itself, or assumed a more benign motive.

Researchers have known for years that many family conflicts are intensified because one member of the family assumes a negative motive behind the behavior of another member of the family. Researchers have also made it clear that children who have been abused and neglected very often assume negative motives for their adoptive or foster parents' acts of discipline. Parents are also vulnerable to assuming negative motives when their child's behavior does not change in response to routine discipline. Partners often do the same toward each other, causing hurt feelings and generating a defensive stance that makes resolution of a conflict much more difficult.

When you think about it, the underlying driver of a child's behavior may be a mystery. Parents frequently describe their child's behavior as strange or as "not making sense." Most parents and their foster or adopted children have very different backgrounds, experiences, and histories of past relationships. Given these substantial differences, and the resulting differences in worldview and experience of relationships, it is not surprising that in these instances the parent may not know the reason for a child's "incomprehensible" or "strange" behavior. The most helpful first response to our child's negative behaviors is to assume that we may not know the reasons for it. Such a stance:

1. Immediately prevents us from responding without adequate thought being given either to the reasons for the behaviors or to the most suitable consequence. A "not knowing" stance slows us down so that we are likely to respond only after first giving suitable thought to what would be the most appropriate response.
2. Communicates to our child our commitment to understand the child's behavior. This demonstrates that we value the child and find the child to be valuable.
3. Conveys to the child that we do not habitually perceive "him" in a negative light with negative assumptions, about which we are so cer-

tain we do not even have to "check them out." We do not "assume the worst."

4. Guides us toward making the best possible response to the behavior.
5. Fosters a "nonjudgmental" stance toward our child that creates within the child a greater sense of being accepted as a person, even if we need to judge the behaviors.

Even if a parent's negative assumptions about the child's motives are correct, it is often likely that the parent has not gone deeply enough into the child's motives to truly understand the child. For example, it may be accurate that the parent's child "just wanted to make me mad." The next question that might be asked is, "What is the reason for having that motive? Why would a child spend much of the day wanting to 'make his parent mad'?" Deeper motives might include the child's fear of the parent's love for the child or the child's sense that the child only has the ability to get a negative response from the parent and that positive responses do not "fit" who the child is and hence make the child anxious or feel empty. We all "expect" to be treated a certain way. When we are not treated in that manner we act, often without awareness, to get the other person to treat us the way we expect. So too a child with a history of Complex Trauma. Expecting to be treated badly, the child may act in ways to evoke care that is congruent with the child's internal image of self, other, and the relationship, which is based on these past experiences, not the current realities. The child may also be convinced that the parent will eventually reject and abandon the child and so try to "get it over with." The child may also be compulsively "testing" the parent's commitment to the child by engaging in more and more difficult behaviors. If the parent is able to understand these deeper motives the parent is often more able to become engaged with the child in ways that will better address those motives and be therapeutic.

Frequently parents react to their child's behavior with sudden anger only to later regret their immediate response. Upon reflection they may decide that there are other explanations for the behavior or that they overreacted to the behavior because of reasons unrelated to their child. Pausing to reflect—to better understand the various reasons for the behavior—is good insurance that we are likely to give the best possible response to our child's behavior. The chapter on "Mindfulness" can be helpful in this regard.

CHILDREN MOST OFTEN
DO NOT UNDERSTAND "WHY" EITHER

Few children have deep insight into their behavior. Children who have been abused, neglected, and abandoned by their parents are most often children who have little insight into their inner lives. They most often are very unclear regarding their thoughts, feelings, wishes, judgments, values, perceptions, and motives. They did not develop the motivation or skill to explore their inner life and develop the verbal skills to give expression to it. Their birth parents did not become sensitive, responsive, or attuned to the meanings of the child's behavior. These birth parents did not respond to their infant's physical expressions or help them to make sense of their infantile intentions. Their parents failed to help them to make sense of all aspects of their world, both the external and internal ones. As a result, these children, as they matured, had very little self-awareness. When they tried to understand their own motives, their understandings were primitive efforts to make sense out of being hit, screamed at, ignored, or left alone. Their understandings focused on their own worthlessness and became experienced as shame. Their understandings of others' intentions focused on the fact that the other would cause them pain and not be interested in meeting their perceived needs. They failed to develop a basic trust in the motives and behaviors of their attachment figures.

Parental efforts to aid their children in developing self-awareness and self-expression need to focus on approaching the inner life of their child much like they would do with an infant and toddler. Their stance needs to be based on acceptance, curiosity, and empathy in order for the child to feel safe and secure and to be relaxed enough to explore and then expose those hidden parts of self. This stance encourages the child to try to understand and honestly give expression to the mostly nameless patterns of thought and emotion that are being uncovered. With this parental stance the child is more likely to experience the sense of safety necessary for the child to be open to the experience of feeling and reflecting upon the child's inner life.

For example, an eight-year-old adopted girl, Melinda, teased the family dog with some food and then ate it herself, causing her almost to be bitten. Her mother scolded her, with her anger mixed with her fears about safety for her daughter. The girl first reacted defensively and shortly afterward expressed distress over why she teased the dog whom she often tried hard to get to like her. She allowed her mother to put her arm around her while she sobbed about the incident. She repeatedly asked "why." While they quietly explored her relationship with the dog, her mother quietly mentioned that Melinda seemed to become upset when she saw her mother pet and play with the dog. When the girl agreed, the mother suggested that Melinda might sometimes wish that she had had her mother's complete love and enjoyment when she was younger. She added that when her daughter saw their dog getting all the "love" from her mother, it reminded her of what she never had when she was young. Melinda quietly said that it was so unfair that she spent so long with no one loving her. She admitted that she did not like to think about it and that sometimes when she saw her mother with the dog, she did think about it. Very quietly she added, "Maybe I want him to have some of my unhappiness. To have somebody be mean to him just like they were to me." Her mother agreed and comforted her further. After that discussion, her mother noticed a definite improvement in Melinda's interactions with the dog.

As opposed to this empathic, curious stance, adopting a more critical, problem solving stance tends to both make the child more defensive as well as make the child's inner life less accessible. Such an approach tends to convey a sense of evaluation and judgment that discourages openness. Such a stance disregards the affective component of the experience, and this experience is central to the awareness of self and its roots in the intersubjective relationship with the parent. This is not an intellectual discussion, but an affective dance of discovery of both self and other.

Thus, when a parent is able to explore the child's motives for behavior and experience empathy for the origins of the problems—which were most likely within terror and shame—the child is likely to acquire a much greater awareness of the child's own motives as well as the motives of the parents in disciplining the child. This leads to greater self-empathy and less shame. Eventually, the child is able to express his inner life with both verbal and nonverbal communication and is less likely to use behavioral symptoms to give expression to it.

It Is Crucial to Differentiate the Behavior from the Self

"I'm not angry with you; I'm angry at what you did." Parents frequently make that statement to their child, and most of the time their child does not believe them. There are two central reasons for this:

First, when parents quickly express anger in reaction to their child's behavior it is very likely that the anger includes the parents' assumption about their child's motives for his behavior (i.e., he doesn't care about his sister's feelings). By including their assumption regarding their child's assumed motives in the reaction to the child's behavior, parents are, in fact, communicating that they are angry with the child, not just the behavior. An individual's sense of self is intimately associated with the person's "inner life," including thoughts, feelings, perceptions, wishes, intentions, and judgments. When a parent judges the reasons negatively and becomes angry with the child as well as the behavior, the child is very likely to experience being judged for who the child is, not just for what the child does.

When evaluating a child's behavior it is wise to stay focused on the behavior itself and the natural consequence of the behavior rather than evaluating the reasons. If "Joey" says that he does not like his sister and then hits the sister, any appropriate consequence should be for the behavior, not because he said that he does not like the sister. In fact, the more that he is able to express thoughts, feelings, and wishes about the sister, the less likely he is to act inappropriately toward her. The child is more likely to voice such expression to inner life when he is confident that his inner life is not being judged negatively. Thus, a parent might respond: "You don't like your sister! Wow, you sound really strong about that! Thanks for telling me! Now I think I understand better how you have acted toward her lately. Help me understand . . . how come, do you think, you don't like her lately?" If a parent wants the child to believe that the parent likes the child—but not some of the behaviors—then it is very helpful to clearly focus on the behavior and not the motives or assumed motives.

Second, the child with significant trauma and attachment anxiety is likely to be characterized by pervasive shame. This state of shame leads the child to judge the child's own behavior very negatively, as reflecting how "bad" the child is, or how "unlovable" the child is. Shame is a child's first reaction to being abused, neglected, or abandoned by his parents. There is no other way a young child is able to make sense of the reasons for the parents' behaviors. As an infant and toddler the child habitually concludes that there is something wrong with self that warrants the maltreatment that the child experiences from the parents. Since the child assumes then that the child's behavioral "problems" reflect this pervasive negative quality about self, when the child's adoptive or foster parents react to the child's behavior with anger the child will be convinced that the parents judge the child to be "bad" as well.

When a child is embedded in a pervasive sense of shame, the child is likely to have difficulty developing a consistent sense of guilt in response to the child's behavior that is hurtful to another. Guilt is an affective response to judging that one's behavior has hurt another person; shame is an affective response to judging that one's self is "bad." This child is not able to differentiate the "self" from behavior. The general response of shame is to hide. The general response to guilt is to want to repair or fix the problem. When the child misbehaves, the behavior is a threat to the child's precarious sense of self so the child has much difficulty facing it. The child is likely to lie, make excuses, blame the other, minimize it, or become angry at efforts to have the child address it. In many ways, lies are just a more sophisticated way of hiding. "Joey" is more likely to begin to accept responsibility for his behavior if his shame becomes less. It is more likely to become less if the parents are able to express empathy for how hard it is for him to address his behavior due to the shame. The child is also more likely to accept responsibility for the behavior if the parents are able to direct their anger at the child's behavior alone, and not allow their anger to be directed at the child's "inner life" as well.

Knowing the Child's Reasons Creates Empathy for the Child

When a parent has a better understanding of the child's reasons for the child's misbehavior, the parent is more likely to experience and communicate empathy for the child's behavior rather than reacting to it with anger. When a parent knows that the child swore at the parent because the child thought that the parent really did not like the child anymore, the parent is more likely to be able to set a limit regarding the swearing while at the same time express empathy for the child's fears that the parent did not like the child: "Billy, I did not realize that when I said that you could not ride your bike that you thought it was because I did not like you. No wonder you got angry with me! It would be so hard to think that your mother does not like you! So hard!"

I am assuming that when we understand a child's reasons for his behavior we will not be uncovering reasons that we and the child believe to be shameful. In this example involving Billy swearing at his mother, the reasons for the swearing that are uncovered will not involve Billy being "selfish," "bad," or "mean." Rather the reasons involve the child's fear that he is not liked and might be mistreated or rejected. His anger was seen as his strong response to a perceived major threat to his relationship with his mother. The behavior of "swearing" might have to be dealt with firmly, but the reason behind the swearing will be met with empathy.

The reasons that we uncover will most often be reflective of the child's early experiences of abuse and/or neglect. Given the circumstances of the child's past, the child's behavior is more understandable and more able to elicit empathy. This empathic response, in turn, will make it more likely that the child will be able to accept responsibility for the child's behavior. The child will be more certain that the child's relationship with the parent is not being jeopardized by the behavior and any resultant consequence. The child will also be more confident that the parent's motives for providing the consequence are not negative. Finally the child will be more able to reduce a sense of shame and allow the child's inner life to be more open to feelings of guilt for misbehavior.

Knowing the reason, we are more likely to know the most appropriate response or consequence. Not knowing "why" a child did what the child did makes it quite difficult to know what is the most appropriate consequence. How serious was the behavior? It is often hard to know the right answer without knowing the reasons for the behavior. What consequence is the most likely to affect a change in the behavior? Again, knowing the reason will provide the best answer to that question.

If a child steals money from the child's parents, what is the most appropriate consequence? Returning the money, doing chores to pay back its value, accepting the need for restitution all may be quite valid first responses. They may be sufficient if the behavior does not reoccur. But if the behavior occurs more than once, is it sufficient simply to increase the severity of consequence? More than likely, a better approach would be to understand the specific reasons for the behavior. The reasons might involve unexpressed anger at the parents, a pervasive sense of shame, a sense of emptiness that might possibly end through buying objects, a desire to become popular by buying things for others, a wish to buy a present for the child's father on Father's Day to ensure that the child will not be abandoned, or a plan to buy a knife to hurt the child's brother who the child believes is loved more than he. Clearly, if the behavior was motivated by one of these reasons it would be very helpful to know which particular reason it was in order to address it. Such a response would be the most effective means of ensuring that the behavior would not reoccur.

For example, an eight-year-old boy whose behavior had been quite stable for close to a year suddenly became verbally abusive toward his adoptive mother. His parents reacted with very clear discipline, and the behavior stopped. The same behavior occurred a month later with similar results and then it happened a third time. The parents were puzzled since his progress appeared to have been significant and the behaviors started and stopped so suddenly with long periods of stability in between. Upon reflecting, they realized that each of the three times occurred during the weekend prior to a business trip that the father would be taking the following week. They wondered if his behavior was his effort to express his anxiety over his father's leaving. He might have been fearful that his father would not return. His behavior may have represented an effort to keep him at home. When his parents explored this with him, he began to cry. He indicated that he never had had a dad who loved him and he was terrified that he would never see him again when he would leave on a trip. His father's understanding and empathy helped the boy to communicate his fears quite openly. His father then thought of some practical things that he could do that would also help to reduce his fears.

It may often be difficult to determine the correct reason in part because often the child is not able to articulate it. At other times, the child may know but have other reasons for not wanting to express it. A parent's non-judgmental stance toward the possible reasons will make it more likely that the child will share underlying feelings and inner thoughts. Such a stance will make it easier for the parent and child to openly be curious about possible reasons and uncover the most likely possibilities.

It is important to note that uncovering reasons for behaviors does not represent a search for excuses for the behavior. A reason becomes an excuse only when it negates accountability. The value of finding the reason is both to prevent future behaviors from occurring and also to resolve conflicts or doubts that are generating the behaviors. The results of the recent behaviors still may require a specific or general consequence. For example, Robert might have broken his brother's toy. Before deciding on the most appropriate consequence for the behavior, the parent is well-advised to explore the reasons for it. Through nonjudgmental curiosity about his motives, his parent discovers that Robert thought that his brother did not like him because he had teased him in front of his friends. Robert went on to say how much his brother means to him and how he fears that his brother will no longer want to do things with him. His fear of the loss of his brother led to his anger at him, which led to him breaking his toy. His parents were able to lead a discussion between their sons in which Robert was able to express his fears and his brother was able to reassure him that he will always want to play with him. Following that, Robert quite willingly offered the "consequence" of buying his brother something from his allowance.

When a child behaves in a manner that has serious effects on others, the child remains accountable for the child's behavior, regardless of the reason. A reason becomes an excuse only when it negates accountability. The value of finding the reason is both to prevent future behaviors from occurring and also to resolve the conflicts or doubts that were generating the behaviors. The results of the recent behaviors are likely to still require an appropriate consequence. When a parent responds to the underlying motivation or cause of the behavior, the child will feel accepted on a very deep level and develop greater trust in the parent's benign and positive motives for any consequence that might follow.

KNOWING THE REASON HELPS THE PARENTS TO BEGIN TO TRULY KNOW WHO THEIR CHILD IS

Children with histories of interpersonal trauma and attachment losses or disorganization tend to be children who often have an assortment of behavioral problems which may occur for quite some time and be quite resistant to change. When this occurs, a real danger is that the parents and other important people in the child's life will only perceive the child as a constellation of symptoms and lose sight of the child underneath. When adults begin to experience the child-as-symptoms, the child is certain to experience self in a similar manner. Being a set of symptoms, there is little means of changing—nor reasons for trying—since the symptoms are the valid expression of the child's identity. Since a child's experience of self is largely derived from the child's experience of the child's parents and significant others' experience of the child, this child is now trapped in a never-ending circle of hopeless reenactment of the perceptions that others have had of the child, starting back with the perceptions that arose from the eyes of the first parents while they were being abusive or neglectful. The child was, and is, no more than a child who deserves to be abused and neglected. The past abuse reflected that, and the current behavior problems confirm that daily.

The development of the sense of self is vitally dependent upon the "inter-subjective experiences" that children have with their parents and/or attachment figures. If any child is ever to grow with a "self" that includes being "courageous," "lovable," "delightful," "honest," "joyful," and "persistent," he needs to have adults who experience those qualities within him. To find such qualities, his parents need to search continuously under the symptoms for the reasons that will both explain them and reveal other qualities in the child which are too fragile to become manifest.

In order for the parent to perceive these strengths and vulnerabilities within their child, they must refrain from making negative assumptions regarding the reasons for their child's behaviors. Even if these assumptions are correct, they tend to be shallow and do not reflect their origins that were steeped in abuse, neglect, and abandonment. Parents must search for deeper reasons, uncover their related vulnerabilities and strengths, and help those reasons to become expressed. During this process the child, at least as much as the parent, will be able to discover positive qualities in himself that can become the foundation of healing and the transformation of self. If parents do not lead the child, or at least accompany him in this process of self-discovery, he will remain locked in a limited and distorted view of self formed around shame and terror.

For example, Jacob is a ten-year-old adopted boy. He experienced repeated abuse and neglect from his parents until four years of age. He then resided in four foster homes until he was adopted at age seven. His behaviors throughout foster care and adoption were characterized by aggression, oppositional-defiance, lying, and stealing. During his fifteenth treatment session, the therapists, with his parents' active participation, were attempting to explore with him the unique reasons that he may have had for recently destroying his parents' new CD player. Explorations of possible reasons for his anger at them were not uncovering anything that seemed to resonate with the intensity of his expression of anger. Connections with his past, while certainly relevant, were not able to come alive in the present explorations. The persistence of the therapist and parents in gently exploring the underlying reasons, not settling for generalities or "therapy-talk," brought Jacob toward a state of distress that verged upon anger whose function it was to hide his shame. This time though, Jacob brought the discussion to a sudden stop by shouting, with an urgency and sense of raw vulnerability, "Why don't you just stop this! Stop talking like you care! Stop lying to me! You know you're going to throw me away! You know you are! Just do it! Just do it!" Then after about ten endless seconds, he added with more anguish than anger, "Please stop lying. You don't care. Please make me leave." Jacob then sobbed. The therapist and parents could so clearly see his vulnerability, his shame, his loneliness. They could not see then his rage or defiance or stealing that seemed so far removed from this little boy.

The therapist broke the silence: "You are so brave, Jacob. You have told us what you are certain is true. That your parents are lying, that they don't care, that they are going to send you away. Send you away. And you are saying just do it. Just do it!"

Jacob's parents then said, almost in unison, "You're not going anywhere, Jacob. You're our boy and you always will be."

Jacob screamed, "No! Stop lying! You don't care."

Jacob's mother then matched his scream with one of her own: "Yes I do! Yes I do! You don't know that! You don't know what I think and feel about you! You don't! I've had to learn that I don't know what you think and feel! And I'm still learning! And I know you don't believe that I love you! I'm crying because you don't! You don't! And I want you so much to feel my love and you're telling me that you don't feel it! And I have to hear you! But you can't say you know what I feel! You can't! I love you, Jacob!"

"WHY! If you do, why do you?"

"Because . . . because . . . you jumped into my heart the moment I saw your picture! And when you walked into our house! And asked me if you could have a bike. And looked at me . . . the way you looked at me. I knew you would never leave my heart. Never leave my house. That's all I know, Jacob. That's all."

Jacob and his mother stared at each other. Their tears fell to the floor while their eyes held contact until mom pulled him to her and he shook in her arms.

This example may be a more dramatic expression of the discovery of the motives that underlie a child's behavior but it nevertheless is representative of the motives that often are expressed within, locked underneath, the repetitive problems. Invariably the reasons for the behavior involve the child's perceptions of the present family that are secondary to his experiences of abuse, neglect, and abandonment.

Parenting the child with a history of trauma and attachment distress is difficult in part because the parent needs to attend to both the behavior and reasons for the behavior without joining the two. While the behavior may require changes in structure, supervision, and specific consequences, the reasons for the behavior nevertheless also require the parent's attention. In responding to the behavior the parent may need to stress clear, calm, and firm presence that enables the child to establish behavioral control and accept the parent's directives. In responding to the child's inner life that caused the behaviors, the parent needs to stress acceptance of the child, nonjudgmental curiosity, and empathy. The inner life of the parent needs to be open and well-regulated if she is to remain open and present suffi-ciently for the child to be willing and able to access and explore his confus-ing and shameful inner life. The parent needs to manifest the self-awareness and self-regulation skills that she wants her child to develop.

BRINGING REFLECTION AND EMPATHY INTO DISCIPLINE

Having presented the value in trying to know "why" her child acted in a certain manner, I would now like to briefly describe "how" the parent might be the most successful in achieving that goal. When turning atten-tion to a child's inner world, it is crucial to begin with a nonjudgmental attitude and with a commitment to understand a child's thoughts, feelings, wishes, perceptions, judgments, and motive, withholding judgment and evaluation until later. Such unconditional acceptance of the inner life of the child makes it much more likely that the child will participate in the process and attempt to both understand and communicate what lies under his behavior. In addition, this emotional-relational stance vis-à-vis the child demonstrates to the child that the parent values the child. This can help a child to feel valued, valuable, loved, and lovable. Within the con-text of such acceptance, the child is then invited to reflect with the parent about the various possible meanings for the behavior. The parent's stance is one of active, open curiosity about whatever may have led to the child's behavior. Upon discovering the roots of the behavior, with the meaning now more clear, often the parent's first response is one of empathy for the child's efforts to manage or resolve a conflict, area of shame, doubt, or fear. In providing empathy, the parent is conveying that the child is safe with the parent and the relationship itself is safe. In feeling safe the child is more open to explore the behavior with openness, rather than defensiveness, and to experience more empathy for himself about his choice to act in a way that is most likely not in his best interest. These two threads—reflec-tion (curiosity) and empathy—combine thought and affect and lead to a more integrative and coherent understanding of the behavior as well as its relationship to the self.

Reflection (Curiosity)

The parent needs to approach the child with an attitude of openness, without judgment, if she is to discover the motives for his behavior. This is communicated both nonverbally and verbally.

The nonverbal tone of exploration is one of relaxed not knowing, a desire to simply understand without judgment, a degree of curiosity that reveals deep interest. The voice itself lacks the usual stern monotone that often characterizes lectures. Such a tone tends to generate defensiveness and withdrawal from reciprocal communication. Rather the voice has a storytelling quality, a somewhat singsong phrasing, that shows interest in knowing the whole story rather than conveying judgment and advice. The facial expressions are relaxed, a bit puzzled and receptive without criticism. The parent does not intrude into the child's physical space. Rather her gestures and posture and position demonstrate one of care, safety, and deep interest. Communication—reciprocal communication—is clearly the parent's primary goal, rather than "finding the truth."

The verbal statements are congruent with the nonverbal tone and demonstrate the same open, inquisitive, stance. The following statements, always said with the safe vocal tone just mentioned, might be commonly chosen:

"What do you think was going on?"
"Tell me about it."
"What do you sense it is about?"
"What is that like for you?"
"What were your thoughts/feelings?" (followed by) "What were your feelings/thoughts?"

With each expression the parent tries to help the child to elaborate:

"So when you thought that I was not going to let you have the treat, you began to feel really angry with me. Did you have any guesses, if I was going to say 'no' to you, why I might say 'no'?"
"Let me get this right. You thought that I cared more for my job than spending time with you—that my job is more important to me than you are! Wow! Have you thought that before?"
"So you were so angry with me for not letting you visit your friend, you decided to show me how upset you were by breaking that cup. Have you been that angry at me before? What's your guess about why I wouldn't let you see him?"
"You mentioned that it seemed to you that I just didn't care about what is important to you. Why do you think I wouldn't care about that? Why wouldn't I care?"

Such open questions, with following questions that are likely to lead the child more deeply into his inner life, often leave the child feeling more able and willing to communicate about himself to his parent. He often has less shame associated with his thoughts, feelings, and motives and is more confident that his parents will not criticize his sense of who he is. Such communications frequently reduce the need for behavior that requires discipline.

Empathy

When the parent has successfully initiated a conversation with her child about his inner life she is often able to understand aspects of her child's vulnerable states that are characterized by fear, sadness, loneliness, shame, and anger. As these vulnerable states begin to emerge, the child often becomes anxious about the emerging affect as well as the uncertainties about how the communications are affecting his relationship with his parents. The most effective and natural way of responding to such anxiety and doubt is by communicating empathy for the child's vulnerable experiences. Again, the communication is the most effective when it combines both verbal and nonverbal features.

The nonverbal expression of empathy tends to convey an understanding of the affective state of the child at the time by matching the nonverbal expressions of affect through a comparable affective state within the parent. When the child's voice is quiet and slow, the parent's voice has a similar intensity and rhythm. When the child is more agitated with some forced speech, the parent's voice becomes more animated and rapid. But the parent does not match the child's anger, fear, or shame itself. Rather, she is matching the nonverbal expression of that affective state.

The verbal responses similarly match the expressions of affect manifested by the child:

> "How hard that must be for you—thinking that I really don't care what is important to you."
>
> "You look so sad. I can understand better now. Sometimes you're not sure if I care about you."
>
> "Wow, are you angry about that! So angry! What makes you that angry do you think? What is *that* upsetting to you?"
>
> "How scary that must have been for you! All alone, for so long! You thought that I forgot about you! I'm so sorry that you thought that!"

By experiencing empathy for her child's affective state, the parent is helping the child to "stay with" the affect rather than denying it. By so doing, the child is more likely to regulate it and express it in ways that will resolve whatever associated factors created it.

By both reflecting on her child's behavior through her open and curious stance and by expressing empathy for the associated affect, the parent is facilitating a similar state within her child. Helping her child to better reflect upon and accept his inner life, she is also helping him to develop greater self-control of his behaviors and choose a more appropriate response to a stressful situation. He is now able to create a flexible response rather than reacting impulsively.

Most importantly, when a parent is able to pause to explore the motives for a child's behavior, she is communicating a desire to know her child better. She is communicating that he most likely has a reason for his behavior that reflects his past and does not represent any shameful part of himself. She is separating who her child is from what he does. In so doing, she is helping her child to rethink who he is and to develop a sense of self that contains strengths and vulnerabilities rather than traits that he had come to be ashamed of during the abuse and neglect of his past. Then, when she needs to discipline his behavior, her child is likely to be able to manage and accept the act of discipline and possibly even turn to her for comfort and support, much as toddlers do when they are securely attached to their parents.

5

Theraplay for Parents

Phyllis B. Rubin

Some of you may not be newly adoptive parents but have had your child for six months, a year, two years, or more. Yet you are still struggling with your relationship with your child. Your child is sullen or rejecting, angry or apathetic. You are missing out on the special closeness and comfort other parents and children seem to have with each other. You yearn for a closer relationship.

Or perhaps you have just adopted a child, and you've found this book to guide you in developing the parent-child relationship you long for. When you first adopt, you and your child are strangers. Your first days and weeks will be focused on learning about each other. What brings delight and what brings anger? What brings comfort and what brings upset? Some children are clingy and cannot let you go. Others are more cautious and may take longer to relax and trust you as their parent. The process of learning to "dance" with each other will follow paths that are as unique as both of you are unique individuals.

For some of you, the dance will proceed easily and you will achieve a relaxed closeness and feeling of confidence with your child. Over time, you will literally fall in love with each other and feel like you are the family you hoped for. But for others of you, the dance may be hard. Your child may remain wary, standoffish, or even fearful of you. You might be getting a lot of anger directed at you. Like your child, you may become wary, cautious, angry, and fearful of trying to make contact. It can be quite difficult to dance if your child doesn't respond as you expected and, instead, resists your efforts. Something, either in your child, in yourself, or both, is getting in the way and you want help.

Wanting a closer, more comfortable relationship is not a selfish wish. It is a genuine need—a need of yours *and* your child's—to be able to hug each other spontaneously; to have moments when your eyes sparkle with delight at each other; to have moments when you feel a glow of warmth and tenderness toward your child and you feel it reciprocated. But how do you get there? Blocked by your child's history of trauma and fear of closeness and, perhaps, by your own ghosts from the past, how do you help the attachment process move forward?

In this chapter, you will learn about how you can use the principles of Theraplay to help build a closer relationship with your child. Theraplay can be helpful to you because it is modeled upon the types of interactions parents naturally engage in with their infants and young children that create the experiences needed to develop a healthy attachment.

Theraplay goes back to the basics helping you reach your child and helping your child accept what you offer.

THE "BASICS" OF BUILDING ATTACHMENT

Theraplay views the building of attachment as requiring four important dimensions. Attachment grows when you care for your child: when you pick up your crying child, when you soothe and comfort your child's distress, when you feed, wash, and dress your child. These are the crucial nurturing experiences that say to your child, "I will watch over you and tend to your needs. You don't have to worry that you will be cared for. You can trust me and the world." Children who have been adequately nurtured grow up feeling special, important, and worthy of love. While research confirms that children need soothing and nurturing, nurturing is not the only way that attachment grows and not the only type of interaction your child needs.

For healthy attachment to grow, your child also needs to experience positive interpersonal play. Theraplay calls this engagement. Without the enjoyment and fun of pure play, there is little motivation for your child to want to relate to you. Fun, happy surprises, and excitement in relationships say, "I have something really wonderful to do with you." And, "Wow, we can sure have fun together!" When you interact with a child in this manner, your child feels special and important. Your child's world, which you represent, is interesting and inviting. Different from the nurturing and soothing which calms us, fun and play increase your child's emotional arousal in pleasurable and healthy ways. Regulated arousal is a necessary experience for us all, helping us to manage the ups and downs of our daily experiences without going to emotional extremes and falling apart as a result.

Children also need to feel protected by their adults. This means that your child needs you to do two things:

1. Take sufficient charge of interactions and situations so that your child doesn't feel undue responsibility for your child's own well-being, without being controlling, engaging in power struggles, or creating distance in the relationship, and without anger or resentment.
2. Set limits and appropriate expectations on behavior so that your child doesn't feel out of control and uncared about or is allowed to wreak havoc in your home; again, without being controlling, harsh, punitive, or angry. A familiar word for this is structure. Taking charge and setting limits can sometimes be hard, yet they communicate a very important attachment message: "I care about you so much that I will stand firm in guiding and protecting you. Because you are a child who cannot always make good decisions, I will make decisions and set the necessary limits that I know you need." Your child must feel you as a positive force, someone who will respond to your child's needs with flexibility and sensitivity.

Lastly, your child needs appropriate challenge. Children are born with a natural drive to explore the world, take risks, and expand their abilities. To do this they need a "safe base" from which to move out into the world, as described in the chapter on Theory in this book. Children need a safe, attentive parent to be in charge, allowing and offering appropriate challenges for them to experience. When you appropriately challenge your child, you are saying, "You can do it! You are competent and strong, and I'm so very proud of you!" Children who have been given appropriate challenges and who are allowed to explore safely are able to be appropriately independent, can initiate plans and projects, and feel competent to face the world.

The Importance of Touch

While other aspects of attachment-building have been described in this book, I want to highlight the importance of touch because touch is the first way that the new human being comes into contact with the world. Tender touch is crucial in developing feelings of love for another and actually triggers love hormones in the body that help us fall in love. It gives the nonverbal message that you are near and available to your child. Without experiences of healthy, safe touch from you, your child, who may be confused about and possibly untrusting of touch, will never learn what healthy touch is. Theraplay is filled with healthy touch, ensuring that you and your child experience this most basic connection.

Emphasizing nurturing, engagement, structure, and challenge, we will paint a picture of how these components look in real life.

The Healthy Baby Scene

Picture a healthy baby with her or his parents. Baby is waking from a nap, and whimpers. Baby whimpers more. Mommy comes and picks Baby up, pats Baby on the back and gently bounces Baby, saying, "It's okay, it's okay." Quickly, Baby quiets. Help has come. (This is the surest way to quiet a baby.) Thoughtfully, Mommy checks Baby's diaper and, sure enough, a change is needed. While diapering, Baby and Mommy suddenly lock gazes. Mommy breaks out in a huge smile and says, "Hi there, cutie!" Baby wiggles in delight at the social interaction and Mommy catches Baby's legs and starts playing patty-cake with Baby's feet. Baby squeals with pleasure.

They play for a bit, and then Baby starts to fret a little. Mommy notices this, feels a tug of mild distress at Baby's upset, and wonders what Baby is trying to tell her. "Listening" to her baby's communication, she realizes Baby must need something else now. So she stops playing and picks up Baby. From long experience she recognizes that her baby must be hungry, so she settles into a comfortable chair and cradles her baby for nursing. Once Baby has nursed for a bit and is calmed by the feeling of a filled-up tummy, Mommy's face suddenly becomes more interesting than the milk. Baby looks up at Mommy who realizes that her baby is now wanting to interact with her. She smiles and says, "There you are! Hi!" and Baby lets go of the nipple and breaks into a delighted smile. Then Baby, with eyes fixed on Mommy's eyes, lifts a hand and reaches for Mommy's smiling mouth. Mommy goes "mmm" and nibbles on her baby's fingers. Baby smiles and giggles, enjoying this relaxed give-and-take. This rhythm of feeding, connection, and intimate play repeats itself a few times before Baby is finished nursing. Now Baby is content and alert.

Daddy puts his baby on the floor for "tummy time," and gets down on the floor himself. Daddy puts a favorite toy a little distance away from Baby, and Baby kicks and pulls up to reach for it. Daddy says, "Come on, you can do it. Here it is!" and makes sure the toy is just barely out of reach so that Baby, with one more kick, will get it and feel successful enough to try future challenges. "Yay! You got it!" Daddy says with his joyful, wide open eyes. "What a smart baby you are!" With his attention caught by the Daddy's strong emotion, Baby locks his gaze onto Daddy's joyous face and squeals with delight.

Daddy continues to play with Baby, showing Baby toys, putting Baby in a Baby gym, carrying Baby around football style, and going to see what Mommy is doing. After a while, Daddy sees Baby bring hands up to Baby's eyes. Alert to this nonverbal communication, Daddy says, "Oh, you're getting tired. Almost time for a nap." After a few more minutes of interacting and eye rubbing, Daddy says, "It's time," and picks up Baby, rechecks the diaper, and then gently puts his baby in the crib. Baby fusses a little. Daddy reads this as his baby saying he needs help with calming down, and puts his hands on Baby's tummy for soothing. Slowly Baby's muscles settle, eyes begin to close, and Baby is asleep.

This baby has had affirming, well-attuned parent-child interactions. The parents sensed their baby's state, read their baby's "mind," and responded to their baby's needs. When their baby needed *nurturing*, they nurtured (changed and nursed Baby). When their baby needed engagement, they played with their baby (patty-cake, nibbling fingers). When their baby was ready for challenge, they challenged (reach for toy). And when their baby needed them to take charge of things, they provided structure by feeding their baby and putting their baby to bed. They held their baby close (touch) and responded sensitively when they met their baby's need for food, play, sleep, and also when they felt the joy of their baby's accomplishment. These attuned interpersonal experiences kept their baby emotionally regulated. This is a picture of attachment-in-the-making, and it is what we replicate through Theraplay.

This child's inner working model of relationships is developing in a positive direction. The child feels good about self, feels able to make an impact on the world, and feels cared for and safe. The child's world is secure and inviting.

Sadly, a child who has not been cared for adequately, who has lost caring caregivers, or has been abused is more likely to have a tenuous, or even absent, sense of self as special, important, and lovable. Instead, the child probably feels the opposite. This child may feel unlovable, unimportant, unwanted, and no fun to anyone. Having learned that parents and adults are untrustworthy and dangerous, this child may feel able to depend only on self.

A child with aspects of this negative inner working model needs your help. You will want to create interactions that will transform this negative model into one that is positive. In doing so, the two of you will get closer to that comfortable sense of family you both need. This is where Theraplay can help.

THERAPLAY IDEAS FOR HOME

Getting Ready

There is no rule about when or how often to do Theraplay games with your child. While you want to have spontaneous Theraplay moments when the spirit moves you, you may also want to create the physical and emotional space and plan for time for what I will call "Attaching Time." Having a comforting, supporting environment for your "attachment moments" is important. Let's talk about how to do this.

Physical Space

Neglected children often have muscle tone weaknesses that make it harder for them to sustain unsupported sitting or standing for very long. As they get tired, they get wiggly (often interpreted as hyperactive behavior) and are less able to engage with you. You want to give them the support they need to free up energy for interpersonal play. Beanbag chairs with or without pillows can be very helpful, allowing children to recline yet to be very well supported. Reduce distractions in your play area so that other things are not visible to compete with you as the play object. *You* want to be in the foreground, prominent, interesting, dominating the view.

Emotional Space

First and foremost, be attuned to yourself. Don't push yourself to play with your child when you are feeling exhausted, frustrated, angry, or otherwise stressed. Instead of feeling fully engaged by you, your child will be feeling your tension. Children "listen" to your nonverbal communication. If you are really feeling, "I don't want to be doing this with you. Something else is bothering me, and I can't devote all my attention to you," your child will hear, "I'm not interesting, special, or lovable." This would damage the attachment process. Instead, choose times when you feel freed up to play with your child.

How you interact with your child is more important than what you *say* and sometimes even more important than *what* you are doing. For an example of this, picture giving your child a kiss on a hurt, but doing it in a matter-of-fact, indifferent, preoccupied, or resentful way. Your child will hear, "You are irritating me. You are a sissy, or not important enough to hold my attention." In contrast, when you give the kiss with a face and a tone of voice that mirrors the pain your child is feeling, your child will feel like Mom or Dad really understands what it feels like deep inside. Your child will feel like you are "in your child's shoes" for this moment. It is just this experience that lessens the hurt. It is your empathy, shared feeling, and willing responsiveness that heals. You have spoken to your child's experience. This is attunement. This is rich emotional connection, and your child will feel, "Whew! My parents do care about me! That's just exactly what I needed."

Often, children struggling with attachment-resistance issues will react negatively to your attempts to connect, even during playful interactions.

If your child is rejecting, avoidant, withdrawing, fidgety, or fighting, you might find yourself feeling hurt and rejected. This experience can activate your own attachment history, resulting in feelings of increasing ambivalence about making attempts to connect again. If that frequently happens, get professional help. We cannot parent and interact with our children in healing, healthy ways when we are feeling negative about our child or ourselves. We start fighting or withdrawing, and that is not a recipe for promoting attachment.

Making Time

Now that you have a physical place and you are emotionally ready to have fun with your child, make real time for it. Plan break time from your usual routine to announce, "Attaching Time!" or "Mommy or Daddy Time!" Attaching Time can occur once in the morning, once in the afternoon, and once in the evening (like cuddling before bed). If you can't do it that frequently, then do it once a day. If you are a two-parent family, you may want to start out with just one of you playing with your child during Attaching Time. This will help your child focus just on you, and you won't have to be concerned with coordinating the activities with your spouse. This doesn't mean that that one parent does all the Attaching Times. You can take turns. You may want to start out with a brief play session of about five or ten minutes with one or two activities. As you and your child get more comfortable, you can add time and games. It can be helpful to end with something nurturing so your child leaves this highly interactive time feeling very cared for.

NURTURING

Achieving a Nurturing Mind-Set

Remember that infants need nurturing, and your child very likely needs the healing of infant-level attachment interactions "done right." If infants are not cared for and attended to, they will die, and your child may have partially died emotionally. You must provide nurturing to bring your child back. Caring for another means protecting, nourishing, and cherishing, literally giving of oneself for the welfare of the other. It means meeting your child's physical and emotional needs. Whether one month, two years, or four, eight, thirteen, or eighteen, your adopted or foster child likely has "baby needs" that went unmet before coming to you. By interacting with your child in nurturing, younger ways, you will create the types of intimate moments that build a sense of closeness, caring, and trust—the ingredients of attachment.

Having just said this, your child's need for nurturing may not be at all obvious if your child is preschool age or older. Even toddlers who have been abused or inadequately cared for may behave in ways that say, "I don't need or want your soothing or tenderness." While cared-for babies mold to their parents, seek eye contact, squeal and smile to signal their need for interaction, or cry for soothing and nurturing, your child may not acknowledge these needs or take the initiative in seeking you out. In the absence of these "green light" signals, you may stop nurturing your child, responding instead to your child's "red light" behavior that says, "Stop! Don't!" instead of listening to your own intuition and good judgment that says, "Do!" It is so important to find ways to nurture your child. Otherwise, your child could become an alienated teen and adult who doesn't interact well with others, who doesn't care much about others' feelings, or lacks the capacity for empathy. And when your child has children, it will be harder for your child to nurture in healthy ways. So *you* need to create opportunities for nurturing your child that will ignite a love affair between you. Be willing and ready to touch, touch, and touch!

Theraplay principles remind us to always interact with children at the level of their emotional, not chronological, age (Becker-Weidman, 2009). This means that if your child crawls into your lap, sucks a thumb, wants to play with your hair, or even nurses on a bottle or sippy cup, go with it! Unless your child is very young, you won't get these opportunities frequently. And you don't want to reject these unmet baby needs when they surface because your child could learn to shun internal feelings of need, and instead develop an unbalanced and possible rigid insistence on independence.

Why meet your child at the emotional age your child is presenting? Why nurture unmet needs? If I do, might the need increase? Actually, the opposite happens. When a need is fully met, it will go away. Needs and wants are not the same, and parents who are wise enough to nurture the unmet need will be helping their child to develop healthy attachments and, eventually, the emotional security that leads to appropriate independence.

How You and Your Child Might Respond to Nurturing

Prepare for being surprised if your child welcomes your lap, your cuddling, and your caregiving. Some children will soak up the nurturing they have such a deep need to experience. But having a bigger child in your lap who behaves more like a baby can be a strange experience for you. It might feel discrepant with what you think is age-appropriate behavior. Hopefully, you will put aside your worry that your child will never grow up and, instead, will remember that your child didn't get nurturing needs met and certainly didn't get them met by *you*! When your child has had enough "young-child" nurturing, you will likely get a sign, just as all children let us know they are ready to move into a new stage of interaction. And even when basic needs are met, all children, even teenagers who haven't asked to be on our laps for years, may regress at times when they experience illness, stress, or loss. And then, you may be surprised to find your daughter's head in your lap with your fingers stroking her hair, or your son's head snuggled on your shoulder. Don't stop nurturing, and don't push your child to grow up. Your child is still learning to let loved ones co-regulate strong feelings. Welcoming our loved one's support is the positive result of a healthy attachment relationship. Remember, when the need is met, it will go away.

Some children when nurtured will have a more difficult time letting go of control because they are deeply frightened. They may avoid most nurturing interactions, may try to nurture themselves (i.e., feed themselves), and may wiggle, strain, and pull away when you try to hug, cuddle them, or bring them close. If this describes your child, be patient, calm, and reassuring. Your child is frightened of intimacy and neediness for reasons originating in your child's past. Do not force your child to accept your nurturing. Try moments—literally moments—of nurturing, like a quick pat on the back, a quick squeeze of the hand, or a partial hug (squeeze of the shoulders with your hands). Approach nurturing in baby steps so that your child is not scared away but can gradually get more comfortable with these types of interactions.

If Problems Persist

If you find it hard to nurture your child, whether it is because your child continues to push you away, or because you have something inside of you that is scaring you off or saying it's wrong, too babyish, or too intimate, you should seek help. (See the chapter on "Mindfulness" for suggestions on what to do.) Negative feelings about nurturing will get in the way of you developing a caring, healing relationship with your child.

HERE WE GO! NURTURING ACTIVITIES FOR YOU!

1. Care for hurts. Have a bottle of lotion easily available for the many opportunities to show caring. Make a "big deal" of caring for hurts whether mild or severe, visible or invisible, old or new. Lotion around the area of the hurt (not on top of it), stroke or dab it with a dry cotton ball or a feather, blow on it, or kiss it. See if lotion feels good to your child, and what scent is preferred. Some children can have an aversive reaction to the feel of lotion, especially if they have tactile sensitivities. For such children, soft stroking can feel like tickling and

will stimulate the excitatory nervous system resulting in activity and arousal, not calm. Instead, try firm, slow, deliberate touch, the type of deep pressure that is calming for most of us. If your child reacts negatively to lotion, then don't use it. Instead, use the other items described above.

For older children, you may hear, "I'm not your baby." You could say, "I know. But we didn't have a chance to do this when you were a baby, and this is what I would have done." Or, "I wish you'd been my baby, and this is what I would have done." (See the chapter on narratives for other ideas.) This may help your child respond to your overtures. If not, don't force it. You've "planted a seed," giving your child permission to have "baby needs," while verbalizing the reason those needs are still there. You are also giving your child permission to get those needs met *and* permission to get them met by you. By doing this, you are creating an opening for nurturing to happen when your child is ready.

2. Initiate interactions typically found during earlier developmental periods. Purposefully recapture for your child and yourself earlier developmental periods—especially babyhood. Try using an actual baby bottle to feed your child water, juice, or milk. (Note: Enlarge the hole in the nipple by cutting an X through the hole with a sharp knife. Older children don't have the strong suck reflex of the infant and will get frustrated with the smaller hole.) Don't let your child walk around holding the bottle; work toward your child being comfortable being cradled in your arms or leaning against pillows and help your child hold the bottle. Sippy cups and juice boxes can be used similarly. Other ways to recapture babyhood is by feeding, bathing, singing, and cradling your child. While you should not bathe an older child or adolescent, you certainly can nurture by sponging neck and arms on a hot day, fanning with a fan, paper, or a big pillow after active games, and by playfully feeding a cookie and watching your child eat it all up! With younger children, play early childhood games such as peek-a-boo, patty-cake, "This Little Piggy," and "Eensy-Weensy Spider" and other one-on-one games with face-to-face eye contact and touch. Adapt these to older children by using finger plays (find them at www.nncc.org/Curriculum/fingerplay.html) and gestures with songs and chants ("B-I-N-G-O," "A Sailor Went to Sea Sea Sea," "Miss Mary Mack").

3. Sing to your child: sing lullabies, happy songs, silly songs.

4. Do some self-help tasks for your child: tie shoes, brush and style hair.

5. Massage your child.

6. Get to know your child in the way that parents learn about their new baby.
   A. Gaze into your child's eyes.
   B. Count fingers, toes, ears, or nose.
   C. Find and admire your child's special spots. Put lotion on them. Take pictures.
   D. Take turns imitating funny faces and noises. Follow your child's lead, imitating your child's face first, then you making a funny face for your child to imitate.
   E. Compare similarities and differences between you in size of hands and feet, color of skin and hair, details of smiles, number of freckles, lines in hands or faces.
7. Show and demonstrate love, don't just talk about it. Remember the song "Show Me" in *My Fair Lady*? It is not enough to tell your child, "I love you" many times during the day. Your nonverbal communication says it all, so develop your own personal ways to show you care.
8. Swing in a sheet. Two parents, or parents and other family members encircle the sheet. Have your child lay down facing up so you can be seen. On cue, everyone picks up the sheet and swings it gently while singing:

> Rock-a-bye [child's name] on the treetop.
> When the wind blows, the cradle will rock.
> When the bough breaks, the cradle will fall,
> And we will catch [child's name] cradle and all.

Or, to the tune of "My Bonnie Lies Over the Ocean":

> My [child's name] lies over the ocean.
> My [child's name] lies over the sea,
> My [child's name] lies over the ocean,
> Oh bring back my [child's name] to me, to me
> Oh bring back my [child's name] to me.
> (Repeat last line twice more)

9. Use ideas in *I Love You Rituals*. This book by Becky Bailey has nursery rhymes, interactive finger plays, soothing games, and physically active games for children from infancy through age eight. The traditional words have been changed to convey positive, upbeat messages.
10. Read nurturing and attachment-promoting books. For little kids or for older children with limited English, *Hug* (Alborough, 2000), and *"More More More" Said the Baby* (Williams, 1990) are perfect for conveying the nurturing relationship of parent (in these books, it is Mom) and child.

11. Have Cuddle Time. Make a time to simply cuddle with your child. This can be at bedtime or anytime. Putting on soft music, reading an attachment-promoting book, singing, or feeding your child are fine things to do during Cuddle Time. You can also tell your child what you will remember about your child from that day: "Today I'm going to remember how your eyes got so big when you caught the ball." Instead of a performance-focused message, like "You did a good job playing basketball," try to give nonjudgmental messages like, "I remember your big strong muscles from our basketball game," and "I love the way you crunched your cookie."

12. Find ways to facilitate face-to-face interactions with tender eye contact. When you feed your child, try to "find" your child's face and eyes with your eyes. Try not to say, "Look at me." If your child is looking elsewhere or looks away from you, say, "Oh no! Where did you go? Where are those beautiful eyes? Let's see if I can find them." Then move your face to be in the child's line of vision; then move again if your child avoids your gaze. Make this very playful and don't persist past two attempts. You want to "woo" your child, not coerce or dominate. You want to communicate your desire for eye-to-eye connection (which is really heart-to-heart connection) so you can feel emotionally closer, while simultaneously being attuned to any fears of intimacy your child may have.

13. Use your child's name. Resist using a generic word, like "son," when you talk to your child. Using your child's name will draw your attention to your child's unique personhood and help your child feel more noticed and special. Tender nicknames are fine. Use your special name for your child in songs, fingerplays, when giving directions, and commenting on daily events.

14. Find ways to be important to your child. If your child shows no need of you, communicate that you want to be involved anyway. Create ways for your child to need you. Use toys that require your help, like blowing bubbles, or blowing up a balloon.

15. Check-ins: When your child is playing without you, practice checking in. Interrupt what you are doing to acknowledge what your child is doing. This may mean a big check-in ("Hey, you're really making a neat picture!") or a small check-in (only making eye contact and smiling). Even a brief moment of connection will tell your child, "You are on my mind whether you want to feel distant from me or not. I'm remembering you, regardless."

16. Feeding: Feeding younger or older children recaptures the direct, concrete nurturing experiences of infancy. Young children often enjoy being fed by their parents at mealtime, snacktime, anytime. Older children will often accept being fed, especially their favorite

ice cream given from a tiny spoon. This can be done as an evening routine, with the child lying next to you on the couch, or across from you in a comfy chair. As you feed the ice cream, talk together without any particular goal; small talk is a relaxing, shared experience that will develop your ease with each other, regardless how anything else went, good or bad, earlier in the day. Even children who are resistant to other forms of play initiated by a parent often enjoy spending time with a parent who feeds them ice cream.

For Older Kids

Play Stack of Hands with Lotion. It is preferable to first lotion everyone's hands, but this game can be done without lotion. After lotioning, you put one hand out toward child, palm down. Have child put one hand on top of yours, then put your other hand on top, then the child's other hand. Slowly move your lowest hand to the top, then child moves child's lowest hand to the top, and so on, higher and higher, until you decide to stop. You can come back down as well. This can also be done with more family members.

Play Weather Report. This is a fun way to get nurturing touch into interactions with your older child. This can be done as a pair (parent-child) or a family. Sit or stand next to your child (or other family members) and turn to the side so that you are facing your child's back (and behind you is someone facing your back). Position yourselves so that you can comfortably touch the back of the person in front of you. Now announce the weather report. For each type of weather you announce, massage and move your hands on your child's back in ways that symbolize the weather. For a sunny day, you can draw a round circle and then the rays of the sun. For rain, start with a drizzle (soft taps with fingertips down the back), then rain (heavier taps with fingertips and some stroking down the back with fingers), thunderstorm including lightning (a zigzag movement on the back) followed by thunder (fists thumping on the back). Snow can lead to a blizzard with wind and sleet (swirls of movement of fingers, hands, arms). Add whatever weather you think of, then end with a sunny day.

ENGAGEMENT

Achieving an Engaging Mind-Set

Children need high-intensity moments of interpersonal play, best achieved through spontaneous, unselfconscious play. I'm not talking about board-game play, nor am I talking about imaginary play that involves creating stories with dolls, puppets, stuffed animals, or other props. These objects take away from the types of direct, face-to-face, emotionally connected, interpersonal play that Sunderland, in *The Science of Parenting*, says are "moments of real meeting between you and your child." As parents of an adopted child, both of you need moments of real meeting so that you can feel you and your child belong to each other. To "really meet" your child, not only must you not use toys and dolls, you must not let your inhibitions interfere with playing! Your child needs to see the child in you, the laid-back yet spirited person who can have fun for fun's sake, without any goal in mind other than having a pleasant time together. Can you relax and turn off your mature, goal-directed thinking? The joyful dance between a parent and child exemplifies a joie de vivre often lacking in a hurt child's experience. Moment to moment enjoyment of each other, experienced during playful times together, is the experience that builds the bonds of security and love. Your joyful engagement can go a long way toward helping to light up your child's life.

Cultivate the art of being appealingly positive. Smile, open your eyes wide, let them twinkle, and let positive, playful emotions show on your face. Think of your child as a small baby who has to learn from you that the world is wonderful and inviting. To do this, *you* have to be enticing and inviting because emotionally hurt and traumatized children generally will not entice or invite you in. Children like yours tend to go about their business, or approach and then avoid, or fight when you try to offer something fun. This behavior can be very difficult for any parent. Birth parents of nontraumatized, healthy children usually get positive responses from their children, and, very quickly, their children seek them out for interaction. It is very hard to keep approaching your child with optimism and hope when you are getting no response to let you know you're on the right track. In fact, it may be hard to see your child as appealing. Parents who have a predominantly positive relationship with their child can cope with things that are normally aversive (poop, mess, vomit, even angry feelings fit into this category) because they feel a strong, protective reaction toward their child. Without feeling attached, aversion can kick in easier and we feel more repulsed, angry, and sorry for ourselves. (If you are already at this point, it would be best to seek help. See chapter 10, "Mindfulness," for suggestions.) Try to see the sad, fearful, upset child, and then respond accordingly. You need to communicate that your child's feelings are okay and that you will be responsive, nurturing, and helpful through the journey toward emotional self-regulation.

How You and Your Child Might Respond to Engagement

The exciting nature of these engaging activities may rev up your child. Be ready for such a reaction with some calming, slower, and quieter activities of a more nurturing nature to follow active games. Your child may ignore your invitation to play, reject your idea for a game and demand to play something else, act disappointed and unhappy with your choice, or look at you with disapproval. This could engender in you the understandable feelings of inadequacy, anger, and resentment for all the planning, hopes, and effort you have put into this. It helps to not take such resistance personally. It is simply your child's defense against past hurts. Invitations to let go of worry and enjoy you or your plans could be causing your child to feel vulnerable to another rejection. Some children have experienced so much disappointment that they no longer ever count on having a good time again, and if they do, it surely won't last. Something will go wrong, even if they have to make it go wrong and get it over with, already. Persist for a while. Your enthusiasm and refusal to be diverted or stopped by your child's resistance may carry the day. If not, you can back up a bit and try some still engaging but more low-keyed, structured activities. (All activities involve more than one Theraplay dimension.) Instead of acting enticing and inviting, try calmer games. Your child may respond.

If Problems Persist

If your child continues to resist your playful efforts, or needs to always control the activities, you'd do well to get some help. Likewise, if you cannot find your playful self, maybe you weren't played with as a child. Certainly, if you find yourself resentful or angry that your child isn't responding, seek out a therapist or try some of the suggestions in chapter 10, "Mindfulness." Negative feelings can be tied to "ghosts" of the past and will be a barrier between you and your child. Attachment won't grow with ghosts in the way.

HERE WE GO! ENGAGING ACTIVITIES FOR YOU!

1. Play This Little Piggy: Gently take your child's sock off. Be surprised at what you find: five wiggly toes! Then, with firm (not tickly) touch on each toe, say:

   This little piggy went to market.
   This little piggy went home.
   This little piggy had roast beef.
   This little piggy had none.
   And THIS little piggy went . . . wee, wee, wee, all the way home. (Firmly move your fingers or hands up child's leg until you get to your child's tummy, giving it a firm-pressure "tickle.")

2. Read *Pete's a Pizza* (Steig, 1998) and act it out, getting to the end and pretending to eat your child up.

3. Make Play Doh moldings of child's hand(s), feet, ears, belly button.

4. Play Toilet Paper Bust Out: Wrap toilet paper around your child, leaving the face uncovered. On the count of 1-2-3-Go, have your child bust out!

5. Play Bubble Pop with body parts: Blow a few bubbles to your child who will pop them with a finger, an elbow, a chin, knee, etc.

6. Play Three-Legged Walk: Stand next to your child with your sides together, facing outward. Tie a scarf around your inner legs. With your arms around each other's waists, walk together to different locations around the room.

7. Play Balloon Balance: Blow up a latex balloon, and balance it between the two of you with no hands, using just your chests, or foreheads, sides, backs, and so on.

8. Play Beep-Honk: Face-to-face, touch your child's nose, saying, "Honk!" Do it a few times with surprise. Now gently tug on an ear and say, "Beep!" in a higher pitched voice. Go back and forth between nose honk and ear beep. Then gently tap your child's chin and make another funny sound, like a raspberry. If your child reaches up to do the same with you, that's just fine!

9. Play Slippery, Slippery, Slip: Sit face-to-face and support your child in a beanbag chair or pillows. Let your child recline into the pillows or beanbag chair. Generously lotion your child's arms. Then "try" to pull your child up saying, "Slippery, slippery, slip!" and when you say "slip," let your child's arms slip out of your grasp. Either you can fall backward, or your child can safely fall back into the chair or pillows. Repeat. This gives your child firm pressure and good tactile feedback to the body.

10. Play Cotton Ball Blow: Hold a cotton ball in your hand, up close and in front of your mouth. Give the 1-2-3-Go cue, blow the ball toward your child, and see where it lands. Then hold the ball in front of your child's mouth, give the cue, and see where your child blows it. Maybe your hair, nose, or your tummy!

11. Play Cotton Ball Touch: Have your child close eyes. Touch somewhere on your child's skin. Child must tell you where you touched. For very young children, let them watch you touch them. Give them turns to touch you and you guess.

12. Sing "If You're Happy and You Know It": Include actions that are interactive (like give high fives, give a hug or wink, jump up together, etc.).

Calmer Games

13. Play Count the Squeezes: This game involves engagement and nurturing and is a focused exercise. Hold your child's hands in yours and gently give a certain number of squeezes, but not more than ten. Your child can count out loud or silently. To make it more difficult, have your child close eyes. Then squeeze other parts of the body like shoulders, elbows, knees, or feet. You can tenderly hold your child's face in your hands and squeeze (like hugging the face with your hands). For very young children, instead of having them count, have them tell you if your single squeeze is big (a long, firm squeeze) or little (a brief, weak squeeze).

14. Share stickers or feathers: Have a collection of stickers or feathers and give matching groups to you and your child (the groups should match in number and color of items). Put your stickers or feathers on your child and have your child do the same on you, matching locations and which colors are used. For example, a blue feather on heads, orange on a shoulder, yellow on knees.

15. Palm Finding: Put powder on your and your child's palms and look for letters or shapes.

16. Charades: Take turns acting out something and the other person guesses.

17. Create a Story: Create a story about something you did together. Alternate sentences as you develop the story, with your child giving the first sentence, you the second, and so on.

STRUCTURE

Achieving the Structuring Mind-Set

In order to understand what a safe, protective, and nurturing parent can be, your child needs to feel you as a strong, benevolent presence. When you use Theraplay's way of structuring playfully, you will be communicating such a presence to your child while helping your child better accept the inevitable limits in life. We all have to learn to live with limits. Theraplay has a clever and effective way of helping a child learn to stay within healthy limits. Rather than structure being serious and un-fun, Theraplay makes it an appealing part of playing with your child.

This is Theraplay's approach to structure: Structure your child by taking charge of the activities you do, but do it in a playful, engaging way. This means that *you* will initiate the games with your child and take charge of

100 Phyllis B. Rubin

making positive, playful interactions happen. Be determined, but do not force. Find ways to persevere. Instead of asking your child, "Do you want to play?" which can invite the answer, "No!" use more engaging language like, "Let's" or "I want to play with you." Your child will hear how invested you are and know that you care.

Cue your child for the start and the end of games. Although you might be tempted to follow your child's lead, it is good practice to have interactions in which *you* take the lead. This doesn't mean that you get to be first. It means that you decide what's going to happen and when the action will start and when it stops. Putting this all together, it means a soundtrack that goes something like this: "Come stand right here on this spot on the rug. Now, get ready! Make a fist (you show how). Oh, that's a good one! Now punch like this (you show child again). Now (you hold in front of him a sheet of newspaper), get ready to punch right here (you show him where)! Get ready! Get set! Go! (Child smashes the paper.) Wow! What a great punch you have and such strong muscles! Let's do it again."

When it's time to be finished with this game, you say, "Last punch. One-two-three-punch! (He punches.) What a great punch you have! Now sit down while I massage your muscles from that strong punching." (You lotion child's muscles or fists, getting in some nurturing.)

Do you hear the parent taking charge? Can you feel not only the power and confidence of that parent's language, but the compelling energy that invites the child to respond to the parent's playful, upbeat directions? This is the beauty of structure through Theraplay. It's actually fun!

How you and your child might respond to structure: Some people are comfortable with taking charge and setting limits. The goal is to make it playful so your child will not feel that limits are only used to thwart and restrict. But what if your child tests or resists? When you say, "go," your child doesn't respond or responds too soon. There are a number of ways you can handle such situations. If your child doesn't respond, you can playfully check the arm that did not punch. "Uh oh, you lost your muscle! Now where could it be?" (And playfully look for it, put the muscle "back," and cue for the punch again.) If your child still resists, you could agree that the muscle is gone, that a punch isn't possible, and you can verify this by giving the cue again, saying you know this won't work because the muscle is gone. You win either way. If your child punches too soon, then you can say, "Uh oh! We have to try again. 1-2-3-(holding your child's arm, then)-Go (and let the arm go and cheer your child's success)." Stay positive and accepting, even if your child steps out of the limits you have set. If your child is persistent, and repeatedly punches too soon, switch your tactics and say "Punch before I say 'Go.'" This is called "prescribing the behavior" or "if you can't beat 'em, join 'em." Telling your child to repeat the "problem" behavior can diffuse the problem and keep you emotionally connected and away from power struggles.

Now some of you may have trouble setting limits for your child. You may feel you should tread ever so gently after all the losses, disruptions, and hard times your child has had in the past. You want your child to love you. It can be tough to be firm when you associate being firm with being a "bad guy" and losing someone's love. If this is true for you, you may be confusing taking charge with excessive strictness or even with abuse. There is a big difference between calmly taking responsibility by guiding your child about how to live within our social norms, and unhealthy and inflexible strictness arising from fears about the dangers that lurk in a child's display of autonomy and individuality. Indeed, you must face your issues about structure because, if you are not able to set good limits for your child, your child will not respect you as the responsible adult. Your child needs to see your strength and confidence in order to develop a healthy dependence on you as the parent. This will not happen if you are unable to structure.

If Problems Persist

If, after trying these structuring ideas, you still feel unable to take charge and set limits, and it feels like your child is taking advantage of you, it is time to find a therapist. The sooner you find help, the better because your child needs to experience you as a force in life. On the other hand, children who persist in resisting your structure may be showing the more serious signs of attachment disorder and PTSD. They must be in control of things, because they do not feel safe, and thus they don't respond to your structure. You suggest one thing, they ask for another. You do the other, they ask for something else again. If this behavior doesn't improve, seek help. Your child's need to control is a version of distrust in the world. Your child feels safe only when in charge because of pervasive fear that stems from very real threatening experiences in the past.

HERE WE GO! STRUCTURING ACTIVITIES FOR YOU!

1. Always structure your play activities. Whenever you want your child to do something (jump, run to you), first say, 1-2-3-Go! Or Get Ready-Get Set-Go! This will help reduce the possibility of your child reacting impulsively and is a very playful way to teach your child to listen for your okay. Even children with little language or English understand the sounds of 1-2-3-Go when you combine it with hand gestures (one finger up; two fingers up; three fingers up; then a gesture to indicate "go.") Don't use this cuing for nurturing though.

2. Play Paper Punch: Tear off a large piece of newspaper. Show how to make a fist and have your child practice punching on the count of 1-2-3-Go. Hold the newspaper stretched open in front of you but slightly to the side of your body. On 1-2-3-Go! see if your child can smash the paper. Wow!

3. Play Cotton Ball Hockey: Sit across from your child with a large pillow between you. Place a cotton ball in the middle of the pillow. On the count of 1-2-3-Go, both of you blow the ball, trying to roll it off the opposite edge of the pillow. Let your child win!

4. Measure your child: This is a great way to learn about your child. Use crepe paper, adding machine paper, or Fruit Roll-Ups. Measure different parts of your child: arms from shoulder to end of longest finger; hands; feet; head as though measuring for a hat; ears; nose; smile. If you use Fruit Roll-Ups as your measuring tape, you can feed your child the fruit after measuring to get in some nurturing. Keep the paper strip from the Roll-Ups as a concrete reminder of the lengths of the parts you measured. These can be labeled and taped to the wall.

5. Play Follow the Leader: Take turns doing some sort of action (jumps, dancing, etc.) and the other copies.

6. Play Hot Potato-Cold Potato: Pass from one to the other a soft ball. Start off very slowly while saying, "Cold potato" as the ball passes from one to the other. Then speed it up while saying, "Warm potato." At "Hot potato!" pass the ball as fast as you can! Mix up cold, warm, and hot speeds. This is great fun for the whole family.

7. Play Row, Row, Row Your Boat: Sit face-to-face, holding hands, with your feet straddling each other's sides. Then lean back and forth singing:

> Row, Row, Row your boat,
> Gently down the stream.
> Merrily, merrily, merrily, merrily,
> [Your child's name] is but a dream.

8. Play Partner Pull-Ups: This is good for older kids. Sit face-to-face, holding hands with knees bent and toes together. On the count of 1-2-3-Go, pull up together and don't let the other fall. You can also try sitting back-to-back, arms linked at the elbows, knees bent and feet as close to your body as possible. Push up together on cue.

9. Use Theraplay structure during the day. An example might be at dinnertime when you might say, "Okay, time to go to the table. Get ready, get set, GO!"

CHALLENGE

Achieving a Challenging Mind-Set

In one sense, your child doesn't need challenge for attachment. Your child has already been challenged enough: (1) by having to adjust to one or more new caregivers; (2) by having to cope with neglect, abuse, rejection, abandonment; (3) by having to take on the responsibility of caring for self or siblings because your child learned that others can't be depended on. Too much of a focus on challenge from you could reinforce your child's independence and self-reliance, which could counteract the attachment process. If you convey that you value independence, your child may learn to shut down dependency needs. Yet autonomy and growth are normal processes that will be active, especially the older your child is. Challenge can address this need.

You can use challenge to recognize, admire, and appreciate your child's competences—again to be a strong, confirming presence to your child—while remembering to always balance this message with plentiful doses of nurturing.

How You and Your Child Might Respond to Challenge

You may find yourself wanting to keep your child close rather than to "stretch" your child's abilities. After all, you are now working on attachment and may not want to see your child so capable and strong because it means less emotional connection and less need for nurturing. Here is where you need to check on whether your child needs to be kept close and nurtured more, or whether *you* need to maintain that level of closeness and dependency. This is about "reading" your child and knowing yourself. If your child allows healthy nurturing, then some degree of healthy challenge can help you keep your relationship well balanced.

Some children are reticent to take risks or show strength. Is your child clingy or timid? If so, there is likely to be a benefit in doing some of the challenging activities described below. If your child accepts nurture, then it is okay to try some light and playfully challenging activities. Start by maintaining closeness during the game, or by having your child in your lap to support playing with the other parent, and then switch laps. Introducing challenge into your interactions will communicate that you have confidence in your child, that life is trusting and safe, and that you support growth and healthy autonomy. If you do this gently and gradually while remembering to also nurture and engage, it will help your child feel stronger.

If Problems Persist

Fear of venturing out on one's own and taking appropriate risks can arise from many sources. There could be sensory, motor, coordination, or other physical factors making your child feel extra vulnerable and clingy. There could be serious psychological factors, like Post-Traumatic Stress Disorder, that make showing strength and courage very hard for your child. I'm not talking about a very newly adopted child, who, while adjusting to having parents, may seek closeness and even need to cling to you. This behavior is normal and promotes attachment in the early phases of your relationship. How long is too long for this behavior to continue will depend on many things about your child, yourself, and your child's history. If clinging and fear of venturing out continues such that you start to wonder and worry, get an assessment of this by a knowledgeable mental health professional, such as those listed as registered clinicians on the website of the Association for the Treatment and Training in the Attachment of Children (www.ATTACh.org).

HERE WE GO! CHALLENGING ACTIVITIES FOR YOU!

1. Play Balloon Bop: Blow up a latex balloon (they don't pop easily). Try keeping the balloon in the air by hitting it back and forth to each other, counting the number of hits. The person who lets the balloon hit the ground can get something wonderful (i.e., nurturing) from the rest: a hug; a wink; a high five. This is a great family game.
2. Play Cotton Ball Race: You and your child kneel down on the floor or get on tummies, next to each other. Place one cotton ball in front of you and one in front of your child. On cue, both of you try to blow your cotton ball as fast as you can to the other side of the room (or a designated ending spot). It's fun to let your child win as much as you can. Have a big hug and a high five ready.
3. Play Cotton Ball Fight: This can be a fun way to safely express mock anger or frustration. Give a bunch of cotton balls to everyone playing this game. On the count of 1-2-3-Go, everyone tries to hit the others with their cotton balls. When you run out of cotton balls, grab more from the floor and keep throwing. Saying things like, "I'm gonna get you!" makes it more fun.
4. Play Running to a Hug: With your child a distance away from you, tell your child to run to you on the count of 1-2-3-Go! Have your arms wide open and catch your child in a big bear hug. Then send your child back to do it again! This combines challenge and nurturing.
5. Play How High (or Far) Can You Jump: Have your child jump as high (or far) as possible on the count of 1-2-3-Go. Measure with adding machine or crepe paper.

For Older Children

6. Play Arm Wrestle: Lay down on tummies, facing each other. Pick right arms up on elbows, and then grasp your child's hand. On the count of 1-2-3-Go, both of you try to push the other's arm down. Of course, you let your child win and delight in your child's strength.

7. Play Thumb Wrestle: Cup one hand together with your child's hand. Lift up thumbs. Lay thumbs next to each other on top of your cupped fingers and move them from side to side as you say, "One, two, three, four. I declare a thumb war." Then try to capture you partner's thumb under yours. Again, see if you can play well enough to let your child win!

8. Play Drawing on Each Other's Backs: This game is for children who are good with writing and reading. The simplest level is for each of you to take turns drawing a shape with your finger on the other's back. More difficult is to write a letter, and even more difficult, a word on the other's back. For words, write one letter at a time. Fill the person's whole back with the shape or letter to make it easier to guess.

For the Family

9. Play Dr. Tangle: With enough people, this can be fun. In a circle, take the hand of someone not next to you. Now find someone else's hand with your other hand. Now, try to untangle the circle without breaking hands. This can entail crawling under or climbing over arms. You should end with an intact circle (with some people possibly facing outward) or, sometimes, with two circles.

10. Play Ball Roll: Sit on the floor in a circle, close together, legs straight out in front of you. Start a soft-textured ball going around the circle on your legs, and no one can touch it with their hands.

11. Play Balloon Toss in Blanket: In a circle, everyone hold the edge of a blanket or sheet. Put a balloon in the middle, and on the count of 1-2-3-Go, see how many times you can lift the balloon and catch it in the blanket. Make it more fun by adding balloons!

Now go have fun with your child and let attachment bloom.

6

The Role of Neuropsychological Evaluation and Intervention in the Management and Treatment of Children with a History of Early Maltreatment

Audrey Mattson

In 2002 nearly a million children were determined to have suffered childhood abuse or neglect (DeBellis, 2005). Children with a history of early maltreatment at the hands of caregivers often experience difficulty forming close relationships, and some abused and neglected children develop symptoms that can be conceptualized as a complex form of Post-Traumatic Stress Disorder. Such children may receive a variety of diagnoses, including Reactive Attachment Disorder, which describes the nature and quality of a child's problems, issues, and manner of relating to others. Some children with attachment problems may also, or instead, receive a diagnosis of Oppositional Defiant Disorder (ODD) because they exhibit significant behavioral difficulties (*Diagnostic and Statistical Manual of Mental Disorders*, 4th ed., American Psychiatric Association, 1994). In addition to these problems, children who have been subjected to early maltreatment are at increased risk of developing intellectual, academic, cognitive, and social-emotional difficulties (Briere, 2002; DeBellis, 2005; DeBellis & Thomas, 2003; Schore, 2003; Teicher, 2002). Many of these problems are neuropsychological in nature, meaning that they are related to changes in the brain's structure or neurochemical functioning.

The neuropsychological problems exhibited by children with a history of maltreatment may reflect the combined effects of a number of influences or factors. These factors include the adverse effect of early, chronic stress on brain development (DeBellis, 2005; Teicher et al., 2006); damage to brain structures caused by the direct effects of physical abuse (American Academy of Pediatrics, 2001); prenatal exposure to neurotoxic substances including alcohol and other drugs of abuse (Streissguth & O'Malley, 2000; Streissguth et al., 1996); and the effects of poverty including poor nutrition and inadequate maternal health care (Picard et al., 2003). A subgroup of children with a history of early maltreatment may also be at increased risk of psychological and behavioral difficulties due to hereditary factors (DeBellis, 2005). This is the case when a child's biological parents suffered from neuropsychiatric disorders with, at least in part, a genetic basis (e.g., depression and bipolar mood disorders). Knowledge about the nature and severity of a child's difficulties, as well as their areas of strength, is important, regardless of the exact cause of a child's impairments in adaptive functioning. This information can help guide the development of a plan that can help lessen the long-term impact of early maltreatment.

This chapter will first briefly review the neurobiological consequences of early neglect and abuse. This will include a summary of the potential effects of early head trauma due to physical abuse and prenatal exposure to alcohol and other substances. Attention disorders and learning disorders are also commonly diagnosed in children with a history of early maltreatment, and these conditions will be briefly commented upon. This will be followed by a brief introduction to the field of clinical neuropsychology; the specialty area of pediatric, or developmental, neuropsychology; and an overview of what to expect if your child is referred for a clinical neuropsychological evaluation. Lastly, some general suggestions are offered for parents raising children with a history of early maltreatment.

NEUROBIOLOGICAL CONSEQUENCES OF EARLY, CHRONIC STRESS DUE TO MALTREATMENT

A child's early social environment and the quality of his early attachments (especially with primary caregivers) has a long-term impact on the child's ability to successfully adapt when faced with new challenges, manage stress effectively, and eventually build a successful life (Cozolino, 2006; Schore, 2003). During the past two decades it has become increasingly clear that early maltreatment whether in the form of abuse (physical, sexual, or emotional) or neglect is stressful to the child and causes a series of neurobiological changes that alter the course of brain development (DeBellis, 2005; Schore, 2003; Teicher, 2002). The experience of early and chronic stress produces (1) alterations in the hormonal response within the body's stress systems, (2) alterations in the development of brain structures, and (3) an apparent reduction in the number and the pattern of neural connections between brain regions.

Chronic activation of the body's stress system causes the release of hormones that adversely impact the body's immune system and cause damage to nerve cells, particularly within areas of the brain important for learning and memory and emotional and behavioral regulation (Cozolino, 2006; DeBellis, 2005; Teicher, 2002). Research also indicates that the large bundle of nerve fibers that bridge the two cerebral hemispheres is smaller in children with a history of abuse or neglect. This indicates that early maltreatment is associated with less communication between the hemispheres and less cerebral integration (Teicher et al., 2006).

As a result of alterations in brain structure and function, children exposed to early maltreatment may exhibit subtle or more severe long-term neuropsychological difficulties in various cognitive domains (e.g., learning and memory; visual motor integration; language; and higher cognition which includes reasoning, problem-solving, and judgment) and in the areas of social and emotional function. The chronic, long-term stress associated with childhood maltreatment is also associated with an increased risk of Post-Traumatic Stress Disorder (PTSD) and co-morbid psychopathology. Oppositional and attention disorders have been associated with early maltreatment, and a history of early abuse or neglect may also be a factor in the development of later personality and mood disorders (DeBellis & Thomas, 2003). Without intervention, children exposed to early maltreatment may also be at increased risk for secondary problems including legal difficulties and substance abuse.

NEUROPSYCHOLOGICAL CONSEQUENCES OF PRENATAL EXPOSURE TO ALCOHOL AND OTHER DRUGS

During the last twenty-five years there has been a growing awareness of the nature and severity of problems children may develop when there is a history of maternal substance use during pregnancy. The first association between prenatal alcohol exposure and damage to the developing fetus was made in 1968 by a pediatrician in France (O'Malley & Storz, 2003). A few years later, Fetal Alcohol Syndrome (FAS) was defined as the presence of known or suspected history of maternal drinking, low birth weight and/or small size, and characteristic physical abnormalities and evidence of central nervous system dysfunction (e.g., learning and behavioral difficulties). The characteristic facial features associated with FAS include a thin upper lip, the appearance of widely spaced eyes, a flat mid-face, a short nose; and indistinct ridges between the nose and upper lip. These are often accompanied by other minor physical anomalies that are less specific. Hearing and visual abnormalities are also more common in children with FAS.

Over the years it has become clear that exposure to different levels of prenatal alcohol, at different time periods during pregnancy, can result in a variety of clinical presentations in children who don't have the complete FAS syndrome. A number of terms have been used to describe individuals who exhibit only some of the characteristics initially included in the definition of FAS. These include Fetal Alcohol Effects (FAE), Alcohol-Related Neurodevelopmental Disorder (ARND), and most recently Fetal Alcohol Spectrum Disorder (FASD) (Streissguth & O'Malley, 2000; Astley, 2006).

Fetal Alcohol Spectrum Disorder (FASD) is a general term that describes the full range of difficulties (from very mild to severe disturbances of physical, behavioral, emotional, and/or social functioning) observed in individuals exposed to alcohol prior to birth. Children with FASD are frequently diagnosed as suffering from Attention Deficit Hyperactivity Disorder (ADHD) and learning disorders. They also may exhibit problems with adaptive living skills, poor impulse control, poor memory, poor abstraction abilities, and difficulty understanding cause and effect. Children and adolescents with FASD also demonstrate a tendency toward high-risk behaviors and later in life are at increased risk for developing secondary problems including mental illness and involvement with the criminal justice system.

Individuals at risk for FASD should be screened by their primary health care provider. If the child screens positively, further assessment at a center that specializes in neurodevelopmental disorders is indicated. Several diagnostic systems have been developed to identify individuals with FASD. These systems generally include quantifiable criteria for rating the degree to which an individual evidences a growth deficiency, FAS facial features, and CNS dysfunction. The risk for prenatal alcohol exposure is also part of the diagnostic criteria (i.e., no risk, unknown risk, some risk, or high risk). Fetal Alcohol Syndrome (FAS) and partial FAS are two medical diagnoses that are still made if a child exhibits more severe effects of alcohol exposure and meets strict diagnostic criteria. Early diagnosis and intensive, appropriate interventions can make a significant difference in the long-term outcome for a child with FASD (Streissguth et al., 1996).

In the case of children in foster care or those who have been adopted with a history of early maltreatment, the risk of exposure to alcohol and other substances is often unknown. It has been speculated that these groups of children likely have a fairly high rate of prenatal exposure. Internationally adopted children, depending on country of origin, face a varying degree of risk. For example, the average rate of alcohol consumption in Russia is about three shots of hundred-proof vodka per day. Rates of alcohol consumption are substantially lower in the Muslim sections of Russia and in Far Eastern countries, such as China, Vietnam, and Cambodia. Screening for FASD is warranted, in the absence of a confirmed birth history of exposure, when there are indicators that raise the possibility of FASD (e.g., growth deficiency, presence of facial features associated with FAS).

A number of substances besides alcohol are also known, or suspected, of being toxic if a child is exposed to them in utero. These include cocaine, heroin and methadone, marijuana, and anticonvulsant medications (Dietrich, 2000). It is known that prenatal exposure to cocaine or other drugs increases the risk of premature birth and low birth weight. It is unclear, however, whether this is due to drug exposure or the effects of inadequate maternal nutrition and health care. Studies investigating the effects of prenatal exposure to drugs of abuse, other than alcohol, have had inconsistent results. Research findings do indicate that babies exposed to cocaine or multiple drugs are easily overstimulated, but it is less clear whether these substances result in any long-term neuropsychological consequences. This is partially because it is difficult to conduct research studies on this topic because women who abuse illegal drugs during pregnancy also usually also abuse alcohol or a combination of drugs. Fetal drug effects (FDE) is one term that has been used to describe children thought to be affected in some way by prenatal exposure to one or more drugs.

EARLY BRAIN TRAUMA

Physical abuse is the leading cause of serious head injury in infants, and homicide is the leading cause of injury-related deaths in children younger than four years of age (Alexander et al., 2001; Bruce & Zimmerman, 1989). Shaken Baby Syndrome is a very serious form of child maltreatment that results from the violent shaking of the infant or toddler. The act of shaking that produces this syndrome is violent, and someone observing would recognize that the shaking was dangerous and likely to kill the child (Academy of Pediatrics, 2001). Caregivers who are under stress, involved in domestic abuse, or abusing substances are at higher risk of engaging in this type of impulsive and aggressive behavior when a young child is irritable and crying. Shaken Baby Syndrome usually involves young children less than two years of age, but it has been documented in children up to five years of age. Over half of infants who are unconscious when initially examined by a doctor die or have profound mental retardation and physical disabilities. Shaken Baby Syndrome may, however, be misdiagnosed especially when the effects are subtle. Signs of Shaken Baby Syndrome vary from mild and nonspecific to severe and obviously due to head trauma. Nonspecific symptoms after a less severe shaking injury may include a history of poor feeding, vomiting, lethargy, and/or irritability lasting for days or weeks. Less severe cases may never even result in a visit to a doctor. Information is not available about the outcome for shaken infants that are not seen by health care providers, but it is quite possible that they may later evidence learning, motor, or behavioral problems with no known cause (Academy of Pediatrics, 2001).

Young children who are exposed to physical abuse and neglect are also at increased risk of head trauma due to other causes, including blunt force trauma and accidental injury (e.g., being struck, falls). Pediatric head trauma, especially when severe, can cause long-term problems including reductions in intellectual ability, academic achievement, cognitive skills (e.g., attention, memory, language, visual motor, problem-solving, and judgment), adaptive functioning, and behavioral regulation (Yeates, 2000). Severe injuries are generally defined as those that result in a period of unconsciousness, or coma, lasting at least several hours and requiring hospitalization.

LOW BIRTH WEIGHT AND PREMATURITY

Children born with a low birth weight (LBW) are also at risk for neuropsychological impairment (Picard et al., 2000). Babies weighing less than or equal to 2,500 grams, or approximately 5½ pounds, are considered LBW. LBW births account for approximately 6 percent of all live births in the United States and occur as the result of prematurity and/or intrauterine growth retardation (IUGR). The causes of LBW births are not well understood; preterm births are generally related to the mother's reproductive history, and IUGR tends to be more associated with demographic factors. Risk factors include socioeconomic conditions, ethnicity, maternal health, smoking during pregnancy, lack of prenatal care, toxic exposure during pregnancy, and complications during pregnancy. The findings presented here are from studies in the United States, but LBW may also be a significant problem among internationally adopted children, such as children from Romania and less developed regions of the world.

The number of LBW births in the United States has remained relatively stable for several decades. There has, however, been a decline in infant deaths associated with extremely LBW (babies weighing less than 1,000 grams or 2.2 pounds) due to the increased availability of neonatal intensive care units. These children are at high risk for medical complications and long-term disability. Picard and colleagues (2003) reviewed the literature regarding children born with LBW in earlier decades prior to the existence of neonatal intensive care units. They report that as early as the 1940s LBW children were described as having varying degrees of neurocognitive impairment during infancy and early childhood. Picard and colleagues (2003) also report that there is a gradient effect between actual birth weight and the extent of intellectual and cognitive impairment in LBW children. However, even heavier LBW children exhibit some differences in cognitive ability when compared to similar children who had birth weights in the normal range. LBW children may exhibit difficulties as they mature in the areas of attention, visual motor function, language development, fine-motor skills, and tactile abilities.

ATTENTION DEFICIT HYPERACTIVITY DISORDER

Attention Deficit Hyperactivity Disorder (ADHD) is a condition that is defined behaviorally. The cause or origin of attention difficulties exhibited by children with this diagnosis is quite diverse. In some cases, ADHD appears to run in the child's family and has, at least in part, a genetic basis. Other children with this diagnosis have a history of pediatric head trauma, and problems with attention and impulsivity are attributable to the trauma. Children with a history of prenatal exposure to alcohol or other substances also frequently receive a diagnosis of ADHD, (O'Malley & Storaz, 2003). Research indicates that when children with FASD have ADHD, their attentional difficulties likely began at an earlier age; are characterized primarily by inattention rather than hyperactivity; and co-occur with a number of other developmental, psychiatric, and medical conditions. There is also a growing awareness that attentional difficulties may be related to later mood disorder. Specifically, children of parents diagnosed with Bipolar Disorder who later develop Bipolar Disorder are often diagnosed as suffering from ADHD prior to the onset of their mood disorder. Children with attentional difficulties and ADHD symptoms are also often identified as having problems with sensory integration (See the chapter on sensory integration in this book for more details).

LEARNING DISABILITIES

About half of the children receiving special education services are classified as learning disabled (LD) (Fletcher et al., 2007). What a learning disability is, however, is not well defined. Until 2004, schools identified children with learning disabilities on the basis of a discrepancy between their aptitude and level of academic achievement. Changes in the Individuals with Disabilities Education Act (IDEA, 2004), however, have changed how school systems are identifying learning disabled students. Learning disabled students represent a diverse group, and LD students may have problems with various aspects of reading, math, and/or written expression. As discussed earlier, children with a history of early maltreatment may exhibit a variety of neuropsychological deficits, including problems with learning and memory, as a result of alterations in brain structure and function. They may be evaluated at school due to academic difficulties and diagnosed as suffering from a learning disability. If your child has been identified as a learning disabled student, it is helpful to get additional information from the school system regarding your child's particular problem areas, the types of educational interventions (e.g., special classes, accommodations) he is receiving, and how he is responding to specific interventions. This information is generally provided to parents during Individualized Educational Plan (IEP) meetings.

Children with a history of early maltreatment, particularly those who exhibit problems with learning, attention and/or other areas of cognitive or adaptive functioning (e.g., social, emotional) may benefit from a referral to a clinical neuropsychologist for a comprehensive neuropsychological evaluation.

CLINICAL NEUROPSYCHOLOGY

What Is Clinical Neuropsychology?

There are approximately 600 ABCN/ABPP board-certified clinical neuropsychologists practicing in North America at this time out of an estimated 75,000 licensed psychologists (AACN, 2006; Yeates & Bieliauskas, 2004). The number of board-certified clinical neuropsychologists who primarily or exclusively work with children represents a minority, albeit a substantial number, of this group. A clinical neuropsychologist is a professional psychologist who has undergone extensive training in the science of brain-behavior relationships. In 1997 at the Houston Conference on Specialty Education and Training in Clinical Neuropsychology guidelines were developed that summarize the content and scope of academic and clinical preparation needed to practice clinical neuropsychology. The Houston Conference guidelines have become widely accepted (Hannay et al., 1998; Yeates & Bieliauskas, 2004). These guidelines specify that training in clinical neuropsychology is obtained by completing a (1) a doctoral-level psychology training program, with coursework in brain-behavior relationships and clinical neuropsychology; (2) a predoctoral clinical neuropsychology internship; and (3) a two-year postdoctoral residency in clinical neuropsychology. The Houston Conference guidelines apply to recently trained clinical neuropsychologists. Prior to the Houston Conference there were several recognized training paths to a career in clinical neuropsychology (Reports of the INS-Division 40 Task Force, 1987).

Board Certification in Clinical Neuropsychology through the American Board of Clinical Neuropsychology (ABCN)/American Board of Professional Psychology (ABPP) is the clearest evidence of competence as a clinical neuropsychologist (APA Division 40 Definition of a Clinical Neuropsychologist, 1989; Hannay et al., 1998). The ABCN/ABPP board certification requires successful completion of a written examination, clinical work sample review, and oral examination, as well as completion of a doctoral training program, internship, and residency in clinical neuropsychology (Yeates & Bieliauskas, 2004). Board certification in clinical neuropsychology is an important credential for the person evaluating your child to have, just like you would prefer the physician who is treating you for a heart condition to be a board-certified cardiologist.

Pediatric Neuropsychology

Pediatric neuropsychology is an area of clinical neuropsychology that is concerned with learning and behavior in relation to the child's brain. This area is also referred to as developmental neuropsychology and child neuropsychology. Pediatric neuropsychology provides a framework for understanding and treating developmental, psychiatric, psychosocial, and learning disorders in children and adolescents (Teeter & Semrud-Clikeman, 1997). Psychologists who work with children come from many diverse training traditions. Although distinctions can be made between child-clinical psychology and developmental or pediatric neuropsychology, many aspects of education and training in these areas overlap (Baron, 2004). Training in both areas includes academic preparation in the areas of child development (e.g., cognitive, social, emotional) and clinical training and experience in the use of pediatric assessment and intervention techniques. The difference between these traditions lies in neuropsychology's emphasis on (1) the link between behavior (including emotional, social, and neurocognitive functions) and brain structures and systems, and (2) the application of this knowledge to individual patients (Baron, 2004; Teeter & Semrud-Clikeman, 1997). School psychologists also share some aspects of training with clinical neuropsychologists, but the services they provide are usually focused on academic issues. School-based assessments are generally conducted to determine whether a child qualifies for special education programs. They tend to focus on the child's level of achievement and the specific skills needed to succeed in school. They do not typically address how the child's difficulties are related to altered brain functions or development, nor do they focus on or address the child's level of functioning in other areas of life.

Neuropsychological Assessment of Children

Children are typically referred to clinical neuropsychologists by doctors, teachers, school psychologists, or other professions who are working with the child. Child neuropsychologists assess children who suffer from a diverse array of neurological and developmental conditions that are known, or suspected, of having an adverse impact on brain function. This includes trauma to the brain (e.g., due to accident, birth injury, or other physical stress), neurological illnesses, and neurodevelopmental conditions (e.g., Tourette's and Fragile X Syndrome). Children with difficulties in learning, attention, behavior, socialization, or emotional control for unknown reason are also often referred for neuropsychological evaluation. In these cases, the evaluation may be recommended to help clarify the underlying cause of the child's difficulties. When the child has a clear history of illness or injury that has impacted brain function, an evaluation is generally requested to clarify the nature and severity of the child's limitations in intellectual, cognitive, social, and/or emotional functioning and to obtain treatment recommendations.

Clinical neuropsychological evaluation of children typically involves collecting information about the individual child's current abilities and behavior and his developmental history (e.g., birth history, attainment of early developmental milestones, medical history, educational history and academic performance, psychosocial history, and history of emotional and/or behavioral difficulties). This information is obtained through direct observation, formal test procedures, parental interview, and review of previous records (e.g., birth history, medical records, school records, prior psychological or psychiatric consultation reports). The length of an examination varies depending upon the child's age and the nature of his specific problems.

Formal testing generally includes the administration of paper and pencil tests, hands-on activities (e.g., puzzles, computerized tasks), and answering a variety of questions. Parents and teachers are also often asked to fill out questionnaires. Children are usually told in simple language the purpose of the assessment and encouraged to try their best. A typical evaluation includes measures that provide information about intellectual ability, academic performance, various cognitive domains, and emotional/behavioral status. Cognitive domains assessed may include attention and concentration, learning and memory, language, visual perception, visual motor skills, fine-motor coordination, tactile abilities, and higher-level abilities such as problem-solving, reasoning, and judgment. The clinical neuropsychologist may have an assistant administer some of the tests. The tests are scored and the results are interpreted within the context of the individual child's history and current living situation. Recommendations are also made regarding diagnosis and treatment. The specific types of recommendations made will depend on the specific reasons that the child was initially referred for the evaluation. After the evaluation is completed, feedback regarding the neuropsychological evaluation results and recommendations is typically provided in person to parents at a meeting scheduled for that purpose. A clinical consultation report, which summarizes the evaluation results and recommendations, is also written and a copy provided to parents upon request.

Several approaches to the clinical neuropsychological evaluation of children have been described. Bernstein (2000) described a developmental neuropsychological assessment approach that seems particularly well suited to the assessment of children with histories of early abuse, neglect, and/or maltreatment. This assessment approach is comprehensive in nature and seeks to promote the development of independence, competence, and well-being at the maximum level for each child assessed. This approach takes a longitudinal perspective, and does not narrow its focus to a specific area of function (e.g., academic skills, cognitive abilities, and school performance). Rather, the goal of the assessment is to promote optimal functioning in all adaptive domains, including social and emotional competence. The clinical neuropsychologist does this by gathering and integrating information from multiple sources about the child's current status in multiple domains (e.g., developmental level in cognitive, social, emotional domains), the child's developmental history (e.g., medical, social, educational, behavioral), and the environments in which the child needs to function (e.g., home, school, community). The goal of gathering and integrating this information is to gain a holistic view of the child and to be able to provide input that will help the child function successfully in all aspects of life (e.g., family and peer relations, academic pursuits, leisure interests).

Several points are central to the developmental approach described by Bernstein (2000). First, this assessment approach views the child as a developing organism that is in a constant state of change. Secondly, it recognizes that the environment places demands on a child, and the nature of these demands also changes over time. For example, societal and family expectations are different for a toddler, a school-age child, and an adolescent (e.g., impulse control, attention span, level of independence). Expectations also vary depending on the situation. Behavior deemed appropriate in one situation, say at a picnic or ball game, may not be considered appropriate in another situation, say at school or church. The developmental approach also recognizes that the child's behavior is the result of interactions between his or her "brain," his or her developmental level and his or her environment. The developmental approach stresses that brain structures and systems are not only important in understanding cognitive functions, but also underlie social, emotional, and self-regulatory behaviors. Lastly, this model recognizes that the development of brain structures and systems is also influenced by the child's experiences within his or her environment, which is compatible or consistent with recent advances in the understanding of the effects of early childhood maltreatment on brain development (e.g., Schore, 2003).

Neuropsychologists who use a developmental assessment approach are able to provide information within a framework that helps clarify for parents, teachers, and therapists how early abuse, neglect, and/or other early traumas may have impacted a specific child and contribute to ongoing clinical management. In terms of clinical management, it is important to provide some education to the child, parents, and involved professionals (e.g., teachers, therapists, doctors) about the general principles of neurobehavioral development and the various developmental challenges (i.e., social, emotional, and cognitive) that all children encounter over the course of childhood and adolescence. Another area of intervention involves the provision of feedback regarding the child's evaluation results. Feedback regarding an evaluation generally includes (1) a summary of the child's cognitive strengths and weaknesses, as well as the practical significance of the child's ability profile (e.g., if the profile pattern raises concern that people may tend to either underestimate or overestimate the child's actual capabilities); (2) a description of, and explanation for, any inconsistencies noticed in a child's performance during testing (e.g., due to distractions or changes in task demands) and how these observations may be relevant to fluctuations in the child's level of performance in other situations; (3) an understanding to the child's developmental course to date, including how any known, or suspected, neurological insult or atypical experiences (e.g., severe neglect or abuse) may have contributed to the child's current problems in adaptive functioning in various domains (e.g., cognitive, social, or emotional); and (4) specific recommendations regarding the need for any additional clinical interventions. A description of the child's pattern and style of attachment behavior can also be helpful, but may be beyond the scope of a neuropsychological evaluation. Such a description can help a parent understand the child's behaviors as being the result of "learned" adaptations to the previous maltreating environment. These ingrained behaviors may be seen in "learned-helplessness" and a lack of motivation, which leads to poor academic performance. It should be added, however, that a lack of motivation or drive may also reflect, at least in part, the behavioral consequence of neurobiological alterations in development as a result of the early maltreatment.

Recommendations based on a neuropsychological evaluation may be related to (1) academic placement or needed classroom modifications (e.g., technology, new seating arrangements, changes in curriculum expectations); (2) intervention strategies that may be effective when interacting with the child in specific situations that the child, parents and/or teachers have identified as challenging; (3) further assessments that may be warranted (e.g., pediatric neurology); or (4) the potential benefit of individual or family interventions to address problems the child is having with peers, or to address any systemic issues that impact the family. The developmental neuropsychological model also often allows the clinical neuropsychologist to identify, or predict, specific problems that may arise down the road (i.e., based on an understanding of the child's unique ability profile and the types of developmental challenges that lie ahead), and recommend specific clinical interventions on a proactive, preventative basis to try to lessen the child's risk (Bernstein, 2000).

How Do I Locate a Psychologist to Provide a Board-Certified Clinical Neuropsychological Evaluation of My Child?

There are several places that you can start when trying to locate a clinical neuropsychologist in your area with expertise in developmental or pediatric neuropsychology. First, if your child has a pediatrician and/or sees a child psychiatrist or psychologist, they may be familiar with resources in your area and be able to provide a referral. If not, and you are located in a large metropolitan area with a university-affiliated medical center, it may have a department of child and adolescent psychiatry or pediatric neurology that has an outpatient pediatric neuropsychology clinic. A directory of board-certified clinical neuropsychologists is also located on the American Academy of Clinical Neuropsychology (AACN) website (www.theaacn.org). If you contact a board-certified clinical neuropsychologist in your area and he or she does not work with children, ask the neuropsychologist to provide, or locate, contact information for several colleagues in your area who do evaluate children. Another potential resource for names of potential evaluators is the psychological association in your state. Some state psychology associations have referral systems and can provide you with the names and contact information for psychologists in your area who provide child-clinical and/or pediatric neuropsychological evaluation services.

It is recommended that when you contact psychologists for information initially that you have a list of questions prepared, so that you can select the provider who best meets the evaluation needs of your child. You may want to ask about the psychologist's education, clinical training, and professional experience in the area of developmental or pediatric neuropsychology. If your child has significant emotional/behavioral issues that need addressing, you may want to know how much experience the psychologist has evaluating and/or treating children who have had similar issues.

If you, or a professional working with your child, arrange for a neuropsychological evaluation, it is also recommended that a list of specific referral questions is provided so that the evaluation adequately addresses your specific concerns.

What Parents Can Do

Caring for a child or adolescent with neurodevelopmental difficulties can be difficult and extremely stressful. As indicated earlier, children with a history of early maltreatment may exhibit a variety of difficulties in adaptive functioning (e.g., cognitive, social, emotional, behavioral). These children are also at higher risk for secondary problems when they become teenagers or young adults including mental illness, legal difficulties, problems with alcohol or drug abuse, and unwanted pregnancies. Early clinical interventions, however, and being raised in a supportive, structured environment can mitigate the effects of early trauma and reduce the risk of secondary problems.

Some general suggestions for parents include:

Practice Self-Care

First, it is very important that parents learn and practice good self-care skills. This serves two purposes. First, parents who practice good self-care are better able to effectively cope with the stress of caring for children with special needs. Practicing good self-care includes getting adequate rest, eating on a regular schedule and eating a healthy diet, exercising, and scheduling time to be alone and to enjoy the company of friends and family members. A second reason to practice good self-care habits is that parents and adult caregivers serve as role models for children. Through example, parents teach children that practicing good self-care is an important emotional regulation tool that can help them cope with the challenges of daily living.

Maintain Records

In many situations parents function as advocates for their children. One thing that can facilitate this process is to set up and maintain a three-ring binder or folder that contains important information regarding your child. This may include adoption records including birth history (if available), early developmental history, medical and mental health history (e.g., copies of any neurological, psychiatric, psychological/intellectual evaluations), developmental/rehabilitation therapy records (e.g., treatment summaries from early speech/language, occupational, or physical therapy interventions); and educational history (e.g., Individualized Education Plans [IEPs] and psycho-educational assessments). The file should also contain copies of any official letters that indicate that your child has qualified for specific programs or special services.

Having these documents readily available may prove helpful over the years, even in the distant future when your child is an adult. Professionals working with adults with a history of early developmental or educational difficulties find it time-consuming and often difficult, if not impossible, to locate and obtain old records. School districts typically destroy special education records after a number of years, and old medical/psychiatric records, if not destroyed, are often archived in storage facilities off-site and difficult to obtain. Having these records available for professionals to review can be very valuable when evaluations are conducted down the road whether for mental health, educational, or legal purposes. In some cases, having records available that document early history may make the difference between your child being found eligible or ineligible for special services (e.g., Social Security disability, special accommodations in college, or vocational rehabilitation services).

Parent Advocacy

In the role of parent advocate, it is important that if you have concerns regarding your child's social, emotional, or cognitive development that you talk with your child's doctors and/or with the special education department in your school district. Ask about the resources and services that are available and the procedures in place to formally request an evaluation. In addition to neuropsychological evaluations, which were discussed previously, your child may benefit from a diagnostic evaluation by a pediatric neurologist or psychiatrist depending on your child's history and the nature of your concerns. These medical specialists can also determine whether any additional medical evaluations or diagnostic tests are warranted (e.g., audiology, electroencephalogram [EEG], brain scans, genetic testing). School districts are mandated to provide educationally based school evaluations which include speech and language therapy, occupational therapy, and physical therapy assessments. School districts have to have diagnostic and intervention services available, but accessing these services can prove challenging in some regions of the country.

Strategies and Interventions

In addition to professional resources in your community, there are many support groups throughout the country and websites on the Internet that provide practical information to parents who care for children with specific issues or developmental disabilities (e.g., Fetal Alcohol Spectrum Disorder, pediatric head trauma, learning disorders, and Attention Deficit Hyperactivity Disorder). Parents are encouraged to access these resources for additional information.

The following are some general suggestions that may or may not be applicable to a particular child or in a specific situation. However, children who exhibit deficits in adaptive functioning, impulsivity, attention difficulties, and poor emotional and behavioral regulation may benefit from these strategies.

Monitor Your Child's Level of Arousal (Energy and Excitement)
and the Level of Environmental Stimulation

Children with problems with self-regulation often are easily overstimulated. When overstimulated they may become hyperactive and have difficulty paying attention, concentrating, or learning new information. They also may have trouble listening and following directions when overexcited. When a child is overstimulated, reducing the level of environmental noise, lights, and activity may help to calm the child. Some children, in contrast, experience a tendency to shut down and withdraw when overwhelmed or overstimulated. It is important to monitor and learn how your child typically reacts in various types of situations, and to track what intervention strategies seem to be effective.

Consistency and Routine

Children with problems with adaptive skills often do best in a structured environment where changes are kept to a minimum. Stable routines that don't change from day to day can help to decrease emotional and behavioral reactivity.

Avoid Abstract Concepts and Keep Information Concrete and Specific

Children with poor adaptive skills and difficulties with self-regulation often do well when parents and educators talk in concrete terms. This means being very direct and not using words with double meanings or sarcasm. This is because the children may have deficits in social-emotional understanding. Depending on the child, it may help to "think younger" when providing assistance or giving instructions. When giving directions to a child be specific and outline what is expected from the child in a step-by-step manner.

Repetition

Many children with developmental difficulties have short-term memory problems. They may forget things they want to remember, as well as information that has been learned and retained for a period of time. Having information periodically repeated, or retaught, may help store it in long-term memory. Important concepts may be remembered better if they are presented orally and in writing or pictorially.

SUMMARY POINTS

Children with a history of early maltreatment may experience intellectual, academic, cognitive, psychological, and/or behavioral difficulties that are due to alterations in brain structure and/or functioning as a result of many factors including early chronic stress, head trauma, prenatal exposure to toxic substances, and/or the effects of poverty. These children are also at higher risk for secondary problems when they become teenagers and young adults including mental illness, legal difficulties, problems with alcohol or drug abuse, and unwanted pregnancies. Clinical neuropsychological evaluation results can contribute to the ongoing management of these children. Early clinical interventions and being reared in a supportive, structured environment can also mitigate the adverse effects of early trauma and reduce the risk of secondary problems later in life.

7

A Sensory-Integration Perspective

Kristen Mayrose

Have you ever had just one of those days when nothing seems to go right? Your alarm clock malfunctioned and you wake up at 7:45 a.m. and need to leave the house by 7:55 a.m. You don't have time for your usual coffee stop and are forced to drink the office coffee (that you do not like the smell of). You get to your desk and realize you have on two different pairs of socks. One sock sinks down around your ankle and the other is tight around your calf, and you become very preoccupied and irritated at the annoying sensations. As the day progresses you hit your head on the file cabinet drawer that was open as you are picking up the papers that seemed to leap out of the file folder that was just removed from that drawer. Reaching for the salt in the cafeteria, you knock over your colleague's drink. At this point, the rest of the day is unproductive because all you can think about is going home so you can "just feel right."

This was a dysfunctional day for our "normally" intact sensory system. The good thing is that you know tomorrow will be a much better day.

Now understand that our children with sensory-integration dysfunction feel like this most days. Nothing ever seems to feel right. They are always uncertain that they will feel better later and most certainly do not have high hopes for tomorrow.

DEFINING SENSORY INTEGRATION: WHAT IS IT?

Sensory integration can be defined as a neurological process that organizes sensations from the world around us for our functional use. There is a significant amount of sensory information surrounding our bodies every minute of the day. For this reason, sensory integration has been characterized as a super highway system. On a highway, cars are merging onto the main traffic pattern, they flow with the traffic and exit when needed. This is similar to the path sensory information takes as it is routed through the body. Like the super highway of continually merging cars, the neurological system continually receives sensory information. This information travels to the brain, where it is registered and interpreted, and then an appropriate response is generated. For example, an aroma is in the air where it is inhaled. This sensory information is then sent to the brain via specific neurological pathways. The brain registers the smell and interprets it. The brain informs that the aroma is a familiar favorite food; the mouth waters, and a feeling of hunger comes.

To create a better understanding of intact sensory integration, let's look at another example of an integrated nervous system: A mom gently touches her child's shoulder and smiles. This touch sensation from mom and visual awareness of her smile creates a sense of well-being and happiness in the child. This information and response is based on past experience of similar situations and outcomes. The neurological system is then able to create an appropriate response from the child such as giving mom a hug, a smile back, or just creating a calm sense of well being.

Development of Sensory Integration

Jean Ayers, the founder of Sensory Integration Theory, states some basic principles regarding the development of sensory integration.

> Most of the activity in the first seven years of life is part of one process: the process of organizing the sensations in the nervous system. . . . A newborn infant sees and hears and senses his body, but he cannot organize these sensations well, and so most of them don't mean very much to him. He can't tell how far away things are, or what noises mean, or feel the shape of something in his hand, or know where his body is in relationship to everything else. As the child experiences sensations, he gradually learns to organize them with his brain and find out what they mean. (Ayers, 1979, p. 13)

It is through our experiences with sensory information that we begin to develop a perception of the world around us. These perceptions and experiences form our responses and the manner in which we conduct ourselves within our world. When the environment surrounding a child is consistent and supportive, it is more likely that the child will develop an appropriate, adaptive response. This means that the child will adapt and learn from these experiences. "When a child acts in an adaptive manner, we know that his brain is organizing sensations efficiently" (Ayers, 1979, p. 14). We observe this when a child learns to focus his attention on particular sensations and ignore others. Movements that were clumsy and jerky in infancy become smoother and direct in childhood. He learns the complicated movements of speech. By organizing the sensations, the child gains control over his emotions. He learns to stay organized for longer periods of time. Some of the situations that upset an infant give an older child knowledge and satisfaction. (Ayers, 1979, pp. 13–14)

Sensory-Integration Dysfunction

So what happens when sensory integration is not working properly in an individual's neurological system? Picture that super highway system: the nicely flowing traffic pattern of information (sensations) coming in and appropriate responses going out. Now picture the system with sensory integration dysfunction as a "traffic jam" in the super highway. The information is still coming in, but there is confusion as to where it is supposed to go, resulting in a poorly adapted response.

To better understand a poorly integrated neurological system, let's look at that example again. A mom gently touches her child on the shoulder and smiles. The child overreacts to her touch. The child may respond by withdrawing, striking back, or verbally lashing out as if mom intruded on his personal space. The child with an integrated system will normally respond in kind, with a reciprocal smile, perhaps leaning into mom's body, or turning to look into mom's eyes.

Why did the child react this way? Did the touch on his shoulder feel like an attack? Was he fully engaged in some project and the touch so startling that he had this overreaction? Whatever the reason, his response did not match the sensation or the intention. This was a dysfunctional response because it was experienced in a way not in tune with the intention (giving affection) or the expected response (receiving pleasure). In this case, over her lifetime the mom has received and given many similar touches, and she would therefore expect the child to interpret and experience her touch in kind.

There have been many studies through the years that have looked at sensory stimulation as it relates to development. In her book, Ayers refers to the studies that look at sensory deprived groups that resulted in poor development and poor adaptive response (Ayers, 1979). Some of these studies are listed in the reference section at the end of this chapter.

There are many thoughts on how and why children develop sensory integration dysfunction. Some researchers feel there may be a hereditary factor. Some also feel that environmental toxins play a strong role in sensory-integrative dysfunction. Both factors may have strong contribution to development of dysfunction. There are some children who lead very deprived lives and have poor contact and interactions with people or things. These children also tend to develop poorly integrated sensory, motor, and learning functions (Ayers, 1979, p. 54).

SENSORY-INTEGRATION DYSFUNCTION IN
CHILDREN WITH TRAUMA-ATTACHED DISORDERS

In my experience, sensory dysfunction presents itself with the children referred with trauma-attached disorders in varying degrees and with different
characteristics.

Those with sensory sensitivity present as children who do not like to
cuddle. They will give hugs and kisses on their terms, but do not like others
to approach them. They often stay to the outside of group situations, not
liking to be in close proximity of others. These children (and adults) also
may have issues with tags in their shirts and seams in their socks. Sounds
can be very irritating and create moody, stubborn behaviors.

Shawn appears as a well-adjusted boy who excels in sports and academics.
He is well liked by his peers. Behind the scenes at home, Shawn is reported
to be very demanding and extremely hard to satisfy. His mother reports that
she must wash newly purchased clothing several times before he will wear
it. When she finds athletic socks, underwear, shorts, and T-shirts that he
will wear, she buys huge quantities. After being evaluated, mom learned
that Shawn was sensory defensive and not just a difficult child. There was a
reason that he was unable to cope and adapt to various sensory information.
This allowed for a starting point for integrating Shawn's tactile system through
specific therapeutic techniques.

There are also kids who present with an underresponsiveness to sensory
information: for example, kids who cannot get enough hugs or who need
to sit almost on top of your lap when next to you. These children tend to
have poor awareness of personal space. They have difficulty sitting still and
attending in school or at the dinner table.

Dylan is a preschooler who is described by his mother as a "too adult child."
He cannot seem to get enough stimulation from the world around him, so
he continually seeks his own stimulation. Following the evaluation, it was
determined that Dylan required significant amounts of physical activity
throughout his day in order to satisfy his sensory needs. It was also vital that
a strong behavior plan was put in place by his counselor and carried out by
his parents so Dylan could begin to monitor his own behaviors and maintain
appropriate control.

Still others present as uncomfortable in their own bodies. They may bump into things and trip over invisible objects as they walk. They are sure to have at least one spill at the dinner table. These children often perform poorly in athletics and have poor handwriting.

> Jon is an adolescent boy who feels pretty poorly about himself. He feels that he is all thumbs, very clumsy, and less than athletic. Because of this, he keeps to himself so as not to be embarrassed. Following evaluation, it was determined that Jon had many poorly integrated sensory systems. His eye/hand coordination was poor as well as his balance. He demonstrated very poor awareness of his body in space, which caused him to often bump and spill things. Following several months of clinic-based therapy, Jon began to gain greater awareness of his motor movements. Spills at the dinner table were almost nonexistent, and he willingly enrolled in a school recreational basketball program.

Signs and Symptoms

How do you know when it is appropriate to seek a referral for a sensory integration evaluation?

If your child presents with poor ability to interact effectively within his environment, whether in school, home, or community, you may begin to think of an occupational therapy, sensory-based evaluation. To further evaluate the need for an assessment the following should be considered:

Does your child have difficulty with:

- Motor Skills
  - Fine Motor (hand skills/writing): Poor use of utensils at mealtime or poor pencil/crayon use, difficulty mastering buttons, snaps, etc., by expected age
  - Gross Motor (large-muscle coordination): Awkward movements when running, trips and falls often, poor body posture, often rests head in hands or on arm when seated during homework, poor endurance
  - Oral Motor (chewing, eating, respiration): Very messy eater, poor tolerance for resistive food such as meat, most often breathes through mouth, speech concerns
- Eye-Hand (catching, throwing, batting, copying, tracing): Does not want to participate in ball games, poor skill at ball games, poor handwriting, difficulty copying from the board
- Perceptual Skills
  - Tactile (over/underreaction to touch information): Needs tags removed from clothing, touches everything in sight, dislikes close proximity of others, very particular about clothing, peels the paper off crayons before use

- Auditory (sound sensitivity, under responsive): Holds hands over ears to protect from sound, makes excessive noise, poor understanding of the spoken word, cannot work in noisy environment
  - Movement (poor awareness of body in space, lacking coordination): Frequently trips and falls, bumps into things and has frequent spills, dislikes playground equipment such as slide and jungle gym
  - Visual (distracted by highly visual environment): Difficulty paying attention due to visual distraction, difficulty organizing written work into neat rows such as in math
- Emotional Maturity
  - Behavioral Control (monitor own behaviors, keep self in check): Overreacts in various situations such as losing at a game or another child chosen first to perform an activity, great difficulty with changes in plans or routines
  - Ability to attend, focus (at home and at school): Daydreams in school, unable to settle self to perform homework, highly distracted with any visual or auditory stimulus

Whether your child presents with one of these symptoms severely, or a few of these symptoms moderately, if the issue(s) is interfering with daily life success, a sensory-based occupational therapy evaluation may be warranted.

THE EVALUATION PROCESS

A referral for an evaluation may come about in a variety of ways. In the school setting, generally a teacher or other support staff may bring concerns to the parent or caregiver in order to generate an occupational therapy evaluation. A parent may also bring concerns to the school and ask for an evaluation to be performed. When following this process, the school is required to look at deficits that are educationally relevant. If deficits found are not felt to affect the child in academics, services may not be rendered.

In the private sector a parent may request an occupational therapy evaluation for their child from their pediatrician. For the concerns mentioned in this chapter, it is more appropriate to request a sensory-based occupational therapy evaluation. Searching online for a provider nearby is appropriate. You will find at the end of this chapter a resource directory of sensory-based therapists.

There are many assessments that can be used by the occupational therapist to identify sensory processing deficits. One of the most thorough assessments to identify sensory-integration dysfunction is the Sensory Integration and Praxis Test (SIPT). This is a lengthy (and costly) evaluation; however, it can give very valuable information regarding strengths and deficits, making treatment planning more accurate. In order to administer this evaluation, a therapist must have additional training.

In addition to the SIPT, the sensory profile is likely to be administered to determine sensory processing abilities and what external factors may contribute to poor functional performance.

Other assessments that look at general fine-motor, gross-motor, and visual skills may also be used and are helpful to see general deficit areas. These are the assessments most often found within the school setting as well as through private evaluators.

In order to determine what evaluation is most appropriate for your child, you must first determine the questions you want answered. Does your child present with learning problems? Are behavior and lack of self-control also factors? What are your primary concerns regarding your child? The occupational therapist should then create the evaluation regime that will answer your questions and lay the foundation for planning therapeutic strategies to improve functional performance.

Evaluation Suggestion for the Sensory Processing Child

A child may display significant difficulty handling the various sensations within the environment. The child may overreact to noises in the classroom or lunchroom. He may have difficulty wearing certain clothing or need tags removed from clothing. Working with school media such as glue or paint may be too challenging to touch. He may overreact when others are near his personal space. Yet he may possess adequate motor skills, seen in abilities on the playground or recreational sports. There are no academic struggles in handwriting, reading math, and so forth. This child performance profile warrants a sensory-based occupational therapy evaluation that consists primarily of the sensory profile, with follow-up to create a sensory diet to help decrease sensory sensitivities. The sensory profile will help determine which aspects of the child's environment are most problematic. This will also help to determine which aspects can be used as a strength when formulating the treatment plan and sensory diet.

General Assessment for Global Deficits

Suppose a child is struggling with many aspects of the academic environment seen in poor writing abilities, difficulty copying information accurately from the board, demonstrates poor coordination in gym class, has difficulty paying attention, and poor skill in retrieving and accurately using information given by the teacher. This child can benefit from occupational therapy evaluations that are commonly used within the academic arena. Some examples of these evaluations include: Bruininks-Oseretsky Test of Motor Proficiency, which assesses gross- and fine-motor skills;

Developmental Test of Visual Perception, which assesses visual perceptual and visual motor skills; Beery-Buktenica Developmental Test of Visual-Motor Integration or the Gardner Test of Visual Motor Skills, both of which assess the ability to integrate visual and motor abilities; Motor Free Visual Perceptual Test (MVPT) or the Test of Visual Perceptual Skills (TVPS), both of which assess perceptual skills without the use of motor skills. For young children the Peabody Developmental Motor Scales (PDMS) may be used to determine fine- and gross-motor status.

These are just some of the commonly used evaluations within the preschool and school-age populations and are not meant to be an exclusive list.

In-Depth Analysis for the Struggling but Not Failing Child

The Sensory Integration and Praxis Test (SIPT) is a constellation of standardized tests designed to measure a child's ability to perceive, organize, and respond to information processed throughout the sensory systems. Skills assessed include visual perception, tactile function, and movement. Skills such as eye-hand coordination, balance, postural control, and motor planning are also assessed. This test is standardized for children four years through eight years eleven months of age.

Formal clinical observations are also performed to determine and assess central nervous system status and biomechanical factors related to learning and desk work performance. The sensory profile should also be done with this type of evaluation to help determine aspects of the child's environment that are interfering with learning.

This assessment is very helpful in assisting in the clinical understanding of children with mild to moderate irregularities in learning and behavior (Ayers, 1991). This assessment is strongly encouraged when the child is demonstrating academic struggles, and general OT assessments are not giving definitive information or guiding the treatment plan.

TREATMENT PLANNING

Once all evaluations are complete and interpreted, treatment planning can begin. An occupational therapist may recommend weekly therapy sessions based on deficits determined by the evaluations. However, one of the most important pieces of the treatment plan is the home recommendations established by the therapist for you to carry over on a daily basis. Parents and caregivers are a vital piece of the treatment plan. It is the caregiver who will be there on a consistent basis to support the environment for the individual child. The caregiver will need to develop an understanding of why the child is acting or responding in a given way. The home strategies that the therapist sets up will help the caregiver to promote improved child response and success.

Often a child who has been evaluated with a sensory integration–based assessment will need a "sensory diet." Just like a nutrition diet is essential for our health and wellness regarding nutrients, the sensory diet is essential for the health and wellness of our sensory system. Some individuals may need to jog on a treadmill in order to begin the day "feeling awake." Some of us need to listen to classical music to relax prior to a stressful meeting. Just as we need different sensory input to make us feel "just right," the contents of a child's sensory diet will vary per each child to make him feel "just right." One sensory input that is often used is a program called the "Wilbarger Protocol." This program is designed to decrease sensory defensive responses to environmental stimuli. Parents will often be asked to carry this over on a daily basis along with the other pieces of the sensory diet. Very specific parent training for this treatment plan must take place and involves a process established by Pat and Julia Wilbarger who are referenced at the end of this chapter.

The premise of the sensory diet is to feed the neurological system with information that it needs to organize itself. For example, if a child has an inability to sit still and spends most of the day running from place to place and room to room, he will have a sensory diet that contains much movement. However, instead of the movement being disorganized, the required sensory time will contain movements that are very organized and that saturate the movement sense so the need for movement will be taken care of in a more appropriate manner.

Kids who may have sensitivity to touch, sound, movement, auditory, and oral sensations will have different types of sensory diets, but one thing remains consistent: Parents and caregivers will be of irreplaceable importance in the daily carryover of the treatment plan.

An Example

James is a nine-year-old boy who had been in foster care since his birth until age five when he was adopted. James was referred for a sensory-based occupational therapy evaluation by his psychologist who was addressing his behavioral and attachment issues. Primary concerns for James included a very high sensitivity to tactile input. He displayed very poor attention in school and at home. James also displayed poor sleeping patterns. He was very hard to rise in the morning, yet next to impossible to get to sleep in the evening. James was described to have a hard time getting along at home and at school. He was overreactive to those around him. Once he was awake, he was in constant motion and he appeared overstimulated by visual information. During writing tasks he would use so much pressure, he would often break pencil tips.

It was determined that since James displayed academic challenges as well as sensory processing concerns, the SIPT and the sensory profile would be the focus of his evaluation process. James had previously been assessed by general occupational therapy assessments within the school setting, but they were inconclusive. Therefore, an in-depth analysis using the SIPT would offer more detailed information.

SIPT evaluation results were weak in many areas; however, the biggest deficits were found in the somatosensory cluster. The somatosensory systems refer to the combined sensations of touch (tactile perception) and awareness of body position (proprioception). The tactile system is responsible for the development of several important learning concepts. These include size, shape, and texture of objects. The tactile system is also key in the establishment of body scheme. Input to the proprioceptive system is registered through joint and muscle receptors. It impacts on one's touch and movement systems and allows the individual to understand his position in space. This affects body awareness and provides feedback about how much force is being used on objects and tasks. Functionally, proprioception influences the student in the areas of spatial relationships, which include reading as well as safe navigation through the environment, pencil grasp, pressure exerted when writing, finger isolation and control, and the visual motor integration of letter and word formation. The sensory profile revealed severe deficiency in tactile processing, auditory processing, movement (vestibular) processing, and visual processing.

The evaluation results helped guide the treatment planning process. Since both evaluations indicated severe deficiency in the tactile (touch) processing area, this was the primary area of initial focus. James was having significant difficulty understanding and interpreting tactile information from his environment. This was the underlying reason for his poor fine-motor skills, his inability to tolerate sensations, his spiraling arousal level, and his poor attention. It was also determined that visual information overstimulated James. This negatively affected attention in the classroom. Through careful investigation it was noted that following video games such as PlayStation and Game Boy, James was very disruptive, anxious, and overstimulated.

Initial treatment planning for James included the following:

- Implementation of the Wilbarger Protocol every two hours
- Complete removal of television and video games

Toward the end of the first week, James's mother received a telephone call from his teacher. The teacher asked if anything dramatic had happened in James's life recently. His teacher reported that James was significantly more attentive during class and much less reactive to his peers. He had only two behavioral incidences all week, which were mild. When James's mother told her of the implementation of the sensory diet, she was eager to learn more and wanted to know how she could support the sensory diet at school.

Expanded treatment planning for the next several weeks included:

- Continuation of the Wilbarger Protocol, with a decreased schedule for frequency.
- Restricted time spent with video and TV.
- Increase in physical activity within the home and school setting. For example, at home James began to be responsible for heavy lifting types of jobs like collecting the garbage, bringing in the groceries, and vacuuming. He also took the dog for an evening walk. At school, James would return classroom library books, be a "book carrier" for a schoolmate with physical disabilities, erase chalkboards, and perform other like tasks.
- Each day, when James arrived at school, he met an aide in the gymnasium for some stretching exercises, followed by a light jog, calisthenics, ending with slow, deep breathing.
- Specific music selections were chosen to help James focus better during homework time. The music that worked best for James contained no words and consisted primarily of drumming and other native music.
- Oral input helped James to focus his attention also. His teacher allowed James to chew gum during test taking. She also allowed a water bottle at his desk.
- Deep breathing was performed both at home and at school. Prior to beginning a new task in school or subject of homework, James performed deep breathing exercises that were taught in therapy. Deep breathing helps modulate arousal levels to enable an individual to focus on the task at hand.
- In his classroom, James's seat was moved to be near the teacher, but to the outside row. This allowed James to be able to do the fidgeting his body needed, but to be less distracting to the teacher and his classmates. James was also given a seating device that enabled him to increase the sensation of movement.
- To help James wind down at the end of his day, following a warm bath, his mom would massage James with a wooden body brush (like those you see in a bath store) on his arms and back. He would then retire to bed, lie on his belly and read a few pages in a book while listening to "bedtime" music (classical, slow moving water, etc.).

The results of James's sensory diet and treatment plan were profound. James began to have increased attention to task at school on a consistent basis. James was notably calmer and demonstrated less-reactive behaviors at home and at school. James began to look forward to school and his responsibilities. His parents felt that James had a more positive learning environment and that James felt greater success, which would help his academics.

PARENT RESOURCES

www.SPDnetwork.org/directory. This is a free directory that the KID Foundation offers of professional and community services for those with sensory processing disorders.

www.KIDFoundation.org. With this website, an individual can access information regarding sensory processing disorders.

8

Art and Attachment

Julie Szarowski-Cox

Throughout history, humans have shown a desire to leave a mark, as evidenced by cave drawings more than 30,000 years old found by archaeologists in various parts of the world. Our earliest forms of a written language were visual symbols. For reasons unknown, humankind has felt the drive to make marks in the same way we have sought food, clothing, shelter, and the continuation of our species. Vick states, "Art making is an innate human tendency, so much so it has been argued that, like speech and tool making, this activity could be used to define our species" (Vick, 2003, p. 6). Whether to communicate with the gods, each other, or just for the sake of expression itself, "mark-making" or art is an essential part of being human (Malchiodi, 2003).

The field of art therapy has in one sense grown out of this innate "drive" to create. Our earliest preverbal emotional experiences in infancy are believed to be stored in the nonverbal parts of our brain, the right hemisphere. Traumatic memories are also believed to be stored in this part of our brain. As a result, creative expression can often access these experiences much more effectively than words alone (Arrington and Yorgin, 2001; Chapman et al., 2001; Hurwitz, 2003; Malchiodi, 2003). Art therapy incorporates the fields of art and psychotherapy, but the use of art in healing has been used throughout history by shamans and clergy in the East and West (Malchiodi, 2003; Vick, 2003). In the early twentieth century, psychiatrists were already beginning to explore the artwork created by the mentally ill. Concurrently, educators were noticing that children's artwork was connected to their emotional, social, and cognitive development. The field of art therapy in

the United States emerged as a distinct discipline by the mid-1940s (www
.artherapy.org, 2006; Vick, 2003). Art therapy in the United States is regulated by the American Art Therapy Association (AATA) and in some states
licensure is required to practice this form of therapy. AATA states:

> Art therapy is an established mental health profession that uses the creative
> process of art making to improve and enhance the physical, mental and
> emotional well-being of individuals of all ages. It is based on the belief that
> the creative process involved in artistic self-expression helps people to resolve
> conflicts and problems, develop interpersonal skills, manage behavior, reduce
> stress, increase self-esteem and self-awareness, and achieve insight. (www
> .artherapy.org 2006)

Making art is an opportunity to make a tangible representation of an
inner experience. In this way it continues to be a powerful form of communication often circumventing our censoring mechanism and tapping into
our unconscious (Hurwitz, 2003; Malchiodi, 2003; Ulman & Dachinger,
1996). Becoming actively involved in the process of making art has also
been shown to change brain chemistry, triggering a relaxation response
(Arrington & Yorgin, 2001; Malchiodi, 2003.) For this reason, art therapy
is particularly well suited for use in the treatment of children with Reactive
Attachment Disorder and for art activities to be provided by parents in the
home environment. Since children are naturally drawn to mark-making
as part of their normal development, the art-making process is a logical
choice for facilitating attachment (Hurwitz, 2003; Proulx, 2003). Making
art at home with your child can be a wonderful way to deepen your mutual
understanding, create moments of shared pleasure along with a visual re-
cord of those experiences (Phillips, 2003). The purpose of this chapter is to
assist parents in understanding normal developmental stages of art as well
as how to create an atmosphere and environment conducive for mutual
enjoyment in the art-making process.

BUILDING THE BRAIN

Children require many different types of sensorimotor experiences in order
to develop their brains. A baby is born with around 100 billion neurons
in the baby's brain. The neurons in various parts of the brain connect (via
synapses) to each other through electrical-chemical impulses and form neuropathways. When parents sing, talk, play with, and rock their infants, they
are developing their baby's brain (Becker-Weidman & Shell, 2005; Hughes,
2006; Klorer, 2005; Proulx, 2003; Rubin, 1978; Siegel, 2001). Since the
brain is use-dependent, in one way it can be thought of as a "muscle"; the
more a neuropathway is used or stimulated, the more an area develops.

In a process termed "pruning," the opposite occurs; the less an area of the brain is stimulated, the more it withers and does not develop. Thus, unused pathways are eliminated. Unfortunately, children diagnosed with attachment issues frequently have missed experiences that contribute to their physical, social, emotional, and cognitive development. While some areas of the brain have a time-sensitive window of opportunity for development, other areas such as the social-emotional parts of the brain can be developed throughout life (Becker-Weidman & Shell, 2005; Hughes, 2006; Klorer, 2005; Malchiodi, 2003; Proulx, 2003).

Creating art with your child is an excellent way to revisit those early experiences and begin creating new, healthier neurological pathways. Art stimulates the brain on multiple levels, providing kinesthetic and sensory input for the brain (Henley, 2005; Klorer, 2005; Malchiodi, 2003; Phillips, 2003; Proulx, 2003). Malchiodi (2003) states, "Art is a natural sensory mode of expression because it involves touch, smell and other senses within the experience. Drawing and other art activities mobilizes the expression of sensory memories in a way that verbal interviews and interventions cannot" (p. 20). Moreover, art activities will give you and your child an opportunity to attune to one another and facilitate your child's renegotiation of early attachment stages (Phillips, 2003; Proulx, 2003).

One of the first attachment stages a healthy parent and child experience is that of shared attention and engagement. The infant is able to communicate interest to a responsive parent through looking, smiling, vocalizations, and reaching for an object. The parent noticing the child's attention will engage with the child in his interest in the object. Children from abusive or neglectful environments who did not have consistent opportunities to attend and engage with a caregiver will manifest a variety of difficulties in their behavior. Younger children may display aggressive tendencies or have difficulties with sleep. Older children may display either a flat disinterested affect, be overly independent, or conversely be continually engaging in incessant chatter in an effort to obtain attention. Behavior of this sort is symptomatic of early problems with the shared attention and engagement stage (Becker-Weidman & Shell, 2005; Proulx, 2003).

Oftentimes in my work with families, it becomes clear that a parent and child have lost the ability to enjoy each other. There can be many reasons for this including the child's repeated tendency to sabotage fun experiences or the parents' stress, exhaustion, and frustration (Harvey, 2003). Regardless of the reason, mutual enjoyment is helpful in facilitating a healthy attachment.

An Example: Martha

Martha was four years old when she was brought to the center by her pre-adoptive mother, Ann. Martha's speech was difficult to understand,

and Ann was overwhelmed trying to manage Martha's many behavioral problems. Once Ann had begun to learn and implement parenting skills that made parenting Martha easier, we began to work more on creating enjoyable experiences for the two of them. In one session, Ann and Martha traced each other's hands and feet. They chose the colors to trace with and then colored in the shapes. The activity involved lots of close contact and laughter as they each were "tickled" by the crayon tracing their feet. I then offered Martha tape to connect the drawings together, which she happily and proudly did with Ann's assistance. Martha continued to draw in subsequent sessions and often requested to tape things together. This may have been symbolic of her desire to be connected to Ann.

An Example: Michelle

Michelle was fourteen years old when she came to treatment with her adoptive mother, Sarah. Sarah had adopted Michelle at age four and had struggled for the previous ten years with trying to find a therapist who could help her manage Michelle's behavior. Traditional therapy didn't seem to work, and Sarah found herself increasingly frustrated with disciplining Michelle. Because of the length of time the problem had gone on, there was very little enjoyment in their relationship. In one session, I brought out finger paints and paper. Next, I encouraged them to play with the materials and make a picture together. Initially, they worked separately on their individual side of the paper, but as they continued, they became increasingly playful and collaborative. Michelle seemed to enjoy the tactile sensation of the paint and used all of her fingers to paint with. Although Sarah expressed discomfort with using a material she identified with small children, together she and Michelle began doing crafts at home. In the process of trying various crafts, they discovered that Michelle really liked to do beading projects. This gave them a fun activity to engage in together.

Repeated experiences of participating in the mutual creation of artwork with your child offer an excellent opportunity to attend and engage together. The most important aspects of this stage are having fun together, eye contact, close proximity, and sustained attention (Harvey, 2003; Proulx, 2003). More detailed suggestions for some art activities are included at the end of the chapter, but below are some easy suggestions to try (Phillips, 2003; Proulx, 2003).

1. Purchase some scented markers and have fun smelling them and drawing together with your child.
2. Get messy with finger paint.
3. Trace each other's hands and feet.
4. Find a variety of pretty colored paper and make a collage.

5. Gather a variety of textured materials, feathers, leaves, and so on, and make a collage.

The stage of shared attention and engagement leads into the development of cause and effect thinking. The infant's first experiences with two-way communication occur during this phase. This is a time when infants begin to gain a firmer grasp of nonverbal communication such as facial expressions and hand gestures. When a caregiver responds positively to a baby's cooing, they are communicating with each other. This type of experience occurring repeatedly teaches the infant that he does in fact have an impact on his environment. The infant learns "when I do this, mom does that." This ability to elicit a desired response from the environment gives the developing child a sense of security and feeling of worth. The parent's consistent responses create a sense of trust and stability for the infant (Becker-Weidman & Shell, 2005; Harvey & Connor, 1993; Hughes, 2006; Proulx, 2003).

In an abusive/neglectful home, this cause and effect thinking is not generally developed. A parent who is inconsistent in responses, alternating between responding, ignoring, or punishing the child, creates confusion for the child. The child's sense of the world being safe and reliable therefore becomes absent; older children will tend to fluctuate between feeling powerless and an exaggerated sense of power (Gonick & Gold, 1992; Hughes, 2006). Children who experience difficulty with this stage may display aggression due to their inability to understand and communicate with the people in their environment (Harvey & Connor, 1993; Proulx, 2003). Older children with attachment problems will have difficulty taking responsibility for their part in relationship problems. They will tend to place blame on others and place themselves in the role of victim (Gonick & Gold, 1992; Hughes, 2006). Remedial development of cause and effect thinking after a child has experienced abuse/neglect is dependent on many factors, including a caregiver's understanding of the cause of this behavior. Even after children are removed from the abusive/neglectful environment, the behavior doesn't change because the children's belief system is still intact. They will continue to misinterpret other's intentions and react based on old beliefs. The opportunity to experience positive feeling states through the use of art will assist your child's development of cause and effect thinking (Hughes, 2006).

At the most fundamental level, making marks teaches cause and effect thinking. When I pick up a pencil and press it onto the paper while moving my hand, the mark made is the effect of that action (Betts, 2003). Children in healthy families are usually very excited by this discovery. Making art together offers parent and child the opportunity to communicate with materials and nonverbal gestures about the experience. The most important aspect of this stage is the development of nonverbal communication. Smiling, showing excitement, concern, and so forth, are all ways to help your child develop an understanding of human relationships and their ability to affect their environment (Becker-Weidman & Shell, 2005; Proulx, 2003). Some suggestions for art activities to assist in developing your child's cause and effect thinking:

1. Draw a picture together without speaking or writing words. Communicate only through your drawing and nonverbal gestures (Landgarten, 1981). Have fun.
2. Take a walk with paper and pencil and discover the textures in the environment together by doing rubbings. Place the paper on top of sidewalks, leaves, benches, and other objects, and rub the pencil over the paper.
3. Bake and decorate cupcakes artistically and then eat them.
4. If your child has a nightmare, draw a new happier ending together.

An Example: Justine

Jack was granted custody of his daughter, Justine (age six) after his ex-wife had been charged with abuse. Justine became very anxious every time she had to separate from her father, even resisting going upstairs in their house alone. In sessions, we worked on helping Jack find ways to manage Justine's behavior as well as addressing some of her fears. Justine loved to draw and soon was able to tolerate short separations during the session as long as she was making art. One session, I introduced the idea of taking texture rubbings from some of the surfaces in the room. Justine loved the idea and explored the room using this technique. Jack reported that Justine began using this technique at home as well, freeing him up to work on other things as she explored her environment within safe distance of him.

In order for your child to feel secure in doing activities away from you, she will need to successfully complete the previous stages. Safely exploring the environment away from the parent requires that communication 'can occur across distances. A securely attached toddler who steps away from her primary caregiver to pick up a new object will be able to stay connected and tuned in to her parent with frequent glances (Hughes, 2006; Proulx, 2003).

Children from an abusive/neglectful home tend to feel very anxious or ambivalent when separated from the primary caregiver. As they grow, these children may prefer activities that are isolating in nature such as watching television, playing video games, or being alone in their room. They will also tend to misinterpret nonverbal communication (Becker-Weidman & Shell, 2005; Gonick & Gold, 1992).

Once a more secure attachment has developed, art is a safe way for a child to experience the environment while maintaining a connection to the primary caregiver. While cooking dinner, your child can be busily drawing a picture for you. No matter how old your child may be, he will display readiness for separate art activities when he generally turns to you for emotional comforting, is following most house rules consistently, and can tolerate short periods of separation without tantruming or acting out (Becker-Weidman & Shell, 2005; Hughes, 2006). Proulx (2003) says in regard to this stage, "The child's connection with the caregiver may now begin to be realized across space, without the need for physical contact, affording the child emotional communication with glances, vocalizations, and affective gestures" (p. 62).

1. Sit across from each other and draw portraits of one another. This activity maintains the connection between parent and child and improves eye contact while creating some distance.
2. Have your child draw a picture about his day to be shared when you have finished a task you need to complete. Allow for frequent check-ins to maintain a connection.
3. Have your child draw a picture for each member of the family.

Cause and effect thinking is linked to a sense of history and a developing sense of self. In a healthy family, a child learns how to affect relationships and direct his actions to obtain the desired effect. For example, when a small child picks up a toy and places it in his caregiver's lap with a smile, the message communicated is "play with me." Children with attachment issues will often be cut off from or have fragmented views of their own history (Becker-Weidman & Shell, 2005; Gonick & Gold, 1992; Hughes, 2006). Because artwork is an actual product of their own efforts they can create a visual history to assist them in developing a sense of self. It can also be a way for them to document their own history and begin a narrative of their new life (Robbins, 1987):

1. Create a family photo album and include artwork as well.
2. Keep your child's artwork in a special place and review it together regularly.
3. Have your child use magazine pictures to create a collage of his goals.
4. Provide an older child with an inexpensive and/or disposable camera to begin documenting his new life.

DEVELOPMENTAL STAGES OF ART

Just as there are cognitive, physical, and emotional developmental stages that children experience as they grow, there are also corresponding artistic developmental stages. As a child's fine and gross motor skills develop, the child will be able to better grasp and control a pencil, manipulate clay, and use other materials. Similarly, as a child better understands the environment, the child's observation skills and symbols will advance as well. When children reach school age, they begin to be interested in what others are creating and often copy or adapt observed symbols and techniques. Emotional growth can be seen in the child's content and metaphors used in the artwork. Children draw what is interesting and important to them, and much can be learned from the process as well as the product of their creativity (Malchiodi, 2003; Proulx 2003; Rubin, 1978).

A child's first foray into the world of mark-making often comes well before caregivers generally allow access to traditional art materials. Children are learning cause and effect thinking each time they make messes with food, put their hands in mud, or play in the sandbox. Placing objects in their mouth, squeezing, rolling, pushing, and pulling are all ways for the child to understand his environment and his ability to influence it. For the child, the kinesthetic experience in this type of activity is often more important than the finished product. His muscles are developing, his brain is learning, and in a healthy environment, he is experiencing reciprocal enjoyment with his caregiver (Rubin, 1978).

As the child's fine and gross motor skills develop and he begins to recognize the self as separate from the environment, he will begin to make marks that are more purposeful. He will begin naming scribbles and other creations. Initially, there is little resemblance that an adult can identify between the named object and that which it represents, but for the child it is the beginning of his use of symbols. From here he will make his first attempts to represent objects, usually beginning with the human figure. Generally, the figures begin with just an attempted circle with eyes and mouth (see figure 8.1), developing into a figure in which there is no separation between the head and body (see figure 8.2). As the child grows, his symbols advance as well, including his representation of the human figure as having distinct parts, head, body, legs, and arms (Anderson, 1992; Rubin, 1978).

Identifying your child's artistic developmental stage can be useful when compared with his growth in other areas. If your child is strong in art, but weak in social skills, here is a strength to build on. If your child is strong with three-dimensional art but has difficulty with two-dimensional representation, this tells you something about your child's preferred mode of learning. In addition, it may be helpful in choosing activities to successfully engage in together. If your child has not been able to advance past regressive play with clay, then you may prefer something less emotionally stimulating such as pencil and paper. Fluid art materials such as paint and clay can sometimes stimulate regression as they can be associated with early experiences with bodily fluids. In regressive play, children may revert to using baby talk, rocking, or using the material in an inappropriate way. They may become excited or aggressive and emotionally disregulated. Sometimes children are able to engage in this behavior and then resume normal play, but other times it may require intervention (Kramer, 1993).

An Example: Stephen

I began working with Stephen when he was eleven years old. Working with art materials was his favorite activity when he attended sessions. After a few months, I introduced clay into our sessions, and Stephen became very excited by this medium. However, although he was able to communicate ideas of what he wanted to create, he could only stab the clay repeatedly, becoming visibly excited and rocking in his seat. Even with my prompting and limit-setting, he was unable to create anything from the clay. After the third session of him engaging in this behavior, I decided it was unhealthy for him to continue in this way. When he requested clay again, I let him know that he would be able to use it again in the future and offered him different materials. I eventually introduced clay again into our sessions, but only after I could see his growth in accepting my limits and managing his frustrations.

In working with children with Reactive Attachment Disorder, I have witnessed a broad range of artistic capabilities. Sometimes even neglected or abused children find a way to continue their artistic development. But just as often there can be delays that correspond with cognitive, physical, or emotional difficulties. The following developmental chart is a basic guideline to the developmental stages of art. As in any other developmental theory, each child may progress through them differently, the stages may overlap, be bypassed, come out of order, or children may be in one stage with drawing and another with clay. There is no need to try to force or teach your child into the next stage of artistic development. As your child develops emotionally, cognitively, and physically, his artistic development will occur naturally (Anderson, 1992; Proulx, 2003; Rubin, 1978). Too much advice or constructive criticism will spoil the fun for you and your child and create emotional distance. It is best to have an attitude of being Playful, Accepting, Curious, and Empathic (PLACE) (Hughes, 2006) with regard to the child's expressive creations. Phillips (2003) stresses that the important point is for the parent to be "nonjudgmental and non-interpretive" (p. 147). Working with your child at his artistic developmental level is an excellent way to attune to his experience (Proulx, 2003).

The following table gives a brief overview of developmental stages in art (Anderson, 1992; Rubin, 1978).

Table 8.1. Developmental Stages in Art

AGE	DRAWING/PAINTING	CLAY/3-DIMENSIONAL
18 months–4 years Scribble Stage (See figures 8.1 & 8.2)	Initial stages, makes marks for the kinesthetic experience. Around age 2–3, will begin to name scribbles, even though they do not resemble any objects in the environment. Around age 3–4, children will begin first attempts at human figures, usually no differentiation between the head and body.	Initial stages, children will simply play, pound, and squeeze clay. They will become interested in rolling it into flat shapes and possibly cutting it out. Will enjoy making marks and textures on a flat piece of clay.
4–7 years Preschematic Stage (See figure 8.3)	Following the child's first attempts of representing the human figure, he will further refine the human figure to include more body parts and detail. Constantly refining representation of other objects such as houses, trees, etc. Chooses color randomly.	Can form clay into a ball, will draw pictures into a flat piece of clay, and will begin to be able to create objects to stand on their own.
7–9 years Schematic Stage (See figure 8.4)	Will develop particular way of representing figures and objects. Drawing will often include a baseline and a skyline. Children in this stage will sometimes draw from several perspectives simultaneously (i.e., top and side or inside/outside). Colors tend to be more realistic.	Will work with 3-dimensional materials using a constructive method of piecing the parts together to form a whole.
9–12 years Dawning Realism Stage (See figure 8.5)	Artwork will begin to have many more details included. Widening gap in the differences between subjects chosen by boys and girls. In classroom situations, children are much more concerned with peers' evaluation of art, and may tend to resist doing art if they feel their artwork isn't good enough.	Continues to work with clay using the constructive method. Will be able to work 3-dimensionally with paper.
12–14 years Pseudo-Naturalistic Stage	Attempts to make human figures look very real and will include sexual characteristics. May become interested in working in a certain style such as cartoons or caricatures. Will begin to use basic concepts of perspective in artwork. Will become increasingly concerned over finished product and critical of own work.	Will be interested in making functional 3-dimensional objects as well as representations of human figures.
14–17 years Adolescent Art (See figure 8.6)	Only those children feeling they have skill in art will progress to this level. Will become interested in learning to draw in perspective and represent light and shadow. Will be able to use color and subject to intentionally express mood. Will be interested in acquiring mastery over different materials.	Will be able to work in both constructive and subtractive methods with 3-dimensional materials.

Figure 8.1.   Scribble Stage, 18 months–4 years

Figure 8.2.   Scribble Stage, 18 months–4 years

Figure 8.3. Preschematic Stage, 4–7 years

Figure 8.4. Schematic Stage, 7–9 years

Figure 8.5.   Dawning Realism Stage, 9–12 years

Figure 8.6. Adolescent Art, 14–17 years

SETTING THE PLACE (FOR ART)

In order to continue implementing the PLACE techniques during creative activities, it is important to structure the environment for the greatest success. Having an area in your house that is a designated craft area is ideal. A room where paint spills and splashes, chalky fingerprints, and dropped clay won't cause problems goes a long way toward containment of messes without stifling a child's creativity. The following suggestions may work for your family and will hopefully give you some ideas that can be adapted to meet your needs.

Room for Art

If you are fortunate to have the space to set aside one room or area in your house for the making of arts and crafts, then you will want to have the space arranged in a way that makes use of materials and cleanup easy and efficient.

As with any child diagnosed with attachment issues, art-room rules and guidelines should be determined in advance by the parents or guardians. In general, it is usually best to build success by starting off with a high level of supervision and structure. Your decision to allow increased freedom to choose materials (or to use the art-room without your presence) should match your child's ability to manage art-room protocols. Just as with very young children, reduced supervision accompanies internalization of your expectations and develops in incremental steps. Open access to the room and supplies should be regarded as a privilege earned through the continuous display of responsible use and cleanup of materials. Failure to comply with the rules should be regarded as an indication that the child is not ready to handle this responsibility.

If you do not have a separate room that can be devoted to arts and crafts, then consider finding another place in your house that can be converted to a temporary art-making space. Art-making should occur in an area where the floor can be easily cleaned and will not be damaged by paint or clay. Vinyl floors work the best in this regard, but hardwood floors or rugs can be protected by purchasing a scrap rug or cloth that can be placed under the work area. When finishing walls, look for paint or wallpaper that cleans easily; usually eggshell or high gloss will work the best. Walls can be similarly protected in the same way you protect the floor. The kitchen usually works well to convert to a temporary art-making space, but you may also want to consider other areas such as the basement, garage, or an outdoor area where a mess will not create any additional stress on the family.

Setting Limits

Art supplies that are messier and could possibly be dysregulating to the child should be stored in an area inaccessible to your child. A basic guideline of a continuum from most to least controlled materials is: pencils, crayons, markers, cutting and pasting, oil pastels, chalk pastels, paint, and clay. Paint and clay have the ability to induce possible regressive behavior in children, so it is best to save those activities for when you and your child can work together. It may also be important to keep items such as scissors and glue in an out-of-reach place.

Initially, it may be best to allow your child to have access to art materials only when you are available to closely monitor the activity. This allows you to create lots of little moments of attunement. The following exchange is an example of the opportunities that exist for engaging and attuning with your child through art.

> Parent and child are sitting at the table together. The child works on a drawing with crayons while the parent sits by and watches.
>
> *Parent:* Wow, you're making your drawing so colorful! I like the colors you're using.
>
> *Child:* What's your favorite color?
>
> *Parent:* My favorite color is blue; what's your favorite color?
>
> *Child:* My favorite color is purple, so I'm going to use blue and purple to sign my name. It's all finished. It's for you.
>
> *Parent:* (Taking the drawing and examining it) Wow, it's wonderful, I love it. I'm going to hang it on the refrigerator! (Looking at the child, the parent smiles warmly and the child smiles back.)

An exchange of this sort would be an indication a healthy attachment is forming between you and your child. In the example, the child is genuinely interested in pleasing the parent. The parent is paying attention and joining with the child in his enthusiasm and happiness about his creation. A child who displays pleasure at your pleasure may soon be allowed to work independently with pencil and crayon.

If, on the other hand, the child becomes frustrated with his creation and destroys it, this would be an indication your child will need your close monitoring to assist in processing his emotions. The following is an example of using ACE (being Accepting, Curious, and having Empathy) in such an interaction.

> Child: These crayons are stupid. I hate this drawing. This is dumb anyway. (Child crumbles paper into ball, throws it on the floor and knocks the crayon box over.)

Parent: (Sitting down next to child and retrieving crumbled drawing) Wow, you really didn't like that drawing.

Child: (Crossing arms and hunching down) It's a stupid drawing. I can't draw.

Parent: (Smoothing out the crumpled drawing) What was the most stupid part of the drawing?

Child: (Pointing with his finger) This part here, I can't draw the car right.

Parent: Oh, so you were really upset about not drawing the car right?

Child: Yeah, I never do anything right. I'm always messing up!

Parent: So you were thinking that you always mess things up. How does that make you feel about yourself—like a good kid or a bad kid?

Child: Like a bad kid, I'll never do anything right.

Parent: So you were feeling like a bad kid and that you would never be able to do anything right. Do you think I still love you even when you're messing up?

Child: No.

Parent: No wonder you were so upset about not drawing the car right! You thought it was just one more thing you couldn't do right and that no one could ever love you. Now I see why you got so upset you crumpled up the paper and knocked the crayon box over. You must have been feeling pretty bad about yourself when you couldn't draw that car the way you wanted to.

Child: Uh-huh.

Parent: I would feel upset too, if I thought I could never do anything right and no one would ever love me. No wonder you were so upset. But you know what? (leaning in and whispering)

Child: What?

Parent: I love you no matter what, even when you think you're messing up. And I really like what you tried to do here, just because you did it and I love you.

In this example, the child is clearly in need of the parent's close physical proximity to handle his emotions. The parent sits down with the child and expresses her curiosity about what precipitated the outburst. Through acceptance and empathy, the parent assists the child in getting to the underlying thoughts and feelings driving the behavior. Many children with attachment issues have this deep feeling of being unlovable, and it manifests in myriad ways. For children with attachment issues, it will take many experiences of this sort with an accepting and empathetic parent in order for them to truly heal (Becker-Weidman & Shell, 2005; Hughes, 2006).

Children with attachment issues can sometimes be wasteful with art materials or constantly wanting more supplies. This unquenchable hunger for materials may be irritating to the caregiver, but it usually stems from a history of the child not having his basic needs for nurturance met (Phillips, 2003). Setting limitations in a caring, compassionate way as well as closely monitoring the child will be necessary until the child develops more trust in his current environment. For example, you could calmly explain to your child at the beginning of an art activity that he has a certain amount of paper, even counting the sheets together. When the child quickly uses all of the paper and asks for more, you can then let him know he can have some more paper next time. Initially the child may have difficulty accepting this limitation, but you can use his response as an opportunity to use ACE with him.

Another way a child with attachment issues may express his negative feelings is through sneaky or destructive behavior with the art materials (Gonick & Gold, 1992). Should this occur, then art-making time should revert back to occurring only when a parent is available to monitor. It is not necessary to take art-making activities away; your child may need your close, attentive monitoring in order to maintain emotional regulation while working with the art materials. Often, children who come from abusive/neglectful homes are more comfortable or familiar with no privileges and a punitive/hostile environment (Hughes, 2006). Falling into the trap of taking away art supplies and activities only allows him to re-create this unhealthy but familiar environment. Consequences for inappropriate use of the art materials should, as much as possible, be natural consequences that correspond with the behavior. For example, if your child uses the crayons to write on the wall when you are not looking, then washing the wall may be an appropriate response. To reduce potential inappropriate behavior, making art time an interactive opportunity may be what is needed until a stronger attachment is developed. It's a benefit to be able to be creative and have fun with the consequences of inappropriate art-making, much the way you would with a two-year-old. Writing on the walls is something that most children do when they first begin to experiment with mark-making. Hanging butcher paper on the walls and creating a mural together can be a fun activity that provides opportunities for attunement and mutual enjoyment. For example, after your child helps you clean off the misplaced drawings, you can say, "I see you'd like to draw this way, so let's do it the right way and hang paper up first." This will help your child move toward a pro-social, attuned creative experience.

Using the parenting strategies outlined in this book, which are based on Dyadic Developmental Psychotherapy (Becker-Weidman & Hughes, 2008; Becker-Weidman & Shell, 2005), will help you to understand your child's inner life. Creating a healing PLACE for your child around his art-making activities will deepen your relationship and provide you with opportunities to increase your and your child's insight into his thoughts and feelings. Being playful with the materials and having fun within a structured environment will give your child the opportunity to experience himself or herself as a lovable, enjoyable, responsible individual. Repeated experiences of this sort can be the glue in the relationship that encourages healthy attachment and begins to heal the hurt and pain.

ART ACTIVITIES

The following activities are suggestions for engaging in art-making with your child. The instructions are not meant to be rigidly enforced, but rather are a guideline for the activity. The most important thing with any of these activities is to create moments of shared engagement between you and your child. It is wonderful to be curious about your child's artwork and use it as an opportunity to learn more about his experience of the world. However, it is best to avoid constructive criticism or interpretation of his work (Phillips, 2003; Proulx, 2003).

Scribble Chase
Provides kinesthetic movement and an opportunity for shared engagement.
Materials: Large paper taped onto table or wall
             Crayons
Directions: Parent and child each choose a different color crayon. The parent begins the "chase" by walking his crayon over the paper leaving a crayon trail. The child follows the parent's line with her own crayon.

Homemade Playdough
Provides kinesthetic movement and evokes early nurturing experiences as the materials are food.
Materials: 1 cup cold water
             1 cup salt
             2 teaspoons vegetable oil
             2 cups flour
             2 tablespoons cornstarch
             Food coloring
Directions: Together with your child, mix water, salt, oil and a few drops of food coloring. Mix dry ingredients and add a little at a time to the water mixture. Put flour on the table and on your hands and knead the dough for a few minutes. Make sculptures with the dough, have a pretend tea party, or cut it into shapes. The playdough can be saved for approximately one month in a sealed container kept in the refrigerator.

Hand-Over-Hand Drawing

Encourages physical contact and nurturing.

Materials: Crayons or washable markers

Large paper taped down to table

Directions: Decide together with your child a picture you would like to draw. Have your child choose a crayon and placing your hand over his, draw a part of the picture. Then reverse, having your child place his hand over yours and using your hand to draw.

Family Goals Collage

Provides an opportunity for shared engagement and discussing the ways your family would like to grow.

Materials: Magazine pictures

Crayons, washable markers, and/or colored pencils

Glue

Children's scissors

Poster board or 18 x 24 paper

Directions: This is a great project in which to include all of the family members. Tape the poster board or paper down onto the table. Discuss what each person would like to see happen for the family in the future. Using magazine clippings or drawing, include each of these ideas into the collage. When finished, display somewhere so everyone can be reminded of the goals.

Dream Vacation

Creates a great opportunity for shared engagement and enjoyment, plus it is a wonderful way to relax.

Materials: Magazine pictures

Notebook or journal

Scissors

Glue

Directions: Look through magazines and catalogues for places you or your child dream of visiting. This can be an ongoing project or just one day. Cut out each picture of your dream vacation and glue it into your notebook or journal. Take turns with your child imaging what it would be like in that particular location. Use all of your senses to imagine what would you see, smell, touch, hear, and taste on your dream vacation. Use your dream vacation book whenever you and your child need to relax.

ART THERAPY WITHIN THE THERAPEUTIC TEAM

Engaging in art activities at home is a wonderful way to facilitate attachment. For some children it will still be necessary for them to work with a trained therapist to process traumatic experiences and express their grief and loss. This is not a reflection of a failure of their adoptive/foster family.

Additional treatment should be sought if you are becoming more stressed by engaging in art with your child. Working with a licensed art therapist trained in treating children diagnosed with Reactive Attachment Disorder and/or trauma may be necessary in order for your child to heal fully. There are a number of signs that could indicate your child is in need of more serious interventions by a trained professional. For instance, if your child becomes overly stimulated by art materials, regressing or acting out, his art products are disturbing or he displays an increase in symptoms of Post-Traumatic Stress Disorder (PTSD), it would be appropriate to consult with an art therapist. A trained art therapist will be able to maintain a healthy balance of emotional release without overwhelming your child's defenses (Henley, 2005). You may also wish to consult with an art therapist if you are experiencing difficulty having fun with or engaging your child in enjoyable activities.

Art therapists can work as a primary or adjunctive therapist within the therapeutic team. In either capacity, an art therapist's role is to design art-based interventions to assist the child and family to develop a closer relationship, enhance coping skills, and express experiences that may be impossible to describe in words alone (Arrington and Yorgin, 2001; Chapman et al., 2001; Klorer, 2005; Malchiodi, 2003). An art therapist using Dyadic Developmental Psychotherapy (Becker-Weidman & Shell, 2005) will be able to incorporate art interventions throughout the treatment to facilitate attachment and stimulate development in the child. For example, art activities can be designed to assist a parent and child to find ways to enjoy each other (Proulx, 2003). Using art therapy during the session also offers an opportunity for the child to express his feelings and thoughts while giving him the ability to safely distance himself from powerful emotions. Children will often use metaphors to express their emotions, which can provide a cathartic release of painful experiences without the child needing to be fully aware of it (Arrington and Yorgin, 2001; Chapman et al., 2001; Landgarten, 1981; Malchiodi, 2003; Phillips, 2003; Rubin, 1978). For example, I once worked with a young girl who was placed into foster care as the result of sexual abuse. Through the use of paint she was able to tell her story. She painted a picture of a wounded elephant and talked at length about where he was hurt and how he needed to be cared for. She painted a box around him to protect him and also gave him Band-Aids and medicine to help him heal. This young girl used the art to communicate her experience of being wounded as well as her experience of healing.

Indeed, working with an art therapist can help both you and your child develop a healthy attachment and heal wounds. The creative process may reveal strengths and qualities previously untapped in both you and your child.

9

Storytelling: How to Use Stories to Help Your Child

Arthur Becker-Weidman and Deborah Shell

Storytelling has been a central theme in creating human connections for thousands of years. It is how we pass on traditions, values, and history. Cultural roles, expectations, and how relationships are managed are all reinforced through stories. Stories also teach the reason for certain actions and behaviors and the consequences of deviations from these expectations. Storytelling is how we create meaning in our lives and the lives of our families. We sit around the holiday table and tell and retell the same stories as a way of reconnecting and strengthening our ties with each other. We tell stories that reflect our religious, moral, and ethical beliefs as well as our personal place within our culture. "Remember the time you climbed the big maple and got stuck?" This may begin a long series of stories that recount how you were the risk taker in the family. The nature of the stories you recall and others recall about you helps define who you are. Stories can also serve another purpose: they can heal by describing what might have been and represent our hopes, dreams, and aspirations. "Putting together large chunks of memories into a story that makes sense can promote health," (Emde, 2003). In this chapter we will describe how stories that you create can be used to help your child heal. The narratives you create with your child can have a profoundly positive effect on your child's health and development (Fivush, 1994; Oppenheim & Waters, 1995; Reese & Fivush, 1993).

We tell stories as a means of making sense of experiences. Experiences, in and of themselves, have no meaning until we put those experiences into a narrative and create meaning. Meaning ascribed to early experiences affects the inner working model and sense of self as competent and worthy, or as defective and unlovable. In addition, as our sense of self changes over time, so do our personal narratives. "Narratives organize the stream of life's experiences" (Emde, 2003, p. 3). It is through telling stories together that we cocreate meaning, shared meaning. It is shared meaning, shared experiences, and shared emotion that create relationship. By creating shared narratives with your child you begin to build a common history of experiences and emotions that can serve as the basis for a healthy and secure relationship. The stories you create with your child help define and redefine your child. These narratives can help your child make sense of the child's past . . . was the child neglected because the child is bad and unlovable or because the first parent was not a good enough parent? Is your child valued and valuable to you? Why did the child end up in foster care and then your home? These very important questions go to the core of defining your child's sense of self and can be shaped by the narratives you create with your child.

Cocreation of Meaning

The cocreation of meaning is the way in which interpretation is constructed between people, creating shared understanding about events in one's own life as well as of the larger community to which we belong. The sharing of emotions (attunement) along with shared attention and share intention are the essential elements of a healing relationship.

Siegel (2001) has described how meaning is developed through the co-construction of narratives between the caregiver and child. It is this cocreation of meaning that allows the child to make sense of the child's relationships, emotions, and internal world. "One of the promising ways to assess security during childhood is by looking at the capacity for the child *and caregiver* [italics added] to work together on building a shared narrative around personal and emotional events" (Koren-Karie, Oppenheim, Haimwoich & Etzion-Carasso, 2003). It is through mutual storytelling that you cocreate meaning for yourself and your child. This is one way to define who you and the child are and what your relationship is with each other. When you describe how you would have cared for the child, had that child been born to you, you are defining your child and creating meaning for that child. Compare these two stories:

One: When you were born, that was the happiest day of my life. Dad was there and we both had tears in our eyes . . . tears of joy. Dad turned to the doctor and said, "Did you ever see such a perfect baby before?" We both laughed. Later that day your grandma and poppa came to visit and brought that bear you still have. I remember just watching you all day. I couldn't believe how lucky I was to have you. When Dad and I brought you home we spent the first day just sitting by your crib watching you. Dad used to get up for your 3:00 a.m. feeding so that I could get some sleep. We were so tired because you never slept more than a few hours before needing to eat, or have a diaper changed, or something. We'd get up, take care of whatever you needed and then would go back to sleep. We were always tired that first year, but so happy.

Two: When you were born I was seventeen and your Dad had disappeared and left me stuck with you. I'd leave you with grandma so I could go out with my friends, but she didn't always want to take you, so sometimes I'd just put a bottle in your bed and take off for a few hours . . . you seemed okay. Boy, you cried all the time; I never could figure out what was wrong with you. I had things to do and no one to help, so what do you expect . . . I guess I wanted you, but you were a pain sometimes . . .

Think about how each story would color a ten-year-old's sense of self and the mother's feelings about her child. These "stories" are actually narratives that reflect the mother's internal representations of her child, her relationship with her child, and her sense of self as a parent. As such, the narrative is a powerful organizing structure that creates the child's internal representations of self, other, and the relationship. When a child has lived either narrative for three, five, or more years, the child's self-esteem, sense of self, feelings of being loved, lovable, valued, valuable, good, and successful will be deeply engrained. In the first narrative, that child will have a largely positive sense of self, the relationship with mother, and of the mother. In the second narrative, the child will have an internal representation of self that is largely negative as unwanted, not lovable, not valuable, and as unimportant. The child will perceive the mother as uncaring and probably not experience other adults as potentially helpful or as potential sources of help, solace, or support.

The creation of a "new" narrative, to replace the largely negative one previously internalized, takes time and effort. Generally people tend to find "evidence" to confirm their personal autobiographical narratives, and therefore they will interpret what happens each day in terms of these internalized beliefs. If the invisible but highly influential sense of self is negative, then that insidious negative sense of self will be reconfirmed again and again. This makes it difficult to change one's autobiographical narratives, or internal working models, as John Bowlby, the developer of Attachment Theory, called these frames of reference (the lenses through which we all filter experiences and relationships). So, as a parent, you will have to really work at helping your child develop new autobiographical narratives. One effective and enjoyable way to do this is to tell "stories" whenever you can. The re-storying (sounds a lot like restoring, doesn't it?) of your child's experience can have the effect of building a common understanding, interpersonal trust, and the development of a relationship based on deeply shared meaning. The building of a new, positive sense of self can be greatly enhanced by having loved ones tell and retell the stories of our lives. Your use of positive attributions describing the child's motives and needs, regardless of the actual outcome, is key to re-storying past events. Changing a negative working model of self can be difficult to achieve when the child makes choices that attempt to "prove" he is unlovable! But, when a parent reinterprets events according to the child's positive intent (to get needs met, for example), the storytelling describes (from a developmental point of view) what drives the child's behavior. Then, the ultimate meaning is altered to reflect a perfectly normal infant/child trying to get needs met as best the child knew how. Describing the effects of years of neglect and abuse, and how the child learned to believe "so this is how the world works," helps the child understand why what the child thought the child understood about himself and the world may no longer apply, although it may have made sense at the time. The world has changed and so must the child's narrative change. The parent can help with this by providing another story that is positive and accepting.

An example of re-storying a child's early experience is described in the following two vignettes. When I met Slava and his parents, we explored his autobiographical narrative. The first story is the one he told us before his parents re-created his story according to their positive attributions and meaning as understood from the point of view of Slava, a good baby in a difficult situation (and later, clever Slava, who figured out how to get his little-boy needs met in the big orphanage without the benefit of parents to help advocate for his particular tastes). His parents were surprised to learn how pervasive negative underlying beliefs about his self-worth were rooted in gleanings he'd put together to make sense of his life. I call the stories "myths" because much of the detail and meaning are inferred. There simply is not enough information to be sure of the exact reason or event that precipitated Slava being sent to the orphanage. However it is clear that if one has spent ten years invested in a negative sense of self, the first story will feel appropriate. Once Slava could internalize the possibility of his life experiences from the point of view that he was not a flawed child, the second story could be accepted as the reflection of an experience largely out of his control, with sad events and inevitable changes. It is only because of circumstance, not because of anything unlovable about Slava, that resulted in his placement in an orphanage in the first place.

TWO MYTHS

Slava's Story #1

I was born in Russia to an alcoholic mother. She already had a son, and she must have loved him very much because he got to stay with our grand-mother and I got sent to the orphanage. I agree with that decision, because he already showed them that he was smart and capable. I was just a stupid baby. The neighbors in the apartment building where my mother lived got sick and tired of my crying all the time and so one night they called the police. They came and got me and put me in a crib in a room with lots of other screaming babies. My grandmother stopped coming to see me and I was there until I was five. Sometimes I wish they'd let me stay there in the orphanage. It wasn't that bad because I didn't know there was supposed to be anything else. My life now isn't so great . . . My parents, you know the ones that adopted me, they'd be better off if I'd never come.

Slava's Story #2

Even though my mother was an alcoholic (and in those days in Russia there wasn't any help for addicts), she kept me with her in a tiny apartment for nine months. It must have been really hard for her because I was little and needed a lot of attention and special care. When I was born there was already another boy (I guess he would have been my brother . . .), but he was three and could take care of himself a lot better than I could. I was only a tiny baby! My grandmother was able to take care of him, but she wasn't strong enough to take care of me, too. Better to put me into an orphanage where at least there was the chance I could get adopted and maybe go and live in the USA. Then I would have parents who really wanted me (why else would they fly all the way to Russia to get me!) and they would have enough money to feed me good food, give me toys and books to read, and they'd love me too, because I was such a cute little boy. I could sing so many songs and I wanted to know how everything worked. Sometimes I wonder what it would have been like if I'd stayed with my grandmother . . . she stopped visiting me because there is a law that babies won't get adopted if they still have a relative living in Moscow. She really wanted me to be adopted and have a safe, happy childhood. She must have been so sad to leave me and not know if I was okay. I want her to know that she and my mother made a very hard decision to let me go. And now, I have a good life. It was really hard to learn how to live in a family and have parents. In the beginning they confused me so much. After they came and got me, they would be so nice to me and the next minute they'd be so mean and say no to me! I had to learn that parents love their kids even when they're helping them make good choices. I don't think my Russian mother was able to teach me that because she was having so much trouble herself. Someday I might want to help other kids who aren't able to stay with the family they were born into . . .

With Slava, as with so many children adopted internationally, there wasn't enough information to know exactly how circumstances transpired. He had come from Moscow, with some papers describing his schedule as well as with a video originally sent by the orphanage to his prospective adoptive parents. We watched it together. In great detail, taking notice of every aspect of what was filmed, we discussed the meaning of what was shown: color and fabrics of the furniture, rugs, wall-hangings, toys, dishes, silverware. We cocreated meaning by talking about "what it was like" for Slava to have been a little boy in those surroundings. We imagined him running and jumping on the mats neatly folded away on wooden shelves. With genuine interest we watched the choppy video of four-year-old Slava eating thin soup with a grown-up sized silver spoon and large white cloth napkin, then changing himself out of his pants and shirt and wearing only underwear, putting himself into his cot for a nap, and later, sitting on the psychologist's lap and being told to sing and smile for the camera. Slava's parents were very helpful by describing what they'd learned about Russian traditions, thereby enriching the meaning of this spectacular video, the singular remnant that links Slava and his adopted family, to his original experiences.

The stories that make up a life narrative may be consistent, coherent, and connected, or they may be inconsistent, incoherent, and fragmented. It is the nature and quality of one's autobiographical narrative that both reflects and creates one's sense of self. Having a coherent autobiographical narrative is a sign of mental health. Creating a coherent autobiographical narrative creates a more integrated and stable sense of self and leads to better mental health and higher levels of functioning. The reason for this is that meaning drives behavior. It is the meaning ascribed to events and experiences, more so than the "objective truth" of the experiences and events, that shapes our experience of those events. An early chronic history of maltreatment can create a sense of self and an autobiographical narrative that is fragmented and in which the self is perceived as "bad," "unloved and unlovable," "unwanted," "not valued or valuable," and as intrinsically defective; a "throw-away" person. The child then takes new experiences that are inconsistent with that autobiographical narrative and either discounts those experiences or "forgets" them. Events that confirm that sense of self, or that are misperceived as confirming this negative sense of self, reinforce the negative autobiographical narrative.

So, what can you do? Creating stories with your child that support a different and new autobiography can help. There are several categories that stories often fall into. Below we describe some examples of stories you may want to begin to use to describe your child's life experiences.

THE CLAIMING STORY

Claiming narratives (Lacher, Nichols & May, 2005) describe the symbolic birth of your child and his entrance into the family. It is the story of falling in love, and children of all ages relish the telling and retelling of this occurrence. Unlike adult love that may lead to marriage, and divorce, the love for a child is unbreakable. Even in death, a parent's love for the child can continue to be felt by the child in many ways, through symbols, cherished items, and stories. Depending on the strength and quality of attachments prior to a parent's death, the well-attached child usually continues to feel lovable and worthy. Yet, traumatized children may not have experienced themselves as special and lovable nor would they know about the unconditional quality of healthy child-parent relationships, not only because it was not their experience to have been loved unconditionally, but also because of their negative internal working model, they may not comprehend why you would care for such a flawed child. No matter what the parental conditions or reasons were for leaving the family of origin, the outcome was that the child needed a new family.

Ideally, your child's birth story will focus on the falling-in-love aspect of your child's symbolic birth into your family. This story is about the first time you saw your child's picture, and when you first laid eyes on your child, touched your child, held your child. It is a description of your child's impact on all of your senses, along with an interpretation of how you felt your child experienced meeting you. You describe your child's eyes, your child's face, your child's hands, your child's voice. You give attribution and meaning to your child's reactions, according to your sense of how your child tried to integrate the experience of meeting you. An important element of this claiming story is to tell your child how you would have done things had you been your child's parent from the very start, in great detail describing how you would have prepared for your child's birth, homecoming, and infancy care when your child was so very tiny, as well as what you actually did to prepare for your child's arrival at whatever age your child really did come to you. Expanding this story to include other family members' experiences with your child's symbolic birth will help root the story in family history. Stories about how an older sibling might have been jealous of the new "baby," and how the parent (you) made sense of it and defended the newest child, helps to create a sense of being deeply wanted, protected, and defended.

Another important aspect in bringing the claiming story to life is in the telling now of how it would have been then when you are in places that remind you of how you would have done things, as well as how you did do things to help your newest addition to the family adjust and feel welcome, safe, and loved. For example, when you're in a department store walking past the baby aisle, take your child over to the bassinettes and say, "This is the one I would have used for you; it has a little spot for the pacifier to rest in so you wouldn't have lost it." Talk about the kind of diapers you would have used, the special care you would have taken to wrap your child in the softest towel (with a hood, of course) after your child's bath, the first shoes you would have bought for your child when your child began trying to walk. Show your child the baby shoes, the overalls, the rattles and pails with shovels. You can even get your child a few cardboard storybooks you would have read to your child before your child knew how to read. When you're in the grocery store, talk about how you would have fed your child, what foods first, and relate it to your child's eating preferences now, for example: "I bet you would have loved bananas when you were little; I would have gotten you a banana to eat while we shopped so you wouldn't have been so hungry looking at all this food. Hey, you still love bananas!" Show your child the baby foods you would have purchased, and how careful you would have been introducing new foods, avoiding unhealthy choices, even going through the candy-free checkout to avoid your child being sad when you said no to your child's perpetual longing for sweets . . .

Describe what he would have been like at age two, three, four, eight, ten . . . stressing normal developmental processes and helping redefine some behaviors as normal behaviors of a developmentally younger child. For example, your child's liking to play hide-and-seek begins with peek-a-boo at six months or so. If your child didn't get enough appropriate child play where your child was made to feel special, your child may still react with glee to being "found," tickled when "the last piggie cries wee wee wee all the way home," even at age ten.

TRAUMA STORY (OR YOUR CHILD'S NEEDS WERE NORMAL)

Part One

Children who have experienced neglect and/or abuse in a family of origin, or in foster care, or in an orphanage may not know that they were and are driven by normal desires to explore and discover the world around them. Unsupervised children may "get into trouble," not because they have malicious motives, but because they have not had the support to explore and learn about whatever has made them curious. Such a child needs help to understand that his normal interests may have led him to experiment without safety, but he was not "bad" for experimenting, even though the result may have been rejection or abuse when discovered by the caregiver and interpreted as a transgression deserving of punishment.

The following story describes a situation that caused great shame and subsequent despair in a child who does not yet know that the child is supposed to experience curiosity, nor does the child understand how to share curiosity with the child's adoptive parents. You can tell your child any number of similar stories, about any emotion your child may need encouragement to explore and resolve. This story helps normalize a traumatized child's underlying desires to learn about the child's world within the safety of the child's parents' unconditional love.

Cora's Happy Ending

Once upon a time there was a little girl named Cora. She had shiny black hair and big dimples when she smiled. Her mother said, "Cora, it's almost time for our story. Please go brush your teeth and then meet me on the couch. I'll be waiting for you with your snuggly blanket." Cora finished placing the last star into her sticker book album and skipped into the bathroom, shutting the door with a loud *slam*. (She liked the way the door said "Fun" when it closed forcefully.)

Cora went to grab her pink toothbrush with the fairies climbing up the handle when her eye caught on Mommy's potpourri container. Something about it looked different tonight, and being the very curious girl she was, she peeked under the lid . . . and then . . . *oops!*

Some kind of thick liquid was sliding onto the countertop. Cora was quick to grab Mommy's pretty hand towel to wipe it up. But it kept on spreading. Now it was oozing off the countertop, dripping onto the floor, splashing Cora's purple bunny slippers and the orange bathmat! Her little heart was racing. She tried to clean things up as best she could so Mommy wouldn't know. After all, she was supposed to be brushing her teeth, not investigating Mommy's pretty things!

"Aren't you ready yet?" Mommy said in a loud voice. Cora began to hurry even more. She looked around the bathroom one last time and then quickly opened the door and ran over to the couch and jumped right into her special spot next to Mommy. Mommy put the bookmark onto the coffee table. She settled back into the cushions, ready to read. Then, just when Cora thought everything was okay, Mommy stopped and looked up.

"Cora, what is that smell?" Mommy sniffed.

"I don't smell anything," Cora said, trying to keep her voice steady.

"Oh, yes, I definitely smell something," Mommy said. "Hmmm. This smell reminds me of lilacs." Before Mommy knew what was happening, Cora jumped off the couch and ran into her room. She slammed the door hard (and this time it didn't say "Fun.") She began jumping up and down on her bed until all the covers bounced off and all the lovely stuffed bears and bunnies went rolling across the floor. "I hate you!" she yelled in her loudest voice. "I know there won't be a movie now. I know it!" she sobbed.

Mommy was at her door, but Cora was crying and yelling and she couldn't hear her mommy softly knocking. But, Mommy knew her little Cora was scared and sad. And when little girls are sad and mad they need their mommies to help make them feel better! Mommy knew how hard it was for Cora when she did something wrong. Mommy knew her little girl worried that she would be hurt or sent away just because she did something wrong.

Slowly and carefully Mommy opened the door and sat on Cora's bed. She began talking quietly, even though Cora was yelling and throwing her bear at the wall. Mommy said the most amazing things!

"I can see you're so upset right now. Hmmm. I wonder if you think you're in trouble. I wonder . . ." Mommy leaned back on her elbow and looked quizzically at Cora. "Seems like you want me to be really mad at you right now."

Cora bounced a few more times, then flopped in a heap on top of the rumpled covers. Mommy said, "I wonder if you were just trying to brush your teeth when something interesting caught your eye. . . . And then before you knew it, your curiosity got the better of you!"

Cora sat closer to Mommy, but she wouldn't touch her. Not yet. What if Mommy grabbed her and . . . And . . . Oh! She couldn't bear to think about it! Cora was even thinking she deserved to be hurt.

Daddy heard all the commotion and brought Cora a glass of water, thinking she must be having such a hard time and might be thirsty after all the crying and yelling. "I hope you feel better soon, honey," he said and went back into the living room.

As Cora began to calm down again, Mommy took her hand gently and talked to her in a quiet voice. "Let's go into the bathroom together and see what you were so curious about."

Even though Cora was still a bit scared, she followed Mommy. Mommy knew her girl was very curious, and she wanted to be able to help Cora learn as much as she could about how things work.

Cora pointed to the potpourri jar, and then Mommy began to laugh. "Oh, I put some scented oil into the container when you were riding your bike with Daddy this afternoon. It must have tipped over when you peeked inside. That's why you smelled like lilac! Mystery solved," she said giving Cora a little squeeze. After she showed Cora how the oil was supposed to make a nice smell in the bathroom, and after they cleaned up the oil that Cora wasn't able to get with the hand towel, they went over to the couch and finished their story. They snuggled up in Cora's favorite blanket.

The next day, when Cora woke up, she remembered what she'd done last night. She began to feel scared all over again. She was sure something bad was going to happen and that she deserved something bad to happen. Cora figured it would be no movie today, because that was what she was looking forward to most of all.

She pouted through breakfast. She gave the dog a kick with her big toe. She didn't want any watermelon, even though it was her favorite.

Mommy wondered what was happening now. She tapped her fingernails on the table.

"Hmmm. Are you still a little worried that something will happen because you spilled the potpourri oil?"

Cora jumped up and ran to the hallway, "YES! Hit me already! I know you want to. I'm bad. I'm wild," Cora yelled as the tears fell. "I don't deserve to go to the movie. I know you won't let me go. I know!"

Mommy sighed, and sat down patting the couch for Cora to sit beside her. The dog jumped up instead, but Mommy told him Cora needed her right now and he'd have to wait till later.

Cora's shoulders slumped as she sat down, wiping her cheeks and nose with the back of her hand. She looked so sad!

"Are you still thinking you deserve to be punished for being curious and then spilling the oil, instead of just brushing your teeth like I'd asked?" She gave Cora a little squeeze around her shoulders. "It was so hard for you when you lived in the foster home. I know you thought they didn't like you, and when you needed to learn about how everything works, you were yelled at and punished. You didn't mean to break things back then, you were just being a curious little girl!

Cora cried, and nodded her head. She really didn't know that it was okay to be a curious little girl. And if she got into trouble and spilled things, that she could say what she did and get help from Mommy or Daddy to fix it. She could even ask before she touched something that interested her, and Mommy and Daddy would help her! But Cora didn't know this yet, not all the time, anyway.

So, Mommy helped Cora feel better. She hugged her, and told her how happy she was to have a curious little girl every single day. She told her how they would explore whatever Cora wanted to know about, and that Cora could ask Mommy or Daddy about anything.

"And," she said in her most reassuring voice, "being curious doesn't have anything to do with going to the movies . . . so . . . let's find your shoes and socks and meet me at the front door!"

Cora smiled, jumped up and hugged her Mommy. Then she found one shoe hiding in the toy bin, and the other in the dog's bed. And off to the movies they went. The end.

Part Two

Having access to your child's files before coming to live with you is an extremely valuable way to help your child integrate the traumatic events that occurred without you being there to help make sense of what was endured. Trauma research tells us that it isn't what happened that makes something traumatic. What makes the difference is the meaning a person gives to that experience. And, meaning-making is a product of shared understanding usually done through storying the event with loved ones who *get* the effect on the child. As your child's parent, you can now re-story the traumatic events of your child's previous life. Even if you don't know all the facts, what you already know about the environment your child experienced will help you to make sense of behaviors your child may exhibit but not fully understand. You can trust your child's behaviors to tell a story. Behaviors exist as a result of what was experienced, even if there were no words to describe what happened.

With the help of a Dyadic Developmental Psychotherapy therapist, you will probably be encouraged to read certain events from the child's file, noting police reports, physician's notes, school reports, and the like. Helping a child to make sense of his negative feelings involves teaching the child that the way he feels about himself and others (such as parents) now is the result of maltreatment, not the child being flawed or bad. Preparing an opportunity to grieve together over what has been suffered and lost reduces the child's shame. The isolation endured during maltreatment becomes diminished once it can be shared with you. The following example describes a story in which the child's very traumatic experience is retold in a coherent manner. This child has been given a new narrative of his experience, authentic because it describes his emotional experience during the event and subsequent set of beliefs derived from an inability to view it other than the way he had been maltreated.

Billy's Story

When you were living with your first parents, Bobby-Jo and Melissa, you were hungry a lot. Your first parents were too young to be together, and they'd never really learned how to take care of themselves, let alone a baby and child. You and your four sisters were left alone a lot by your first parents; they didn't know how to take care of you and your sisters. Bobby-Jo and Melissa used to fight a lot with each other and hurt each other; maybe no one ever taught them what to do when they were upset or angry; maybe they'd been hit as kids and saw their parents hit each other, I don't know. But I do know that they'd hit each other, and the police often came to the home. They also must have lost their temper with you and your sisters because one time when the police came to their house they found you with a broken arm and had to take you to the hospital. You were only three years old! It makes me sad now when I think about a sweet little boy all alone sometimes, frightened when the big people yelled and fought, and when they hurt you. That hungry little boy with a broken arm all alone in the hospital; so scary. After the hospital you went to one foster home for a short time and then another home for about six months. You must have been so upset; all these new people, strange homes; new smells and foods, different rooms and rules. It was so confusing for you. No wonder you were angry! Then, you were told you'd be going back home. You were happy because you'd really missed your first mom and dad; of course you missed them, even though they scared you sometimes and were mean, you knew they were "momma" and "dadda." But that didn't last long, and by the time you were four you were back in foster homes; four different homes until you came here when you were six, remember? All those homes . . . you began to feel that no one wanted you; that something was wrong with you; remember? You'd used to say all the time, "I'm stupid," "I'm dumb," "I'm bad." I felt so sad for you when you'd say those things because I realized that you believe them. That was how you made sense out of all those moves and why you never stayed anywhere very long and why you never got to go home to "momma and dadda" again. You thought it was your fault; that something was wrong with you. I was so sad that you thought that. I understood why you'd feel that way. You were too young to know that your momma and dadda were too young and had too many problems to take care of you and your sisters; so you blamed yourself. You were too young to know that all those homes were temporary until the social service people could figure out if your momma and dadda could become the sort of parents you deserved and you could go home to a safe home or if you'd go to another home to be adopted . . .

It is through stories that we make sense of our world, ourselves, and our relationships. The stories we tell our children help them organize their experiences into meaningful narratives that help create a sense of self as loved, lovable, valued, and valuable.

10

Mindfulness

Miranda Ring Phelps

In this book we have given a lot of attention to the state of mind of the attachment-resistant, traumatized child. We've talked about using PLACE as the model attitude in which you can experience freedom to apply healthy, healing interactions and strategies that will help you and your child live together with less reactivity and negativity. This chapter will present the concept of mindfulness, which is a state of mind that you, the parent, can learn and practice while applying PLACE (being Playful, Loving, Accepting, Curious, and Empathic) (Becker-Weidman & Shell, 2005; Hughes, 2006) during the difficult moments of parenting. We hope to provide you with some helpful tools to use when you might become reactive and ineffective in promoting a healing environment.

Mindfulness is a practice that has become familiar to many people in the Western world, having become incorporated into many mental health interventions as well as classroom use. Calming the mind and effective affect regulation are related abilities, essential for healthy everyday coping with the ups and downs of living in the world. In many ways, the teachings of mindfulness correspond to recent brain research findings about how healthy people use their brain to elicit calm, thoughtful states of mind. Siegel (2003) describes "interpersonal neurobiology" as a convergent view of science, which includes findings from his research about the neurobiological effects of attachment, emotion, and narrative as well as from studies in the fields of anthropology, communications, social psychology, and neuroscience. What has emerged is an awareness of "a larger reality" described by varied fields of research indicating a complicated, intertwined, interpersonal flow of information, based in actual experiences, that affects one's sense of self, the other, each other, and the relationships we have. In other words, we affect each other in ways that change how we see, feel, and experience ourselves and each other, on an ongoing basis throughout our lives. As the parent of an attachment-resistant child, learning ways to utilize your state of mind to achieve a healing relationship with your child has the potential to change your child on a cellular level, by "growing" new neural pathways that represent actual positive interpersonal experience.

Now, back to you, the parent seeking help in achieving a calm state of mind, willing and able to affect such changes that will increase your overall sense of happiness and coping abilities. Let's continue on our journey toward the attainment of mindfulness.

Picture this scene: You wake up with the intention to be kind and nurturing to your six-year-old granddaughter (let's call her Natalie). You want to understand her emotional life and to build a positive connection no matter what behavior she sends your way. Then any one of a thousand things happens: you discover she has smeared poop on the walls in her room; or she has cut off the cat's whiskers or stepped right on the collie's back; perhaps worst of all, she looks right into your surprised eyes and shrieks, "I hate you, I hate myself, I hate everyone!" and bangs her head against the wall.

How in the world do you, a mortal human being, after all, find the wherewithal to return to your good intentions, to your kind heart, to your unconditional love of the child? How do you keep from allowing this hurt, traumatized and now infuriating child to derail your efforts to parent her in a positive, nurturing way?

One answer is cultivating the tools to attain the calm, thoughtful state of mind called mindfulness. Mindfulness can offer a sense of perspective, some balance, an ability to see both your child's perspective and your own clearly. The practice of mindfulness can help you to develop a nonreactive space inside yourself, a way of feeling your emotions and seeing your thoughts in a moment of intensity or crisis without acting impulsively (possibly, hurtfully) on them. Rather, you can have the ability to make a choice about your actions, a wise choice, a choice you won't regret.

Most of us have many responses that are almost automatic. According to the Vietnamese Buddhist teacher Thicht Nhat Hanh, these are called "habit energy." They are habitual ways of responding, mostly formed during childhood, that happen quickly and without much consideration. Habitual responses operate in neurobiological concert with emotions and cognitions, often driven by emotional upset and experienced as our mind/body's neurobiological response to perceived threats. Attachment behavior is universal and innate, but the ways we learn to overcome (and hopefully survive) threats will vary according to the situations presented to us. For example, if someone threatens or hurts us, we are likely to flee, freeze, or attack, either physically or emotionally. Depending on the situation, we might take off running, remain motionless, or punch the offending person. We might defend ourselves with sharp words, cry, run away, or plan revenge (punishment). The style of therapeutic parenting taught as part of Dyadic Developmental Psychotherapy, Playful-Loving-Accepting-Curious-Empathic parenting (often referred to as PLACE parenting), requires an ability to offer a relationship-building response to whatever difficult, defensive, provocative behavior your child displays. Mindfulness is a discipline that can make the kind, wise, playful stance of PLACE parenting actually seem possible.

WHAT EXACTLY IS MINDFULNESS?

Germer, Siegel, and Fulton (2005, p. 7) describe mindfulness as "awareness of present experience with acceptance." Other authors have definitions that are slightly more elaborate or that emphasize one or another aspect of mindfulness: "keeping one's consciousness alive to the present reality" (Hanh, 1975, p. 11); "remembering to bring a wholehearted attention to each moment" (Feldman, 2001, p. 168); "moment-to-moment, nonjudgmental awareness" (Kabat-Zinn & Kabat-Zinn, 1998, p. 120).

Elements of mindfulness that are stressed over and over include a present-time moment-to-moment awareness that is both internal and external, encompassing one's own thoughts and emotions as well as what is occurring in one's surroundings; nonjudgment; staying in the here-and-now rather than mentally sliding back to the past or careening ahead to the future. It involves developing the "watcher" or "observer" within yourself, the clear awareness that does not change with your changing emotions and situations.

Let's revisit the previously described hypothetical, very distressing situations that may be occurring between you and "Natalie." Here is how mindfulness might help you out.

Let's take the first scenario, every parent's nightmare. . . . Let's say that you go to wake Natalie for breakfast and school, only to discover her busy smearing poop on the wall behind her bed. . . . Let's say you become aware of every fiber of your nervous system shrieking some variation on, "This is unbelievable! This is horrible! I can't believe she's doing this! (and then . . .) What a little monster! (and then . . . you hear yourself yelling) This has to stop NOW!" Yet, PLACE parenting advises you to find a way to respond to the situation using the attitude of playfulness, love, acceptance, and curiosity to achieve empathy.

Mindfulness can benefit you at exactly this point in time, before your voice starts yelling or your arms hit, shake, or otherwise cause physical or emotional harm. Mindfulness can offer you some tools. Mindfulness allows you to reflect on the situation: Having already practiced for this very moment, you will take some deep breaths, and simply observe the whole situation for a few moments. You will not respond as if this is a threat and therefore you are not frozen, nor are you running away, not attacking. Your calm, complete observation would include your own feelings (recognizing rage, frustration, perhaps even self-condemnation), your own thoughts ("I can't do this anymore"; "Is she still going to be doing this when she's ten years old?" "We'll never have a normal relationship, a normal household."), as well as what might be going on inside Natalie, the underlying emotion that resulted in such an activity (becoming aware of the sad, pleased, guilty, defiant expression on her small face, wondering how her past is being replayed in the present, remembering how much she's been hurt, how unable she is to meet her needs in regular/acceptable ways at this point in time).

Just that ability to take some breaths and to become aware of thoughts and feelings without acting on them can make an enormous difference. Your deliberate, slow breathing can calm the alarm centers in your brain, utilizing your own neurobiological networks to explore and rework the meaning of the scene before you; by altering its meaning from an emergency requiring an alarm response to one of consideration for your child's state of mind, you control the response you give. You can experience the internal freedom to choose an action rather than being emotionally propelled into a habitual response. So, perhaps, just perhaps, you might envision yourself in a relaxed state, shaking your head, laughing, and saying, "What in the world are you doing?" Or perhaps you roll your eyes and say, with some humor, "Whew, it smells bad in here! Come on; let's get you into the shower."

Choosing Skillful Actions

A few months before this writing, we had a gathering of parents who had been working with the PLACE parenting model with their children for lengths of time that ranged from a few months to a few years. There were many inspiring stories told that day that involved a parent stopping, stepping out of habitual reactions, and approaching his child with warmth and wisdom.

Laura, a single mother with three children, one of whom is a boy with autism, talked about her quirky, humorous way of diffusing situations that come up with her fourteen-year-old daughter, Tasheena. In the past, these would lead to lengthy struggles.

Now it's different:

> Tasheena used to be unbelievably argumentative. You could compliment her, and she would argue the point with you. You could be giving her a conse-

quence, and she was going to argue with you. It would be so frustrating! And we would butt heads like two bulls in a china shop. It's very rare now because I've found ways to change the energy completely. Now we laugh, we giggle. I'll make a funny face at her now. She'll be so mad at me, just ranting and raving, and I make a face like this (makes a grotesque monster face). And she loses it and cracks up. Then, okay, it's over. So, a lot of times it is just something simple like making a face at her. Then, we're both done.

Jo is raising a granddaughter whose rage covered a deep and pervasive fear. In her years of attachment work, Jo has become resourceful and able to stay in charge. In order to do that, she said,

I have had to (learn to) just stop. There are times I've had to shut myself in the bedroom for a minute or two to gather myself. But one thing that Kaylee particularly does like is when I'll just pick her up and throw her on the bed and start tickling her. And we both get over (whatever was going on) really quick. She loves to be tickled . . . tickled and hugged and loved. And that's broken many a tense situation, the giggling and laughing. But that doesn't come easy. That comes from working for a time and being able to stop yourself (when things get intense) to make it better.

Jody, the mother of nine children, seven of whom live at home, six of whom were adopted after her husband's niece was unable to care for them, described a recent incident with her nine-year-old daughter, Jahmera. In this case, she was able to not only break through a painful pattern of destructive and automatic actions and reactions, she was able to show her love for Jahmera in a way her daughter could accept and take in. She said the moment was so powerful and others in the family all stopped, and for a rare moment, her busy household was silent.

It's very chaotic in my home, especially when everyone comes home from school. And just the other day, Jahmera had "set me up" and I lost it. I didn't even think of how I should play this one out. And then I realized how I totally lost it in the middle of it while she was crying and just sobbing. I realized that I had "lost it," so I just grabbed her and hugged her and held her. And I just breathed with her, you know, and didn't say anything. And just hugged her and loved on her until her sobbing stopped and there wasn't even a gasp anymore. And then I just said, "I love you," and it was over.

If cultivating mindfulness allows you to make a response like that rather than exploding in anger and despair, you will have accomplished something wonderful. You will have transformed the situation from one that repeats the "habit energy" of both you and your child into one that builds a healing brain-to-brain interaction of positive experience through the relationship between you and your hurt child. You would deserve a chorus of congratulations all around for that difficult and courageous act. Of course, achieving mindfulness in difficult situations without practice isn't realistic, just as entering a competitive athletic event without preparation probably wouldn't result in a medal, either.

DEVELOPING MINDFULNESS

A Few Deep Breaths

Most well-established routes to mindfulness work with the breath. Practicing slow, deliberate breathing, focusing on the breath intake, then the exhale, for a few minutes or so several times each day, when nothing in particular is upsetting you, will begin to strengthen neuropathways in your own brain that represent a calm, thoughtful, present, observant state of mind. Being able to call upon this state of mind during painful, chaotic, confusing situations is the very simplest way to step back and pause so that you may respond in your chosen healing manner. Now, let's imagine returning to the scenario described at the beginning of the chapter. . . . You discover Natalie riding on your beloved collie's back as he yelps in pain. Your first step, of course, is to prevent further damage by separating the girl from the dog. At this point, a few deep breaths may allow you to calm your agitated emotions, keep you from yelling, and help you to take Natalie aside for a "time in" together. Your calming breaths will have given you just enough self-soothing and emotional space to help you reinterpret the situation, so you can be calm with Natalie, and relaxed enough to talk effectively with her about how her actions hurt the dog. Knowing Natalie's limitations with regard to lack of empathic awareness, or other underlying motives involved in this event (and it will be essential for you to be calm enough to allow your brain access to this awareness), will help you in the future to prevent (as much as you can) opportunities for inappropriate interactions between Natalie and the dog. As discussed elsewhere in this book, when a child is unable to calm or regulate himself or herself, then the parent can do that for and with the child. In order to do that you must be calm, reflective, emotionally engaged, and mindful.

Formal Meditation

Meditation is another way to learn and practice mindfulness. There are a number of simple meditation practices which, when done on a regular basis, help to develop the capacity to stop and reflect before taking action and to choose one's action skillfully. Here's one. Find a comfortable place to sit with your back straight, not leaning on anything. While the traditional posture is on a pillow on the floor, either cross-legged or with one's legs beside the pillow—and many people like this posture—you can also meditate fine sitting in a chair. It helps if your surroundings are quiet, though an occasional sound is not a problem. Bring your attention and awareness to your breath as it goes in and out. Some people focus on the nose; some on the belly. Either way, the effort is simply to follow your breath.

Staying with your breath is easier said than done, however, and you, like everyone, will find that your mind has jumped to various thoughts that inevitably arise. You may find yourself riveted to an intense emotion, reflecting on something from the past, planning or worrying about something in the future. When you notice this, just label it "thinking" and return to your focus on your breath, in-out, in-out. Once again, sometimes before the first two breaths have passed, you will notice that your attention has shifted to a flood of thoughts. Again, gently, bring your attention back to the breath.

Meditation is called "practice" because you are practicing bringing your attention back to the present moment (your breath is occurring in the present moment) over and over and over. In many ways, how you accomplish this is a "microcosm" of how you approach other challenges in your life. Are you harsh with yourself, judgmental with yourself, scolding yourself for not getting it "right"? Noticing that is important. Once you have noticed it, you can make the effort to be gentle with yourself as you return from your busy mind to the simple, present-time activity of focusing on your breath.

According to attachment theory, and evidence brought from the convergence of much scientific research, the neurobiology of empathy begins in infancy, developing from the actual experience of how others have cared for us, which becomes internalized and eventually is expressed as compassion for others. First, we were demonstrated compassion by our parent's consideration for our bodies and our feelings, then we developed compassion for ourselves, and then we had the neurological material, based on actual experience, to develop compassion for others. Having compassion for yourself goes a long way toward building a foundation upon which you build empathy in your child. Self-examination is valuable here; are you harsh, self-deprecating, hopeless? Can you reinvent interpretations so that you begin to describe problems without self-hurt? Can you begin to model this for your child, so that her behavior makes sense in terms of the way she "sees," based on experiences of herself, parents, you, the dog? An awareness of how you treat yourself is the first place to begin.

There is a variation of this first meditation practice that you might enjoy and find useful. That variation is to notice the content of your thoughts before bringing your attention back to your breath. Are you reliving some difficult moments with your child? Are you mentally arguing with your mother, who is judgmental of your parenting? Are you feeling excited, discouraged, worried? Just take a few moments to notice what is in your thoughts without dwelling on it; no need to make a judgment about the thoughts; no need to experience the effects of these thoughts in your body.

Observe, without reacting. Then, let the thoughts go, and simply return to an awareness of your breath.

How Meditation Works

As simple as these techniques appear, they have large implications. Each offers the experience of separating thought or impulse from action, of simply sitting with difficult emotions, and of cutting through the often "solid," reactive quality of thoughts. By noticing how thoughts arise and change, letting them go without physical reaction, and coming back to the present moment via attention to the breath, you will be practicing a helpful way of responding to the daily surprises of parenting. Let's look at each in more detail.

Separating Thought from Action

What are the benefits of separating thought from action? Here is an example. Perhaps you find yourself sitting in meditation soon after your child has yelled, "I hate you, I hate myself" and banged her head on the floor. Noticing your thoughts, you find that you are preoccupied with what to say to her. You notice yourself rehearsing a little speech about how she hurt you, then return to your breath. Thoughts come up about wishing she could just relax once in awhile. You return to your breath. You find yourself imagining a conversation where you tell her everything that is special about her, while she turns her back on you and walks out of the room. You return to your breath. Maybe by the end of your short meditation period, perhaps fifteen minutes, you have a clearer idea of what you would like to do. Maybe you would like to just sneak a little hug and say, "I love you." Maybe the right words, something simple and from the heart, have come to you. The point is that in separating first thoughts from action, you avoid clumsy, impulsive actions and often move to something deeper and wiser.

Sitting with Difficult Emotions

People often go to extreme lengths to avoid difficult emotions, both because they are painful and also, because they can force us to face some hard realities. Intense fear, anger, hurt can push us to impulsive actions in order to alleviate the feelings. So, just sitting in meditation with these emotions is likely to be a whole new, somewhat frightening experience. Yet, the experience may be different than you imagine. For example, suppose your local Department of Human Services has put you in an impossible bind. They have encouraged you, Natalie's grandparent, to take her in. Yet, because you are "family," they will offer no help or financial support. You are feeling stretched financially and are full of outrage and righteous indignation. You plot many possibilities for revenge: yelling your anger at the worker; writing a letter to the editor of your local newspaper; putting the child into foster care just to make a point.

As you sit in meditation, trying to focus on your breath, you quickly become aware of the pounding knot of emotion and of all the thoughts that surround it. You return to your breath, in-out, in-out. Soon, you become aware of the fury of emotion and the vengeful thoughts once again. You make the effort to return to your breath. But then something interesting might happen. As you repeatedly make the effort to return to your breath, you may notice your thoughts and feelings shifting. When you become aware of your "thinking," you may be thinking of something else, perhaps something completely unrelated. So, the intensity of and obsession with the anger may shift. You also may find that other things happen. Perhaps you start to have different thoughts about what to do. Perhaps you feel a little more empathy for your worker, seeing the bind she herself may be in. Perhaps you continue to think that a letter to the editor is a good idea, though the content changes a bit, to a letter that is less rageful and more effective. Perhaps a creative solution emerges that you've never considered before. Perhaps none of these occur: you just realize that you can bear the level of emotion you are feeling; it comes and goes; it won't kill you. Your internal emotional container has stretched a little. You are a little larger, a little more flexible than you thought.

Changing Your Perception of Thoughts

Cutting through the solid quality of thoughts is another powerful aspect of meditation. Let's look at how this works. We often regard our thoughts about things as "true" or "real" without realizing how these thoughts shape and limit how we see and react to things. For example, suppose Natalie is assessed and one of the diagnoses is Oppositional Defiant Disorder. Perhaps you have some abuse in your own history and begin to worry that your six-year-old granddaughter will become a threat to you, that you won't be able to handle her.

In meditation, these worried thoughts will probably arise. You notice them, let them go, and return to your breath. They come back ("What if when she's twelve she corners me in a room and hits me?" "I'd better even lock up the butter knives," "I'd better tighten up on her before she starts running the house."). You notice the thoughts and return to your breath.

By regarding these thoughts as "just thoughts" and being aware that they come partly from your own painful history, you become more able to set them aside and see Natalie as she is now, moment to moment, day by day. You might become more able to see the vulnerability beneath her tough

stance and choose skillful, effective ways to respond. Then again, you might
see that your concerns have a real foundation in the present and take extra
precautions. But by seeing your thoughts as "just thoughts," you become
more open to the many aspects of your child and to a wider, more flexible
range of responses yourself.

Informal Meditation

You may be reading this thinking that it sounds good for someone who
doesn't have much else to do. Perhaps you are juggling a busy family that
includes a child with significant attachment issues. Perhaps you are working outside the home too. How in the world can you introduce meditation
into an already overstretched schedule?

Some people come to value sitting meditation so much that they find
a way to make daily time for it. Perhaps they watch less television; maybe
they get up a little earlier. That's one way.

Another way is to bring that quality of returning to the present moment
into particular activities. Some people choose the ring of the telephone or
red traffic lights or walking downstairs as a reminder to return to notice
thoughts and return to the present. Daily chores like cooking, washing
dishes, cleaning bathrooms are a regular part of practice at Zen centers
and can be a regular part of your practice too. Sayings like, "when washing
the dishes, just wash the dishes" help to remind you to stay with what is
happening in the present. Eating is often done on the fly in our busy lives.
Yet, mindful eating (eating in silence, bringing awareness to the taste and
texture of the food) is a powerful practice and may be a possibility if you
are perhaps alone at noontime and have a few quiet minutes.

Thicht Nhat Hanh's tradition uses a "bell of mindfulness" on retreats.
When the bell rings, everyone stops, takes a few breaths, and brings their
attention back to the present moment. The website, www.mindfulnessdc
.org, offers mindfulness bells throughout the day via your computer as a
way to practice stopping, taking a few breaths, and returning to the present
moment. So, even modern technology can help.

In their reflective and helpful book, *Everyday Blessings, the Inner Work of
Mindful Parenting*, Myla and Jon Kabat-Zinn give a lovely description of the
kind of shift in perspective that mindfulness can foster:

> How we view what is happening, whether it is with judgment and disapproval
> or with openness to trying to see beneath the surface, strongly affects our
> relationships with our children. Viewing our children's difficult behavior in a
> more nonjudging, compassionate, and open manner allows us to remain their
> ally and keep a heartfelt connection with them even when we don't like how
> they are acting. (p. 77)

This description of acceptance, of trying to understand the feelings beneath the behavior, certainly echoes what we aim for in PLACE parenting.

Earlier in the chapter I mentioned a gathering of parents talking about their experiences with their complex, often-difficult children. With the help of a videographer, this group made a DVD of our dialogue that we titled, "It's always working on me that's the ticket: Parents' Experiences with Parent-Child Attachment Therapy." The first line came from something Jody said she had realized: that only by working on herself could she become the parent Jahmera needed.

Developing mindfulness is a powerful way to work on and for yourself. Mindfulness can give you the discipline and freedom you need to parent a child who is still recovering from her early life. It can allow you to stop before you become reactive and hurtful and to bring emotional warmth and freshness to each interaction with your child. More than that, "remembering to bring a wholehearted attention to each moment" just might bring you a depth of inner development and growth of spirit that is likely to enrich your whole life.

11

Raising a Child Who Exhibits Sexually Reactive Behavior

Ash Lednur

There is probably no diagnosis a parent can hear that elicits quite the reaction as when one is told by a professional that his child has Sexually Reactive Behavior (SRB). The term itself is mysterious and doesn't lend itself to any real description. The word "sexual" seems to jump out and for most people probably conjures up images of sexual predators. The truth is that there is so much about raising a child with SRB and Reactive Attachment Disorder that intertwines and overlaps, it becomes difficult to tease apart where one diagnosis ends and the other begins. And is it necessary to even know? Intellectually interesting, perhaps, like understanding why most people are right handed while others are left handed. But in the day-to-day reality of life, they are just labels that help my partner and me refer to our son when we are in the position of trying to explain the challenges of his maladaptive behaviors.

Nevertheless, without understanding Reactive Attachment Disorder (RAD), I would not even begin to be able to help our son with SRB, and without our family therapist, I wouldn't understand Reactive Attachment Disorder. In essence, if I hadn't crossed paths with our therapist who specializes in treating Reactive Attachment Disorder, I would not have been able to help my son in the crucial ways he has needed. The fact that our family therapist and I sort of stumbled across each other (because she worked with my son in a different capacity and recognized his Reactive Attachment Disorder), speaks to how lost many children and families must be who aren't fortunate enough to have connected with someone like we have. I don't use the word "connected" lightly. I believe that in order to do this work effectively, one must have a real connection with a family therapist. Our therapist has endless compassion and insight. She mentally energizes me when I feel emotionally spent, and she challenges me to look at situations from a perspective I wouldn't have considered on my own. For these reasons, and more, our therapist has my everlasting respect, admiration, and a very special place in my life and heart. This work is intimate and draining; without a strong connection to one's therapist, I have serious doubts regarding the sustainability of this life-altering work.

Essential Ingredients

Support: Therapist, Post-Adoption Groups, Understanding Friends and Family

Connection: Ongoing weekly (or daily) opportunity to feel understood, to vent, to gain perspective, a connection to the deeper meaning of becoming a healing presence in your child's life.

THE IMPORTANCE OF CONNECTION

In addition, I also believe that I had to have a strong connection with my challenging child. This connection is difficult to articulate, except to say we were undoubtedly meant to be mother and son. Yes, when my partner and I began this parenting journey, I was eager to be a mom, enthusiastic and hopeful. Without being blessed with a strong connection, I have no doubt my enthusiasm would have waned. The very first time we met our son, my partner and I took him out to a Chinese restaurant. The strangest thing occurred while eating our meal. We had chosen a cozy table in the corner. My son was sitting directly across from me, with my partner to his left. At one point, during the dinner, I was looking at them across the table, and time seemed to stand still; I felt that we were somehow suspended in the moment. I felt some spiritual presence; and while looking at our son and my partner, I had the undeniable feeling that we had known him forever. That somehow, we had not "just met." As I sat there, taking in the moment and pondering the rationality of what I was feeling, our son looked up from his wonton soup, stared directly into my eyes, and said, "Have I met you somewhere before?" I still get chills when I replay the situation in my head. I replied, barely able to speak, "It sure feels that way, doesn't it?" He said, "Yeah, it does."

My commitment to our son was and is infinite. There is not anything I wouldn't do to help him feel safe, be successful, and build positive relationships. After a particularly challenging time with him, I think back to that magical moment across the dinner table, and it helps me to reconnect mentally with him. It gives me a different mind-set and allows me to do the repair work with a positive feeling instead of staying stuck in anger or frustration. I suppose it is akin to the absolute "falling in love" that new parents have with their newborn child; the feeling that sustains parents when their kids drive them up a wall. Not having had the millions of newborn experiences with our son, I am grateful for our defining moment, which felt like a predestined bond, a divine message that we are now and forever "meant to be."

When my partner and I first met our son, we were clueless as to what the realities of life would be. Now, eight years later, we feel like old-timers, and our life together just is. The adjustments we've made are a way of life, and we rarely consciously think about them, sort of like tying one's shoe . . . you just do it and it becomes the routine, the norm of life together. Yes, my son has been a tough kid to like at times. He's been a master at pushing me away and saying or doing outrageous things that do not reflect our values.

TOUGH BEGINNINGS

Having said that, my son's early life was a blueprint for disaster. He suffered verbal, physical, and sexual abuse as well as profound neglect beginning the moment he came into the world with a birth mother who refused to hold him. He was tortured sexually, night after night, by a man who was supposed to be a father figure to him, and he witnessed countless sexual acts between his biological mother and the monster she called her boyfriend. Any trust my son had that people weren't "out to get him" in one way or another was repeatedly shattered. The only kind of physical attention that didn't require being hit or having to kneel on painful objects was his body being used sexually. He, like all children, needed and wanted to be touched, held, and loved. The problem was the types of touches he was given were either physically painful or sexual in nature.

When we first met our son, his anxiety level was off the charts. He was impulsive, with very poor boundaries, and had to relearn information and many tasks a healthy nine-year-old would have already mastered. He seemed perpetually confused about time and didn't know the order of the months of the year, or what holidays followed what season. He didn't know how to shower or the fact that we put clean clothes on following a shower. But most importantly on the long list was that there was parent/child touching filled with love that wasn't sexual. My son had difficulty tolerating conversations about abuse or neglect, and he would become extremely silly, laughing and appearing to have ADHD (which is not one of his diagnoses).

He could, however, ramble endlessly about animals and found that subject to be a safe distraction from his real life. He was extremely superficial and his affect rarely matched his feelings. He was "disconnected" internally . . . a survival skill he learned to spare himself having to feel the true horror he endured. I recall a drawing he made when he first came home to us. He filled the paper with smiley faces and had written "Hi" almost everywhere on the paper with the exception of one spot where he wrote the word "Help!" He was, in the only way he could at the time, crying out for someone to see through his façade of smiles and silliness and truly help him to feel again. There were times when my son would spill over information to me (when he was feeling safe or perhaps just overwhelmed) wanting me to write down a variety of horrible memories he carried with him so that he could "get them out of my head." It was almost like he needed to clear space in order to let new feelings in.

NEW BEGINNINGS

Slowly, we began to see a change in his anxiety level, and this correlated with the connectedness he was beginning to let himself experience. The ability to feel such profound sadness for my son's early experiences with physical contact helped me to deal with the inappropriate sexual behaviors he resorted to when stressed or triggered. This again speaks to how closely related responding to a child with Sexually Reactive Behavior and Reactive Attachment Disorder are—feeling empathic frees you from feeling angry or frustrated. It also helps to remind my partner and me not to personalize our son's setbacks. This was, and still is, a work in progress, as far as responding in ways that are therapeutic instead of allowing myself to be drawn into a power struggle or become angry if our child does something unsafe. Reminding oneself that responding in anger will not change the behavior, but showing empathy for why the behavior exists will model the empathy many of these children lack. Also, I know that if my son feels empathy and grieves for the little boy he once was, who was so mistreated, he is much

---

Empathy

1. Feeling empathy frees you from feeling angry or frustrated.
2. Responding in anger will not change the behavior. Showing empathy for why the behavior exists will model the empathy many of these children lack and will connect you and your child in a deeper way.

less likely to identify with the abuser and will live a life being a protector from, rather than a perpetrator of, abuse.

SAFETY

The strategies we use, although commonplace to us now, did not always feel that way. I recall the suggestion that we put an alarm on our son's bedroom door at night to ensure everyone's safety. At the time, the suggestion sounded so bizarre, and a sign of defeat. Would my son ever be able to have the freedoms other children enjoyed? He had invented a convincing story about sneaking out of the house, and he exhibited various unsafe behaviors with our family dogs. I kept telling myself, "It's crazy to have to lock your kid in and install an alarm system." I worried he'd feel like he was in a prison. The truth is, he readily accepted the idea and still does. We quickly realized he needed the extra security. It reminded me, in an odd way, of the old movie *The Wolfman*, who asks to be locked in a room because he couldn't trust his own impulses. More importantly, what we also realized is that the alarm goes both ways. Sure, my partner and I have a key, but our son still has anxiety over someone somehow taking him away from us. And let's face it: It was at night when the real-life monster would sneak into his room and into his bed. In our home, his room is a safe haven, his bed is never invaded, and he can sleep knowing he will be okay. The alarm is an added security blanket for him. Sometimes when we learn that a child has Sexually Reactive Behavior we are so busy focusing on what he might do, we forget to focus on why he may do something unsafe and what we can do as caregivers to protect him. Often times, we overlook the range of effects his experiences in a previously maltreating environment have on current behavior. Because of their history and consequent misunderstanding of healthy interactions, children with Sexually Reactive Behavior are vulnerable to abuse as well. It makes perfect sense to me now that my son feels more relaxed knowing we will set up an environment that focuses on everyone's safety.

Close Supervision

Constant supervision ensures safety for your child. Your child's sense of vulnerability is the result of your child not knowing how to be safe or who can be counted on to provide safety. Your constant, vigilant supervision provides the environment your child needs to learn that healthy people do not exploit children or allow children to be exploited by others.

Another benefit from feeling empathy for my son is that it has helped me progress through some stumbling blocks in my relationship with my own mother. To a much lesser extent than my son, I was sexually abused as a youngster by an older brother. Although I do not choose to socialize with him, I have, because of my relationship with my son, grown to understand my mother's continued love and contact with him. I spent several years being angry and not understanding why my mother would continue to spend time with him after she was aware of the abuse I suffered. My mother had tried to explain to me that although she hates what he did to me, she couldn't stop loving him. I now understand that kind of mother's love.

Having been victimized as a child gave me some level of understanding and a deep compassion for my son's suffering. I know what betrayal feels like and how confusing it is when someone who is supposed to "look out for you" becomes the one to guard against. I also found myself struggling at times when I recognized the behaviors my son displayed and saw the potential for my son to become the victimizer. I cringed at the thought of my son repeating the abuse he suffered and becoming my worst nightmare, so to speak. Because of this, I have always spoken candidly to my son about the effects of sexual abuse. Although I have not shared my own past, I have reminded him that the choices he makes have consequences. Also, encouraging him to grieve for himself will deter him from wanting to inflict any suffering on others. We have spoken about the fact that a choice to abuse can never be taken back. The fact that I believe my brother is genuinely sorry for his actions does nothing to negate the fact that his actions caused me a great deal of pain that took years to overcome. Because of my past, I am hypervigilant, which I believe is crucial to my son's safety as well as the safety of others. In an odd way, past sexual abuse has helped to pave a more enlightened path, giving me an intuition, the ability to recognize red flags, and to respond in ways that help my son live a healthy life.

The constant supervision we provide has allowed our son to experience himself and his interactions with others in a nonsexual way. This fortunately has become his norm, unlike when he was a young boy and nearly every interaction had a "sexual spin" put on it. He now knows there is a different path he can take, and he is aware that there are healthy and appropriate ways to express one's sexuality. He now knows that nonerotic intimacy should have been showered on him as a baby and a youngster. Again, Sexually Reactive Behavior and Reactive Attachment Disorder therapy mimic each other so closely, in that you are always looking for ways for your child to experience themselves, you, and the world in positive ways. You work constantly to not set them up for failure by putting them in situations they aren't prepared to successfully negotiate. I can recall a profound statement made by our therapist: "You don't teach a child by giving them a test. A test measures what you've already internalized and know." This was particularly challenging in the public school setting. I found myself having to explain and reexplain the limits we set on our son. We were continually faced with people who judged what we knew was the right thing for our son. Luckily again, we have been blessed with our therapist, who attended more meetings than I can count and gave me articles and books to offer the team. It has been stressful at times but being assertive, proactive, and prepared has helped a great deal. I must also add it helps to be fun-loving and enjoy playing hide-and-seek, doing crafts, going on hikes, baking, and a variety of other interactive activities with your child. When you have a child with Sexually Reactive Behavior or Reactive Attachment Disorder, you come to recognize that because he can not handle the freedom of others his age, you will oftentimes take on the role of playmate.

When you accommodate your child, you limit his ability to make poor choices, so that seeing himself as a failure or a bad person lessens. Your child's issues do not continue to be the sole family focus. In short, you find creative ways to help your child experience life as a good thing. Paramount to this success is always having a plan, a safety net, and a way to experience wonderful moments but first doing your mental checklist of safety. For example, we don't avoid visiting people; we have a safety contract with clear expectations our child must follow. Prior to the visit, we go over the rules and have had our child sign a safety contract. This, we've found, helped our child to take it more seriously and allowed us to refer to it if need be. One fundamental rule, to this day, is that our son knows he is not to "disappear" from our sight. He needs to stay within eyesight, and if he wants to go off somewhere, he checks it out with us first. As he's gotten older and made progress, if we know he is with older children with good boundaries, we have allowed him to "hang out" for brief periods of time, with several check-ins. If we have children sleeping over at our house, my son is either in his alarm-safe room or on a blow-up mattress on our bedroom floor. We don't avoid going to the movies or outings with cousins. Our son just knows he is not to go into the public bathroom until it's "his turn." His cousins have just accepted the way it is, without question as well. We just

---

Play, Fun, Flexibility

These are the necessary and essential ingredients that ensure daily enjoyment of our lives together. **Play** helps us to make positive interpersonal connections that transcend abuse and neglect. Mutual enjoyment or **fun** helps us to develop and maintain perspective. **Flexibility** implies a deep acceptance of each family member's unique, special place in the family and honors who we are, no matter how we have come to be ourselves.

say, "Okay, it's your turn now, if you have to go." No one has ever said, "How come he can't come in with me?" If they had, we would just respond, "We like to encourage privacy in our family." Did any of this in the beginning feel like mental gymnastics . . . you betcha!

ACCEPTANCE

I think the turning point, at least for me, came when I allowed myself to grieve for the child I had envisioned. I had expected to be able to give my son all of the freedoms I enjoyed as a youngster. Having sleepovers, or even daytime visits with friends (without parental supervision), camping out in the yard or the living room with my sisters or having a clubhouse, were just some examples of freedoms I enjoyed and carry fond memories of to this day. I came to realize that because my son was abused, and therefore lives with the scars that damage caused, he will not have these experiences the way I had envisioned. I was sad for him and for myself. However, once I stopped measuring what I thought he had to have by the good times I had growing up, and began accepting him for who he is at the moment, limitations and all, I was able to stop trying to make him fit into an unrealistic mold. I found, too, that with this acceptance came a profound decrease in my own anger, frustration, and disappointment. I was, and am, still determined to be creative so that my son can enjoy some of the things I did as a child; however, I no longer feel the same sense of urgency I once did. He doesn't need to meet a deadline, and it's never too late to have a happy childhood.

Acceptance

Acceptance of your child's limitations doesn't mean your child won't ever change. Acceptance is synonymous with deeply loving your child. By accepting who your child is and how your child came to be who the child is, you are validating your child's experience as a hurt child. It is the attitude you need to take to think creatively about how to protect your child, to provide what your child needs in the way of extra support, to help your child heal.

We continue to make up for lost time, and in some ways our son has amazed us with his progress. He is truly the most resilient person I know and has my eternal love and admiration. Yes, we ponder when and if the external controls that have helped him so much will ever be obsolete. We worry about the future and if he'll make his way in the world and be okay, but what parent doesn't? Our main focus is no longer on the effects of past sexual abuse. We see our son as so much more than that. He is creative, artistic, gentle, and sensitive. He is clever and has a witty sense of humor. He has a thirst for all sorts of knowledge, about plant life in particular. He continues to be very young for his age, which has been a blessing for him, and us, because he isn't leaving the safety of home anytime soon. We spent so long working with our therapist to first understand, and then reach our son, that in some ways, we feel, our life with him is just beginning.

12

Parenting the Child with Attachment Difficulties

Karen A. Hunt

OUR JOURNEY TO ADOPTION

Our family's story is described in chapter 10 of *Creating Capacity for Attachment* (Becker-Weidman & Shell, 2005), so I'll only briefly outline it here. My husband and I adopted Dima at the age of three years, nine months from an orphanage in Moscow, Russia. Dima had been placed in the orphanage directly from the hospital at two and a half months of age. Our son had a good first year at home until the loss of his Ukrainian babysitter triggered an intense grief reaction, which was later diagnosed as Reactive Attachment Disorder (RAD).

Dima's treatment is also described in some detail in the above mentioned book. In this chapter I will instead focus on parenting a child with Reactive Attachment Disorder and on parenting the child that has been successfully treated. My perspective comes from parenting a child who resolved his RAD at the age of eight and who is presently in his teens. The parenting model I use has been shaped by my personal experiences (both successes and failures), experiences shared by other parents, my education, and my training in the complexity of Dima's multiple diagnoses.

FACILITATING ATTACHMENT IN CHILDREN

It's important to recognize that the bonding process can be started prior to the placement of a child in your home. Visits are beneficial in helping the

195

child to adjust. Whenever possible visit initially on the child's turf, where he is most comfortable. At the point that we were adopting, Russian law dictated that we meet our son before proceeding with the paperwork. This gave Dima an opportunity to acclimate to the changes that would turn his world upside down. To facilitate Dima's connection to us, we sent over a small album full of pictures: pictures of Mama and Papa, his new house, his new bedroom, his toys, and his dog. The book was worn, evidence to us that Dima had frequently looked at it. When Dima met us, the orphanage staff showed him the mama and papa in the book and explained that they were us. Before heading back to the States we left Polaroid pictures of Dima and us together, to add to his album.

I knew very little about attachment when we started our adoption journey so I missed many of the early signs that something was potentially amiss. Initially Dima seemed to settle into his new life without any qualms or concerns. I didn't realize at the time that this is not necessarily a good thing. Children who have faced a major disruption in their life and who have left something worth missing will likely grieve. The more typical reaction would be for the child to be upset, to be sad, and to protest. Regressive behavior and tantrums can also be a component of childhood grieving. Even infants have been known to show indicators of grief.

Parents who bring home a child who has behavior problems should not jump to fearing their child has major attachment issues or psychiatric problems. Newly placed children are going through a lot. Imagine suddenly being taken from everything you know to a very strange land where everything is different and having no say in the matter. Imagine never seeing your friends, your bed, your family, or your things again. And in this new life, the people dress differently, you are dressed differently, they talk differently, and you can't communicate with anyone. Even the food is different. A child should protest and feel sad and angry over changes like this in his life. Even if your past life was neglectful and abusive, it was still familiar. Change, even change for the better, is a very stressful process.

OUR EXPERIENCE WITH DYADIC
DEVELOPMENTAL PSYCHOTHERAPY

Dima was seven and a half years old when my husband and I first met with Art, the fifth therapist in our journey. We had completed a battery of assessments, and I remember worrying that yet another therapist was going to say that Dima had Attention Deficit/Hyperactivity Disorder (ADHD). I felt relieved that we wouldn't have to worry about Bipolar Disorder since only a few items were marked on that questionnaire, and all of those I had pretty much chalked up to Reactive Attachment Disorder.

Art confirmed the diagnosis of Reactive Attachment Disorder (RAD), ruled out ADHD, and felt sensory-integration issues were a contributing factor to the behaviors we were struggling with. Much to our surprise he diagnosed Dima with Bipolar I Disorder. It took months for that to sink in and for me to fully accept that diagnosis and my child's need for medication. I remember feeling that we were at last on the right path. For the first time since my son had started therapy more than two years earlier, we were with a therapist who got the full picture—not a picture I liked, but it seemed that the missing pieces to the Dima puzzle were coming together.

Being involved in therapy with Art was absolutely amazing. Dima was not always willing to work in therapy. Art seemed to know intuitively when to push him a little harder and when to stop therapy for that day. There were times when I wondered if Dima was at that point of no return, and yet Art would try once more. As he started to heal Dima and help us help Dima heal, Dima would often pull it together and continue to work in therapy. It was astounding to see that my son really did want to do this hard work and really did want to face issues that he had worked so hard to bury during his younger years.

THERAPEUTIC PARENTING: A PARADIGM SHIFT

I will not write much in this section about specific attachment-parenting programs and the techniques they recommend. You can read about that in this book! It is my belief that anyone raising a child needing that level of therapeutic parenting should be doing so under the guidance of a skilled therapist.

Reading everything I could get on attachment greatly helped with understanding my son and how to parent him. I took the low-budget approach and ordered many of these books through my local public library. Most libraries have an interlibrary loan program and can search across the state for a book you are interested in. Over the years I have also purchased books for my own personal library and often loan these out to other parents. Some material is also available in video/DVD format for the more electronic learners.

An important element of attachment parenting is for the primary parent to take care of himself before beginning any therapeutic work with his child. There is no way a worn-out, unsupported mom or dad can orchestrate a healing environment, day in, day out, 100 percent of the time. I could have never done this with the added stress of work and outside responsibilities. For five months I was off work and didn't burden myself with expectations of home-cooked meals or a spotless house. My son went to bed early, and I got a nice long soak in a hot tub. I kept well connected with friends and family over the phone. We lived more than two hours from Art's office, fortunately within a reasonable commute of my parents' home. To make the weekly trip for therapy less stressful on me, we always stayed overnight with family. It was refreshing to have someone to visit with, and to relax with family.

Another beneficial resource both in learning about RAD and in obtaining parenting support was the use of the Internet. Of course, part of the problem with relying on the Internet for information is the unknown validity of cyber-sources. When it comes to attachment information the most reliable source is the Association for Treatment and Training in the Attachment of Children (ATTACh); the website is www.attach.org. Any sites you can link to from ATTACh, or any therapist affiliated with ATTACh should be a safe source of information.

Through my research, personal experience, and the support of others involved in attachment parenting I came to shift my perspective from traditional parenting to that of a therapeutic parent. To me the most important element of attachment parenting is to develop a healthy parenting paradigm. Children with RAD often do not heal in environments that are harsh or that are focused on punishment and discipline. All parenting techniques must flow from a sensitive, loving, and genuinely caring attitude. Every interaction, everything you say, even discipline needs to be framed with a caring and endearing overtone.

Much of this I learned through trial and error, and from the support from my son's therapist. I just was not able to be a perfect therapeutic parent 100 percent of the time. I learned to live in the moment. I learned that when I yelled at my son, Dima would quickly back into a corner and prepare for a fight. I came to realize that rather than nagging, it was preferable to frame myself as Dima's ally, someone trying to help him. For instance, rather than demanding that Dima do his homework, I can comment that he should do his homework now so that he has time to play after supper. This way I'm the good guy trying to make sure he can build with his Legos before bed.

Initially this was difficult for me to master. I was fortunate to have been raised by "good enough" parents. But when we were disciplined, we knew we were in trouble. Mom's firm tone and the look in her eye were enough to know she meant business. My mother had six children to keep in line and ran a tight, though loving, ship. Mom did not mess around, and we knew she meant business when she yelled. I still catch myself falling into a dogmatic disciplinarian mode when overstressed. When my son still had attachment disorder, slips like that were costly. He'd regress or rage, but I would catch myself, add in the nurturing, and he would settle down. Now Dima is secure enough in his attachment with me to usually handle my parenting regressions.

Kids with traumatic pasts vigilantly look for "evidence" that they are under attack, that they are not lovable or worthy of love. Parent well for a month and then in a weak moment admonish your child harshly and things could backslide. Your child may see that weak moment as evidence of your true feelings showing through.

I also learned that part of the essence of a healthy parenting attitude is to remember that the nastier my child is, the more he has been hurt in the past. His behavior is less about me and more about his hidden pain. I always strive to see the cries for help in Dima's aggression or defiance. It is so easy to be goaded into an angry response by the extreme behaviors our children can display. Children with Reactive Attachment Disorder may engage in behaviors rarely seen in any other group of people. The seeming intentionality of their actions and the continual sabotaging of any efforts to show them love can and will wear down even the best of parents. I had to force myself to see the hurting child behind all of that behavior. Initially this did not come naturally and had to be something I consciously pushed myself to do every time I felt my anger rising.

Once I understood that my son had an altered view of the world and once I thoroughly understood things from his perspective, I was then able to apply reinforcement principles based on his template. I had failed previously because I assumed my son was like all other kids and I reinforced him like all other kids. Indeed, my son was not rewarded by time with me, by trinkets, or by stickers.

Many children are parented using the behavior modification concept of "time-out." Most parents only have a cursory understanding of this technique. They send a child to his room and call this "time-out." Technically "time-out" is "time out from positive reinforcement." For most American children their rooms are highly reinforcing environments full of computer games, posters, toys, and even TVs. In order for time-out to work, we first have to accept that a child is reinforced by staying in the situation. When it comes to children with histories of abuse or neglect, the child may not be reinforced by staying with his parents. As a matter of fact what is reinforcing or at least familiar to these children may be isolation. They may feel more comfortable being alone.

I find it preferable to use a technique called "time-in." In fact I think time in is likely a preferable technique to use with most children. With time-in the child is still directed away from the activity where he is causing problems. The parent remains calm and simply directs the child to come and sit by him. When I first started using this technique I found it necessary to stop whatever I was doing and have my son sit with me on the sofa. Due to Dima's resistance it was essential to give this approach my undivided attention. I would sit quietly and say nothing while Dima squirmed and pouted.

But gradually he would relax and soften. Sitting close to him, I was able to feel and sense his relaxation and take this as a cue to start processing the situation and his emotions. I was also demonstrating that while I may not be happy about his behavior, I was not rejecting him.

As your child comes to accept time in, you can then apply it to any setting. With a more receptive child, parents do not need to stop what they are doing. Dad may be cooking dinner when the child starts kicking the dog in the next room. Dad can simply advise the child that he will need to be with him in the kitchen. When out in public and your child is starting to make poor choices, simply move closer to him or call him over to you for some unrelated discussion (such as reminding him of the time or applying more sunscreen). This gives your child a break from his behavior, a little parental affection, and helps to step back into the situation more appropriately.

Last year, to encourage initiation of chores and daily tasks, Dima had a whiteboard on the refrigerator. At our weekly family meeting we discussed schedules, and plans for Dima's week were outlined on the whiteboard. In the morning my son and I would talk over his schedule for the day, and he would determine what chore needs to be done before supper. These chores were likewise written on the whiteboard. Dima would get a larger allowance by self-initiating chores after school, and I encouraged him to write a reminder note to himself (thus developing a good compensatory skill). Gradually this system was phased out to increasingly more independent initiations of responsibilities. Now, at age fourteen Dima is able to figure out independently if some basic chores such as running the sweeper, electric broom, or unloading the dishwasher need to be done simply by noticing the environmental cues (having a shedding dog helps here!). On my part it usually just takes a simple verbal reminder in the morning to have a chore done before I get home from work.

REFRAMING A DREAM

When I was first told my son had Reactive Attachment Disorder, and again when I was told he had Bipolar Disorder, my first thoughts were "no way, there's been a mistake." Dima didn't cleanly fit what I had read about RAD because he could be so engaging. I knew the therapist just needed to get to know him better. I remember telling Art in an initial appointment that as he got to know my son, he would see that Dima loved me; it was just that Dima became insecure in that love at times.

After denial comes anger and then bargaining. Parents may seek out someone to blame or become resentful toward their child's previous caregivers who neglected him. We may appear hostile or irritable to others. At some point we decide "Okay, my child has this condition, but I'm going to do 'x' and he'll be fixed." We may vacillate between these stages. One minute we may be bargaining and the next find ourselves angry or in denial again. But eventually, many of us reach that final stage and a level of acceptance: peace with the totality of who our child is, disability and all.

From a personal perspective I found myself repeatedly going through the various grief stages. I met my son on a two-minute video clip made prior to his third birthday. While his motor skills delays were evident I saw that beautiful smile that bridged the ocean between us. And just as an expectant mother dreams about her unborn child, I anticipated the future for my little boy. And of course all my dreams were Pollyanna. I did not dream of medications, trips to therapist offices, or psychiatric hospitalizations. I pondered all the fun things, pleasant things, and joy that we would have together.

Two months after starting the adoption process my husband and I boarded a plane to Russia. Over the course of four days we spend several hours with Dima. It was apparent that Dima has some developmental delays. His awkward motor coordination reminded me of the kids I have worked with who have cerebral palsy. Okay, I shift my dreams. I am already deeply in love with this little boy. Two months of watching that video clip every day had solidified my bond with Dima. By this time he was my son already, emotionally although not yet legally.

At this point there is no denial. I decide I can handle this. When we get Dima home he'll get the best medical care, the best therapy, and my dreams will still come true. And I bargain with my God. Please keep my little boy safe until we can bring him home. And please, God, let him have "normal" intelligence. I'm ashamed to have even thought this. My career is working with people who have developmental disabilities, and here I am bargaining with God to please not let my son be mentally retarded.

And six months after first setting eyes on that beautiful smile on the TV screen, we were on our way back to Russia to get Dima and to start living our dream. Once out of the orphanage, Dima's curiosity and desire to learn were very evident. Yes, my boy was obviously quite bright. He soaked up everything we exposed him to like a little sponge. Motor delays were still evident, but I was convinced that all Dima needed was time and he'd catch up. And for our first fifteen months at home I was living in a state of dream-like bliss. Dima blossomed under our nurturing umbrella. His little body caught up so rapidly both physically and developmentally that I lost sight of the fact that he was still delayed.

And I stayed in that state of denial for the first year Dima was with us. Sure I noticed that many developmental milestones were still lagging behind. I noticed that his feet didn't leave the ground. At four, with much encouragement, Dima would hold my hand and jump off the bottom step of our stairway. And we would practice and practice this little jump every time we used the stairs. And I reveled in his progress, unconcerned about his delays. I felt he was making progress and would eventually "catch up." And sure, I noticed that Dima was too clingy and too obsessed with me to be typical for his age. But I justified this to myself, as Dima had spent most of his life without a mom. I remained in denial, believing that adoption myth that once my child has been with me longer than he was in the orphanage, things would even out.

MAKING PEACE WITH LABELS

Having a child with disabilities means that parents will eventually have to face the quandary of labeling their child. Giving the problem a label will likely bring on a mixture of emotions. A parent may feel a sense of relief to know that there is a real name and real condition to describe all the turmoil they have been dealing with. A label gives the parent something to research and learn about. But with a label also comes sadness. Our child has a diagnosed "disability," something that may be there forever. Accepting a label means accepting an altered dream and possibly an altered future for our child.

Dima has many labels, which is ironic because I have always been one to dislike labeling. The fact is, labels dictate treatment. Without labels we would not be able to benefit from the path well traveled. Instead we would wander about in the forest likely lost forever. Getting a proper diagnosis can be tricky with behavioral disorders. There is much overlap in symptoms and it takes a skilled practitioner to tease them all out. Dima's behaviors could as easily be labeled Oppositional Defiant Disorder (ODD) as they could Reactive Attachment Disorder. And in actuality his first diagnosis actually was ODD. But treating my son as if he had ODD achieved nothing. Until we applied a treatment specifically for RAD Dima did not improve. In actuality, Dima was getting more and more emotionally disturbed with traditional care and parenting.

Dima also has Bipolar Disorder. Knowing this is a medical condition helps me to accept that medication is part of what is needed to stage him for success.

Knowing the correct label also helps to guide parenting techniques. We can research the diagnosis, read up on parenting advice, and join e-lists to learn from other parents. And we can help our children to master their disorder rather than let it control them. Without the label I might punish my son for behavior that is beyond his control. For example, managing mania is all about safety in the here and now. So if my son is in a manic rage we will stay home, keep stimulation to a minimum, and focus on safety. Raging based on other labels might be handled differently.

Parents aren't the only ones who need to make peace with the child's diagnoses. Kids with disabilities usually know they are different. They know this without anyone telling them. I believe strongly in giving kids the appropriate labels when we do have them and then explaining what that label means in kid-friendly language. Of course the information provided needs to be developmentally appropriate and not necessarily very detailed. I find it best to go over the basics and then simply and honestly answer any questions they might have.

Over the years I have learned that what kids imagine is wrong with them is usually much worse than the truth. Kids are often quite relieved to be told they have a certain condition. Many children with disabilities think they are "stupid."

Dima figured out at a very young age that he does not understand things like other kids do. My son knows there are times when he just cannot control the choices he is making, no matter how badly he may want to. Dima knows he can't control his body the way other kids can. And the other kids know it too. At summer programs, I noticed my son would turn over his papers so that other kids couldn't see his delayed work. No one told my son he had problems with fine motor skills. Dima decided on his own that his work didn't measure up. I have actually had elementary-age children ask me what was wrong with Dima or tell me that he needs medicine for "being hyper."

Sometimes parents find themselves facing criticism for discussing a diagnosis with our children. Even some educators and some therapists still operate under the presumption that children function best when oblivious to their disabilities. Other than kids with limited intellectual and social awareness, I have yet to meet a child who did not already know he was different. Sheltering my son from knowledge that he has disabilities would leave Dima to his own imagination to figure out what is "wrong" with him. How will my son ever learn to accept all that makes him who he is if I as a parent stay in denial of an important part of him? How will my son develop a healthy sense of self-esteem if I do not discuss his disabilities with him? And how will my son ever make peace with these labels if I am not open about them and do not demonstrate healthy attitudes for him? To not talk about these things with my son tells him that his labels are so horrible they cannot be discussed.

The bottom line for me is that my son needs to be at peace with himself, all of him: the silly/theatrical part; the talented/musical part; the easily frustrated and quick to shut down part, the overactive/sensory seeking part; and even the manic/sometimes violent part. He needs to accept all this, while also recognizing that he is truly a wonderful, sweet, and caring person. Dima has had to face a lot in his fourteen short years. Life has not always been very fair to him. Despite all of that he is a wonderful, sweet (well, okay, most of the time) kid. My son will become whoever he is meant to be because of some of the hardships he has faced. Last year Dima was described by his teachers as being the most moral boy in his class. I am sure part of that comes from knowing suffering himself. Perhaps without such harsh beginnings this aspect of who Dima is may not have been as fully developed. My son has a great future ahead of him, and no label can take that away.

And despite all his labels, my son has also done some amazing things, more than many adults have accomplished. I think his early years of abuse/neglect have resulted in a really caring and sweet kid. In fifth grade Dima and a friend went to their principal and got permission to set up a hat day at school. They raised over $500 for the children who had been terrorized in Beslan, Russia, earlier that year. And in 2005 Dima was able to raise over $300 for hurricane relief by holding a carnival at our church. And it's not just the big things that show how caring my son has become. Recently an older woman in my church told me that she was carrying some items out of the church hall one day when my son was walking home from school. He went up and offered to help carry these things to her car. Quite an accomplishment for a child previously diagnosed with RAD!

WHAT ABOUT THE SENSORY STUFF?

Most of the parents I have been in touch with parent kids with multiple diagnoses. This seems especially true of the post-institutionalized kids. In addition to Reactive Attachment Disorder, it seems that many of these kids have some degree of sensory processing impairment. So prevalent is this issue that some attachment knowledgeable therapists screen for Sensory Processing Disorders (SPD).

School obviously can be quite a challenge for a child with sensory processing deficits. Most educators are unaware of this neurological condition. Imagine a child trying to learn cursive handwriting or trying to organize the columns of numbers in a math problem when he had a very poor awareness of what his hand is doing. Imagine that child in a classroom when he cannot tolerate sitting still for more than ten minutes or the child who must move and fidget just to pay attention and concentrate. What about the child, sensitive to touch, who is standing in line between two sensory seekers who keep bumping her? Most often children's disruptive behavior, their poor frustration tolerance, or their volatility is blamed on their personality or on poor parenting, rather than being seen as the outcome of a medical condition.

As children reach the tween and teen years they are less likely to desire using anything that looks "adaptive." Dima will not even use a tripod pencil gripper, as he is sure his peers would know its purpose is to address disability-related needs, rather than for fun. Taking a tactic from teen culture, I work with Dima on using sensory "cheats" to get the input he needs. "Cheats" are tactics teens can use to beat their favorite video games. Tying your approach into the teen's cultural milieu is beneficial in combating resistance. In church I work with Dima on "cheats" such as using isometrics by alternating the crunching of his left toes, then his right. That combined with movement when permitted helps to get Dima through the hour-long service. My hope is that if this strategy is successful for church, then Dima will be motivated to self-implement such techniques to get through a tough class at school.

Children love coming to my home as Dima has some of the most interesting toys. Other than the doorway swing, one would never guess the sensory nature of his large repertoire of gadgets. My family room has a mini-trampoline in front of the TV. There is an exercise ball to use as a chair and an air-filled punching bag. On the bookshelf is a bin full of whistle toys, several of which require deep respirations (very calming for Dima, who is usually in a state of overarousal). Fortunately many of these respiratory gadgets are silent! Another tub is full of fidgets: stretchy lizards, gooey balls, weighted balls, and so forth. A smaller basket of fidgets sits on the dining room table where Dima does his homework.

In the CD rack are selections of classical music and drumbeats. Depending on the need to calm or to energize we select accordingly. There are headphones to help isolate the sound and block out outside noise when needed for improved concentration. On the sweeper is a set of headphones to help Dima block out the sound of the motor when doing this chore. Another set of headphones can be used at concerts or when taking tests at school. They create a subtle white noise which helps to block out other auditory distractions. These adaptive headphones tone the volume of the noisy concert hall down to a tolerable level while still letting one enjoy the nuances of the music.

Dima's bedroom is cleaner than the typical teen's. My son vacillates between having many things on his walls and dressers to having his room sparsely furnished, depending on how Dima's system is tolerating visual input at that time. Dima has a fifteen-pound quilt on his bed. Since getting this weighted blanket Dima's rocking in bed at night has been eliminated. Dima's blankets are soft due to his intolerance of scratchy fabrics. You will not find any corduroy in his closet. Pants tend to fit loosely around the waist, and we are experimenting with compression shirts and shorts to see if their input may be calming to Dima. Long-sleeve shirts must have very smooth seams at the wrist, and any irritating tags are cut out of his clothes. Watches, a wallet, and necklaces sit on his dresser, unused due to their irritation.

Our bathroom has a linoleum floor, and I purchase machine-washable terry bathmats. Dima prefers large soft bath towels and has to step out of the shower to dry; otherwise he cannot keep his balance and keep the towel out of the water. Dima has to dry off quickly as the feel of water dripping on his skin is highly annoying. One year a young swimming instructor was irritated by Dima's "behavior problems" because he kept falling into the pool. Rather than keeping the children in the water, her preference was to have them sit on the side while she demonstrated a technique, then get in the water and try it out, get back out and watch the next technique. With no access to a towel Dima likely became irritated by the dripping water on his skin. From a child's perspective, falling into the water would seem like a good solution to his sensory problem.

Dima also has an intense need for movement. Sometimes he is very resistant to sitting at the supper table, sitting in church, or sitting to do his homework. He just messes and fidgets with everything imaginable. You can remove everything possible to fidget with and Dima will still fidget. He is biologically driven at this point so there is no sense in fighting it. We have a sensory seat cushion Dima could choose to sit on. Or if he can't sit at the supper table appropriately, Dima can choose to take his food into another room where his disruptions won't bother anyone else. It's imperative to frame such a statement in a caring and nurturing tone rather than punitive. Allowing Dima to fidget if he really needs to without permitting a disruption of everyone else's meal is a win/win for everyone. Dima can also take a movement break. Sometimes with schoolwork I may have my son take a fifteen-minute break and go outside to shoot hoops. When he comes back from the break, Dima is usually able to work appropriately.

Sometimes Dima would get *very* oral: singing, humming, chewing on his shirts, or sucking his fingers. Reminding my son to get something appropriate for his mouth helps (gum, jerky, crunchy snacks, a piece of hard candy). If I notice Dima engaging in inappropriate oral behaviors I may set a bowl of carrot sticks, nuts, or pretzels by him. Dima naturally gravitates toward what is needed to address these internal drives. If I just point-blank ordered Dima to be quiet, it will never happen. But if I permit him to choose an accommodation, Dima quietly does his work.

THE TANGLE OF PARENTAL EMOTIONS

Parenting a child with Reactive Attachment Disorder is likely to bring out emotions you never thought you would be capable of. Many parents of such a challenging child report sometimes feeling intensely negative emotions toward their child. Some talk of moments when they wish they had never parented that child. Many parents at times have an overwhelming desire to just give up, which then brings on an enormous sense of shame and guilt. After all, parents imagine something must be wrong with me to not be able to love my own child. It's common for parents to question their own abilities and parenting skills, despite success parenting their other children. And while it's typical for all parents to occasionally have these difficult emotions, the depth and ferocity of these feelings is considerably heightened in those parenting a behaviorally challenged child.

Many parents have also reported feeling dread when preparing to come home from work every day. There is a frightening intensity to the desire to linger at work just a "little longer." I have felt this myself during my son's most difficult times, and have heard this sentiment echoed from others parenting behaviorally challenging children. I suspect this emotion may occur in a large number of parents, and may actually be a way of determining just how overwhelmed a parent may be. Home, a place that is supposed to represent relaxation and comfort, instead often brings up thoughts of dread and anxiety.

What compounds the pain of all of these energy-draining emotions is that many times we do indeed make parenting blunders. We take the bait and take our child's behavior personally. How do you not when the child you simply want to love is hurling insults, cursing at you, and meets your gaze with an intense look of hatred. Few understand the challenges of parenting a child who never, ever lets you get close, unless it's in public and he wants to con the observers.

What makes Reactive Attachment Disorder more challenging than many other behavioral disorders is the often lack of connection with one's child. Parents of most children generally get to feel the reciprocity of love. Maybe not all the time but at least occasionally they will get a glimpse of true love from their child. Love is definitely a one-way street when parenting a child with RAD. It is very difficult indeed to keep oneself in love with another being whose main goal in life appears to be to destroy any semblance of affection.

Parents of children with significant behavioral difficulties report that they rarely find themselves supported by others. They feel like they are always under a microscope and blamed for their child's problems. Quite often neighbors, fellow church members, school personnel, family, and even friends feel they could do a much better job parenting this child. These folks may feel they are showing empathy and understanding, but we parents will see right through all that to the blame and criticism. Since we already are blaming ourselves, we are even more sensitive to perceiving blame from others.

Often the well-meaning advice of others is actually quite hurtful. When we seek support or talk about our kids, many try to normalize what we are saying. So many parents have reported that they could have screamed every time someone echoed, "Oh, that's normal, all kids do that." Normalizing our kid's behavior implies that if we just were more effective in applying normal parenting principles, our kids would be fine. Comments like this often stem from that blame-the-parent mentality. Many times, these folks may mean well but unless they have parented a child with RAD they really do not understand what we are coping with. What these advice givers fail to recognize is that while our child's behavior may appear to be normal on the surface, the intensity, duration, and frequency of the behavior morphs way outside the realm of typical behavior. So while any child may become angry when asked to brush his teeth, a child with RAD may go into a full-blown rage, culminating in destroying the TV set and injuring the parent.

As parents of such challenging children we should take the time to help family and friends truly understand before casting judgment on them. Give them a video to watch, or a book or article to read on attachment. But also understand that not all people are open to seeing, believing, or understanding information contrary to their already established views of life. Many parents report alienation from people they have known for years, people who had previously respected them and thought highly of them. Then add a child with RAD to their home and suddenly the parent is seen as incompetent.

It can feel very lonely parenting a child with Reactive Attachment Disorder. That is, until you find another parent in the same shoes. And that is where I feel that truly lifesaving support lies. Parents of children with RAD desperately need to connect with other parents in this parallel universe. It is all but impossible to fully understand the devastation of this disorder until one has lived with it. During those early days of treatment I was lucky to be able to participate in a parent group facilitated by my son's therapist. I cannot stress enough the value of sitting in the same room with other parents who intimately understand what you are feeling and going through. Unless a parent finds an avenue to vent his fears and worries, those emotions have the potential to undermine his therapeutic parenting efforts.

MANAGING YOUR OWN "STUFF"

As mentioned previously, many of us find that our "issues" get tangled up in the attachment work we do with our children. We are all a product of our past experiences. Our history creates a template in which we filter everything that happens to us. Likely we first learned about this in the context of our children; due to their harsh pasts they view the world through a distorted template. Part of the therapy process for our children is to help them develop a healthier frame of reference to experience life through.

During Dyadic Developmental Psychotherapy many parents become aware of how easily our children figure out and repeatedly trigger our buttons. Issues we were not even aware of suddenly surface. And much like our children, we are not always directly aware of the connection between our reactions and our past. We may have been repeatedly burned by the hot stove throughout childhood and yet not understand our aversion to cooking as an adult. It's more likely we blame our children, as our behaviors seem to be a direct reaction to their antics. For many it's only through the guidance of our children's therapists that we first make this connection. It is important to accept that these are our triggers and we are responsible for them. These triggers are rooted in our past and are not our child's fault. We must take responsibility for mitigating the impact of these triggers, so that they don't negatively affect our emotional stability or that of our children.

For parents who were victims of abuse and neglect in their own childhoods, the triggering mechanisms may make more sense. All those repressed fears and anxieties of childhood come back into your face under the repeated stress of parenting a difficult child. Traumatized children develop deeply engrained pathways that jump from an experience to fight/flight mode. Even after years of calm, years of not triggering a reaction, the pathway still exists. Etched into a parent's brain are all the experiences of their childhood. Just as we cannot erase our children's harsh past, we cannot erase our own past experiences. Over and over I have heard parents tell me that for years they went through life with minimal impact from their traumatic childhoods. Many parents have weathered the parenting of typical children without difficulty; then enters the child with Reactive Attachment Disorder and the parent falls apart.

For parents like me from fairly mundane childhoods one might think we get off easy. However, we all have "issues" from our past. Some may have heavier issues than others, but I have yet to meet someone with such a pristine childhood that he is free of any "baggage" from his past. Some of us are perfectionistic; some are people pleasing; some lack assertiveness while others are overly aggressive in their approach. All can create issues that may surface and create difficulties when parenting a child with Reactive Attachment Disorder.

Fortunately I started to address my faulty templates as a young adult, prior to parenting. Being a stepparent gave me further practice at curbing these traits. My skills were further honed by working as an advocate for people with disabilities and as a supervisor of direct care staff. And yet they remain a part of who I am (don't ask how many times I have changed wording in this section alone). While I can reduce the impact of these templates on my life, I still find them surfacing from time to time. Knowing my "issues" and recognizing them as they surface are the two most important elements to reducing their impact on my life.

And then Dima entered my life. For the first year I felt like a competent parent as he blossomed. Dima grew tremendously both physically and developmentally during those first several months at home, before grief issues triggered both his bipolar and attachment disorders. I feel very fortunate to have had that first year of success with Dima, as during that time I was able to experience myself as a competent and successful parent. Then RAD turned our world upside down. The perfectionist in me fell apart. I could barely manage to get myself through a day with this child let alone do the things I felt were important such as clean my house, maintain a garden, or make homemade dinners. I had learned to temper these desires long before Dima entered my life. To see my household fall below a standard I felt was acceptable, however, and to see my child falling apart despite my parenting efforts were definitely triggering feelings of ineptness. Over the years I have heard many other parents echo these exact same sentiments.

Nothing can make a parent feel more incompetent then living with a child who has RAD. And yet if we do not watch out for these emotions, they will drown us in pessimism and despair. While we certainly may have many good reasons to complain, wallowing in self-pity rarely helps anyone feel better. Depression is common among this group of war-weary parents. I too have had those moments where there appeared to be no hope, where I felt the best my child's future could offer was a jail cell. I am sure part of what was mixed in there was that feeling that I was not "perfect" enough in parenting my child.

For a long time I was convinced that if I just explained things enough to others, they would get it. They would understand my parenting perspective and see that I was doing the right thing. In other words, they would see me as a competent parent. And again I struggled with overcoming that template to develop a healthier perspective. No longer do I feel driven to "make" others get it. I will offer the basic information as I feel it is appropriate and let it go. No longer do I feel that the right article or the right words will help a teacher, a neighbor, or a colleague understand life in my shoes, just as I truly cannot understand what it is like to parent a more typically developing child.

These desires and these issues will still be triggered in me from time to time. They are part of who I am, something I need to stay at peace with. By setting an example, I can help my son make peace with his own triggers. I can model a pathway to a positive life, no matter what issues from the past continue to haunt him. A part of modeling a healthy lifestyle for us parents may be to reach out and accept professional help when needed. Many parents of children with RAD go to therapy for themselves. Parenting in general is tough enough, and tenfold so when parenting a child with RAD. It is a sign of strength, not weakness, to recognize and be willing to reach out for support in fulfilling one of the most important roles of your life.

The "stuff" from our past is not necessarily all negative or impairing. Someone who is cautious because of past hurts may very well protect himself from a potentially abusive situation. Someone whose temper easily flairs up can use the preliminary stages of anger arousal as an alert system and implement some stress-reduction measures. My desire for perfection is a skill I can call upon when the task at hand demands high standards. My job requires a high level of organization and accountability. Using my perfectionistic skills I have developed follow-up systems to assure important tasks are not forgotten. My desire for peace and harmony has led to the development of good diplomacy and negotiation skills, another important trait in my field of work.

THE ROLE OF PARENTING PARTNERS

Having both parents involved in treatment also helps the support parent to understand how difficult the role of therapeutic parent is. The support parent will need to step in and carry much of the workload the parents previous shared. This can be especially unsettling when Dad is working eight or ten hours a day and comes home tired and drained. Mom's been home all day, and yet the laundry is not done, dinner is not ready, and you could write an essay in the dust on the furniture. If Dad is involved in treatment, he will better understand just how difficult therapeutic parenting can be and will probably be grateful that he gets a break while at work.

HOW TO NEGOTIATE THE SPECIAL EDUCATION SYSTEM

Children with special needs can receive accommodations through two different types of plans. Children who meet the disability criteria will qualify for an Individualized Education Plan (IEP). These children generally require some type of specialized instruction to remediate their disabilities and to gain the benefit of their education. Children with IEPs can be in a special education placement or in the regular education classroom.

Another avenue to obtain accommodations for children with special needs is through Section 504 of the Rehabilitation Act. These plans are for children who often previously fell through the cracks. A 504 plan could permit a child in a wheelchair to use the elevator, or permit a child with a hearing impairment to have a note taker. It is often easier to obtain effective accommodations for children with obvious disabilities, versus the more interpretive and less-understood hidden disabilities often found in children with RAD.

What qualifies a child for an IEP or 504 plan can vary from state to state and even between school districts within the same state. Quite often the nature of the disability has to impact the child's access to an education or his ability to learn in order to be considered for an accommodation. A child with a disability who can manage to get Cs is often deemed to be receiving the benefit of his education and thus not in need of accommodations. For parents this can be very frustrating as they are the ones to deal with the emotional backlash when these overwhelmed children arrive home from school.

With school districts, talk doesn't matter. It's what you put into writing that really counts. A parent can have dozens of conversations with the special education coordinator, principal, or teacher regarding their child's disabilities and need for services. None of that legally counts until the parent puts his request in writing to the special education department. I encourage parents to make a written request for a "full educational evaluation." That way the district can have your child evaluated by the school psychologist, speech therapist, occupational therapist, or physical therapist as warranted. It's also important to realize that the special education coordinator serves as a gatekeeper to services.

There is a good chance the team evaluating your child may not have experience with attachment issues. They may misinterpret symptoms of attachment disorder. They may see the charming child and conclude there are no underlying mental health needs. Parents have the right to ask the district to consider any outside evaluations they have. I would highly recommend bringing in documentation drafted by any outside professionals your child works with.

If the school district decides your child is not "exceptional" and thus not in need of special education supports and services, this in not the end of the process. If you disagree and feel your child needs an IEP or 504 plan, then you have the right to ask (again in writing) for an "Independent Educational Evaluation (IEE) at public expense." The school district either has to agree to pay for this or go to mediation to prove it is adequately addressing your child's needs. Once an IEE is approved by the school district, you can choose which professional licensed in your state to take your child to, and the district must consider the results of this evaluation valid. The key to getting services for a child in a school setting is not how many labels or diagnoses they have, it's demonstrating how those disabilities impact his ability to learn. And remember, we are talking about getting at least a C grade, not maximizing his potential.

You can also ask for a "functional behavioral assessment" (FBA). This brings in a psychologist who specializes in behavior management to evaluate your child and his behaviors as they impact the child's ability to learn. One of the best things I did when my son was very unstable psychiatrically was to ask for a functional behavioral assessment. I was lucky that our district works with a good team for this, and it truly was the turning point of his year.

The experience of the behavior specialist with your child's diagnosis is critical. If the practitioner does not understand how attachment issues are manifest in school, they may not accurately interpret your child's behavior. For instance, they may recognize that a child with RAD has behaviors at school that are driven by a desire for attention and escape. But unless you dig down deeper and get to the cognitions that drive the child's need for attention, you won't respond in an appropriate manner. The typical adult response to attention-seeking behavior is to give it as little attention as possible and to increase the attention being given when the child is appropriate. But for kids with attachment issues, whose drive for attention is driven by cognitions which say they are a worthless piece of dirt, that just doesn't work. These kids need—*must*—get your attention when they are at their worst. They need affirmation of their worthiness, despite the behavior. Even with these kiddos, however, we still strive to increase the positive attention when they are appropriate. The job of a behavior specialist is actually quite a complicated process with many factors needing to be considered.

While few people want to take their school district to mediation or due process, it's helpful to prepare for this while hoping it will never happen. It is important to keep a paper trail of your efforts to work cooperatively with the school. It can be helpful to send a follow-up letter after a meeting, to spell out your understanding of what was agreed to. While some parents prefer certified mail, I find it easiest to hand deliver the letter. You can ask the secretary to date stamp the letter and then make a copy for yourself, or simply notate on your copy the date, time, and who you gave it to. Guidelines for both mediation and due process can be found on your state department of education website, and parents should be provided with a copy of their rights during the initial evaluation process. A good website for insight into the legal issues involved in special education can be found at www.wrightslaw.com.

Keep an organized file of your child's records. I recommend using a portable system such as folders or a ring binder. Put your child's papers in chronological order, organized by topics. Put all school reports, report cards, progress reports, and evaluations together. Also include all outside evaluations. Keep all of your original documents together and unaltered. Make extra copies, if needed, to write notes on. Bring the binder to all meetings, as you never know when a certain document might come in handy to back up your request.

Weaving through the special education maze can be a very emotional process for parents. You have the right to bring support people to the meeting. This person can just be there for moral support, or to help guide you through the process. Some states have advocates who can attend meetings with parents. It's important to come to the meeting calm and well-prepared. Pull together copies of what you believe will be relevant documents and articles, highlighting or underlining key points you want to make. Have a list of questions or concerns that you wish to have addressed at the meeting, and paper to take notes on (or have your support person take notes). Dress professionally and you will feel more confident. Take some time to relax and unwind prior to the meeting. Guard against being pushed to respond emotionally as you risk being less respected by the IEP teams and being less able to rationally present your position.

SCHOOL ISSUES DURING TREATMENT

My encounters with our rural school district have been difficult, to say the least. Dima is the only post-institutionalized child in my community and therefore one of the most complex children in the regular education program. Dima's belligerent behavior once his disability issues are triggered contributes to the unaware writing him off as behavioral, as spoiled, or as having an "attitude problem."

Dima entered the public school system with a 504 plan which provided for a variety of accommodations including a full-time aide to assist with managing his behavior. Fortunately when Dima started school the principal was very receptive to his needs. This man did not hesitate to put a classroom aide into my son's 504 plan. Dima was blessed with an aide who, although untrained in mental health or attachment issues, had the right knack for managing him. And his kindergarten teacher was a veteran foster parent and familiar with the chaos a child like Dima could create.

Dima was to start second grade when we began Dyadic Developmental Psychotherapy with Art. When Art wrote a letter to the school recommending that Dima have homebound tutoring during the early phase of his therapy, there was no problem getting this approved. My guess is that the district was relieved to not have the burden of this difficult child, if even for a short while.

Once Dima returned to school he did well. We started him back to school slowly, one class at a time. Dima would initially regress and struggle with being away from me, but then would adjust and settle in. In all, my son was out of school completely for four months, and it took an additional two months to get him back up to full-time status.

Communication between parents and teacher is essential to minimize triangulation. Dima had a communication logbook between home and school. E-mail was not offered during his elementary years but would have been an excellent source of communication. Now in middle school, e-mail is our preferred mode of communication.

During Dima's elementary school years we were blessed that many of his teachers seemed to be receptive to at least some degree to information on Dima's multiple diagnoses.

To better stage the new teachers and my son for success, I ask for a transition meeting before the new school year starts. This is a meeting between the special education coordinator, last year's teachers, Dima's teachers for the upcoming school year, and me. It's a time to go over his 504 plan, go over strategies that did and did not work in the previous year, and to provide training in my son's multiple diagnoses. This is also a good time for the district to set up training for the teachers on your child's diagnosis. Many parents struggle over how much to tell the school about their child's disabilities. I eagerly look forward to the day when I can just send Dima to school like any other child. I am also realistic in accepting that such a day may not come until after his graduation. For now, I feel it is unfair to send Dima into a situation likely to strain his disabilities without making an effort to prepare the adults and stage him for success.

CHILD PROTECTIVE SERVICES

Parents of very challenging children may at some point find a child protection worker knocking at their door. Unprepared, this can be a devastating event. I feel that if parents foresee this possibility, hopefully it will lessen the emotional kick that usually results from such an encounter. Foster parents are routinely offered training on how to cope with false allegations of abuse, something lacking in the training of parents through adoption.

I personally would recommend cooperating with any CPS investigation. As a parent, I feel well-educated and capable of caring for my child in a manner that is best for his needs. I am fortunate to also have professional backing for my parenting approach.

PARENTING THE ATTACHED CHILD WHO HAD REACTIVE ATTACHMENT DISORDER

Ending Therapy

While Dima was highly resistant at the start of therapy, he ended treatment on a more ambivalent note. My son was eight and a half years old and had been in Dyadic Developmental Psychotherapy for ten months. Dima was excited because he knew he had made dramatic progress. Dima knew in his heart that he no longer needed therapy. But it was also a sad and scary time for my son. Dima had come to trust Art and in turn me in ways he had never trusted before. Insecurities were kicking up. Was he really ready to make it? Could he continue to do well without seeing Art?

The end of therapy was also a mix of emotions for me. It was a coveted day I had looked forward to during all those long winter months of traveling to snowy Buffalo, sometimes twice weekly. Months of intensive parenting 24/7, then slowly weaning Dima and me back to the school and working worlds. It was hard to believe this day was finally here. Like Dima, I, too, was afraid. Art had been my parenting coach for those long months. He had been patient when I made mistakes. He had walked me through the intense parenting protocol, moving at a pace I could actively put in practice. Art helped to reframe my perspective and attitude toward parenting in a way that fostered healing in my son. I went from someone who had to sit and reread the parenting material while my son raged, to a parent who intuitively responded in a nurturing and yet authoritative manner. In the early days it had been Art's voice or Daniel Hughes (whom I had heard speak a few times) that I heard in my head. Somewhere along the way that voice became mine.

Confident as I was in my skills, I was still unsure about stepping into this alone. While therapy sessions had tapered off to every two or three weeks, they were my safety net. Fortunately for Dima and me, Art chose to leave the endings loose and open. It was reassuring to know guidance was only an e-mail or phone call away. A few months after finishing therapy, my son and I had lunch with Art. This helped to cement Dima's understanding of their ongoing connection.

As I stepped back into that world of typical parenting, I was uncertain of how to proceed. There were no books or manuals; no Dr. Brazelton to say how one should parent a child with resolved attachment disorder. I knew my son would struggle with routine parenting and yet also knew he did not need the intense therapeutic parenting package that had served us so well months earlier. Dima was now attached. He trusted me and felt safe with me. My son turned to me for support when feeling weak or insecure. And yet I knew those insecurities lingered under the surface—maybe not the insecurities of Reactive Attachment Disorder, but I knew those early years would be part of who he is forever.

Many have asked how I can truly know that Dima's attachment disorder is resolved. At first I could not have answered that question with any certainty. I was more trusting of Art's opinion then I was of my own instincts. Dima's improvement had been gradual, with many ups and downs.

One of the first differences I noticed was the change in how Dima reacted to a rough day at school. Before treatment, a rough school day meant aggression and distancing behaviors once home. After completing treatment

Dima would come home and perhaps be a bit clingy if he'd had a rough day. Or my son might ask for a bottle, which had been part of our reconnecting ritual in the early days of healing. Dima actually sought out my comfort rather then rejecting it. And sure there were still times when he regressed, but they were infrequent and readily resolved by nurturing.

Over time I also noticed that Dima was able to get some of his emotional needs met by others besides me. When attachment disordered, Dima was obsessed with me. He hovered around me and would not permit anyone else to care for him. My poor husband would face the "wrath of Dima" if he did things the slightest bit differently than I did. While this tendency was still there for quite a while after therapy ended, at least we were able to start working on it. With encouragement Dima was receptive to doing things without Mom being present. Important to note is that all kids have a tendency to prefer things Mom's way or to have Mom's blessing over something. Again, we are not seeking perfection here, just a reduction to a more normalizing level of this behavior.

Emotional Scar Tissue

My personal experience with the Reactive Attachment Disorder "scar tissue" covers my son's life from ages eight-and-a-half to fourteen-plus. I have gained additional insight from parent support communities and from the work of professionals in the attachment field. The parents I am most in contact with are those of children with a complexity of issues in addition to RAD. The balance of advice that I present in this chapter will be geared toward parenting these more challenging children.

When a child has successfully resolved his Reactive Attachment Disorder, what is left behind is something I call the "RAD scar tissue." For these more involved children the attachment issues typically do not totally disappear. The child does not go on to live a life as if his abuse had never occurred. It would certainly be unrealistic to expect this, especially given all we have learned in recent years regarding the neurological components of attachment, abuse, and neglect.

Essentially I view the RAD scar tissue as the residual neurological issues that remain after the child has developed healthier ways to respond to life's ups and downs. It is the neurological pathway carved in the traumatized brain.

I found this to be true of many situations in the five years since Dima has resolved his RAD. For example, my son attended the same summer day camp from kindergarten through around fifth grade. The last year he attended this program it had a new camp director. Fortunately Dima attended with a full-time therapeutic staff support because within two weeks he was decompensating behaviorally and we pulled him from the program. I later chatted with parents of typical children who said that while their children remained stable, they also complained about the camp.

Parenting a child with RAD scar tissue requires flexibility. At times your child will not need much nurturance, other times he may require many of the attunement activities you did during Dyadic Developmental Psychotherapy. Even though his attachment disorder is resolved, there are times when Dima does still regress. When he's feeling more insecure, such as the start of a school year, I am always home when he arrives back from school. I transition him back to the sitters or to being alone when he is ready.

When I was in school and my schedule changed frequently, I would write into Dima's homework journal where I was for the day. Even now he benefits from knowing what time I'll be home each day. Dima is stable enough presently to be home on his own for a short while after school. Due to my fluctuating schedule Dima does seek affirmation each morning of what time I plan to be home. And if delayed, I am always sure to leave Dima a phone message. If I am out of town I always make sure to call Dima in the morning when he's eating breakfast, when he first gets home from school, and again at bedtime.

Over time though, the hold Dima's RAD scar tissue has on him has greatly weakened. Most recently my son went with his school music department on a trip to Disney to perform. Dima remained behaviorally stable in the days leading up to the trip with no signs of angst. Of course knowing Mom, Grandma, and his aunt were all flying down to see him perform probably helped to keep any anxiety at bay. Dima called me several times on the first few day of his trip, and we ran into each other several times as various school groups performed. Then suddenly the calls stopped, and Dima did not call again until the day he returned home.

Dima's chaperone shared with me that for the first day, he stayed close to her. Gradually he went off more and more with peers. Dima's RAD scar tissue may have been slightly overwhelmed by stepping so far away from his secure base. But he was able to find a natural support, a surrogate secure base until he felt more comfortable. And better yet, within just a few days he was feeling secure and confident enough to step out and enjoy himself just like any other fourteen-year-old. Best of all, Dima came home, we talked and talked about his trip, and life went on. No relapse behavior, no RAD scar tissue inflamed, just a fun trip with lots of great memories.

Teaching Your Child to Manage His "RAD Scar Tissue"

The RAD scar tissue can leave your child with a sensitivity to shaming experiences, a sensitivity that could carry into adulthood. Some children may continue to have difficulties with trust or feeling safe in new situations. It is my hope that as a child matures he'll learn to recognize when the RAD scar tissue is inflamed and use self-directed methods to settle it down. For many of our children it may be late adolescence or adulthood before they can implement these techniques on their own.

Parents can teach their child stress management techniques which will arm them with the tools needed to manage stressful situations. These could include deep breathing, exercise, taking a walk, jumping on a trampoline, reading, drawing pictures, or any of a wide array of activities people engage in to calm and self-soothe. While young children may not recognize the need to calm themselves, parents can walk them through the process, encouraging more and more independence over time.

Likely most of us were directed to start teaching these techniques to our children during their therapy. If not, you can start with a discussion on stress and what things people do to manage stress. Present stress as a normal, everyday thing that all people need to learn to manage. Dima was probably eight or nine when we first did this, so we used a thermometer model. Basically you just draw a large thermometer on the page and label zero at the bottom, up to ten at the top. Most children are familiar with temperatures and that the higher the temperature, the hotter things (or emotions) are. On our thermometer, we ranked stress on a scale of zero to ten.

I started the discussion by talking about how I felt with mild, moderate, and severe stress and wrote these alongside our thermometer. I then talked about what I like to do when feeling the various levels of stress and again wrote these down. Next Dad completed his. When it was Dima's turn we tried to have him generate answers on his own. When he was stuck we would suggest things that other children might say, being sure to include ideas we knew matched his strengths. Dima surprised me with how well he did in this activity. I'm sure the previous months of attachment work probably made this easier for him.

We then had a discussion about the things that many children do when feeling stressed. We talked about physical activities as exercise is a well-known stress reducer, about soothers such as soaking in a hot tub, music, or reading. We also talked about interpersonal relationships that can benefit calming such as talking to a friend, a parent, or trusted adult. And we talked about enjoyable activities such as coloring or building with Legos, as distractions also help to reduce stress. I recommend making a list that the child can be directed to reference in the future.

All of these stress-reduction activities set the stage for developing a more refined and mature stress-response system as our children get older. While an eight-year-old may jump rope for exercise, a teen may enjoy aerobics, shooting baskets, or rollerblading. A young child may like soaking in a tub to relax, while a teen may prefer to listen to his favorite music. And while younger children may like doing crafts, an older child may prefer woodworking, creative writing, or knitting (which is now quite trendy). And into

adulthood many people manage stress by joining a fitness center, taking
yoga classes, gardening, or regularly scheduling dates with their spouse and
friends.

Again and again when Dima has regressed, the answer to his escalation
in behavior has always been "increase the nurturing." In seventh grade,
when working with a local non-RAD savvy therapist, Dima decompensated
significantly in the face of the middle school transition. His Bipolar Disorder became unstable, and Dima was sleeping through his morning classes
and becoming belligerent in his afternoon classes. By the end of the second
marking period Dima was failing all of his academic classes. I had attributed all of his problems to Bipolar Disorder and parented as is appropriate
for that diagnosis. Dima's local therapist at the time did not have much in
the way of parenting advice.

At a loss for what to do, I send a brief e-mail to Art. His simple reply,
"Increase the nurturing," was like a bell going off in my head. How I could
have forgotten that, I don't know. I was nurturing Dima much as I had
months before—more than most thirteen-year-olds need but not enough in
light of the tremendous stress he was facing. Most kids struggle at the start
of middle school so it's no wonder Dima struggled even more. So increase
the nurturing I did, and very quickly Dima stabilized at home. Sleep patterns and behaviors were still an issue at school and didn't fully resolve until Dima completed the transition to his new bipolar medication. Yet again,
"increase the nurturing" was a big part of Dima's stabilization.

Dima continues to benefit from a little more structure than typical teens.
For me it has just become a natural part of parenting. But I really think any
child would benefit from some structure, although this often seems to be
lacking in today's society, especially for teens. When he is psychiatrically
stable, I can decrease the structure without Dima decompensating. Usually
when something tugs at his RAD scar tissue, Dima's struggles serve as a reminder for me to drift back toward more structure and nurturing.

The Role of Therapy after Therapy

Upon the completion of therapy many children are able to maintain for
quite a while without ongoing therapy. There will be times when everyday
life becomes difficult and challenging. A typically developing child with
healthy attachment from birth may struggle from time to time, but will
muddle through with naturally occurring supports.

After completing Dyadic Developmental Psychotherapy, Dima continued his enrollment in the Wrap Around program. In our state this program
is available for children with mental health diagnosis and provides for mo-
bile (in-home) therapists, behavioral consultants, and 1:1 TSS (Therapeutic
Staff Support) services. As Dima continued to be dependent on oversight

from a nurturing and yet authoritative adult, the presence of a TSS at summer and after-school programs was beneficial. How much of this is due to residual RAD versus the complexity of Dima's other diagnoses is hard to say. Over time therapeutic supports became less essential, and within a few years we were able to discontinue services. For many teens being able to touch base occasionally with a guidance counselor at school or with an outpatient therapist seems to provide an appropriate level of support during the post-RAD adolescent years.

Parenting the RAD Scar Tissue along with Co-morbid Diagnosis

Dima's story is complicated by his multiple diagnoses. My connection with other parents of children with RAD is mostly with those parenting post-institutionalized children. It's hard for me to say if our experiences are typical of all children with RAD or just typical of this very intense group of kids. My assumption would be that very few children have RAD as their only diagnosis. The environmental issues that lend themselves to the development of an attachment disorder are also likely to promote the development of other disabilities. A profoundly neglected child experiences many other issues such as malnutrition, sensory deprivation, and post-traumatic stress issues which also etch their mark on the developing brain.

The children I am most familiar with carry an alphabet soup of diagnoses along with Reactive Attachment Disorder. Many are also diagnosed with conditions such as Depression, Post-Traumatic Stress Disorder, Sensory Processing Disorder, Central Auditory Processing Disorder, and institutional autism. International adoptees may suffer from the impact of malnutrition and poisoning from the leaded gasoline fumes that permeate their communities and their food sources. Medical disorders (such as rickets or polio) rarely seen in American children can also be present in this population of children.

The complicated neurology of many alcohol-exposed children makes attachment work more of a challenge. A child whose memory is significantly impaired by fetal alcohol exposure is less able to learn from the natural consequences which are a component of attachment parenting. Many parents report that each day is like starting anew, that the lessons learned yesterday often do not stick with these kids. Some have referred to these children as having "Teflon Brains." A child with significant developmental delays or autism may be less able to engage in the work it takes to overcome attachment disorder. This is not to say that one should not work with these children; less able does not mean there can be no progress, just that it could be take more effort to achieve smaller increments of success. Most children with attachment disorder will fare better with the nurturing parenting style of attachment parenting. And immersed in natural consequences, many neurologically compromised children will show improvement.

When working with a child who has multiple diagnoses it is important to understand the interplay between the various disorders. One diagnosis compounds another. Each disability has a certain level of impact on a person's life. You don't simply add them together to get the total impact on a child. The effects of multiple diagnoses are multiplied upon each other. The more labels a child has, generally the greater the struggle with each individual diagnosis. Of course there are exceptions to this rule. I know of children with such unstable Bipolar Disorder that this alone significantly impairs their life. But if these same children had additional diagnoses, their life would be even more significantly compromised.

Attachment work with Dima was complicated by his multiple diagnoses. And yet his resilient personality and desire to succeed helped him overcome RAD despite these obstacles. My therapeutic parenting had to work in unison with all of his diagnoses. These same principles apply to post-RAD parenting. There continues to be an interplay between Dima's attachment security and his bipolar cycling. Most of the time Dima is very secure in my love and in his lovability. Even if his sensory or auditory systems are overloaded he still seems to understand this. But rock his bipolar and some pretty RAD-like behavior can result. The intense shame Dima feels over his manic-driven behaviors inflames his RAD scar tissue. Things do not improve for Dima until I take a dual approach of addressing both the bipolar and attachment needs.

Dealing with Bipolar Disorder in combination with attachment issues can be quite a challenge. I'm not sure how much of a role the bipolar cycling played in Dima's RAD days. Certainly the depth and length of his raging, while triggered by attachment issues, was probably fueled by bipolar instability. This would help to explain periods where the raging was minimal and other periods where the raging dominated. It would also explain his pattern since age five of decompensation in the mid-fall months. In our case, RAD played a dominant role in Dima's life from age five until nine, while the bipolar issues have been more dominant from age eleven onward.

School Issues with the Post-RAD Child

Since resolving his attachment disorder, Dima has made significant progress in his school-based behaviors. His other disabilities still dictate a need for accommodations and special supports, but minor in comparison to the days when my son was attachment disordered. For the most part Dima is a respectful student, eager to please and compliant with requests. By fifth grade we were able to phase the classroom aide from Dima's plan.

As children get older, it's often beneficial to teach them to advocate for their own needs when in school or other settings outside of home. Help your child understand that if a teacher does not follow his 504 or IEP plan it may not be intentional. The teacher may have just forgotten. As you get into the higher grades teachers are often working with a hundred or more students, of which there could be twenty-five or thirty different IEP/504 plans. Practice with your child asking for help appropriately. Teach him to approach a teacher with a positive attitude. When he is given a difficult assignment, help your child brainstorm possible solutions and practice approaching the teacher with a suggestion.

An older child may benefit from attending his IEP meetings, depending on the teaching team and the child. In some cases the atmosphere of these meetings can be disability and problem focused rather than strengths focused. Teachers may use the opportunity to point out to the parents all the child is doing wrong. There may be a tendency in some districts to blame the child or the parent, rather than look at disability issues and accommodations. With the right team and the right focus, however, it can be very empowering for the child to be part of the IEP process.

The transition to middle school is often a difficult time for emotionally challenged children. Dima had a very rocky transition with high anxiety that sent his bipolar disorder spiraling out of control. This in turn inflamed the RAD scar tissue. Most typical children struggle during this time, so it just makes sense that our children will struggle even more. I have often said Dima is a good barometer. If he can weather the storm, then more typical children should do well. If he cannot, then likely many others are suffering in silence. Children go from highly supportive elementary teachers to those who suddenly expect skills like organization and initiative. Many schools expect these skills to develop without overtly teaching them. Even typical children struggle with remembering everything from their lockers, with getting to class on time, with remembering what classes have which homework. Typical kids will eventually settle in and pick up these skills. Not so with kids who have neurological glitches, especially if their executive functioning skills are impaired. These children needs to be actively taught these skills, starting in elementary school and continuing through the middle and high school years.

Handling Tough School Assignments

In adoption and foster care circles parents often talk about those "dreaded" school assignments. Family trees, immigration reports, and units on genetics can be difficult for any child from a nontraditional family. Add in attachment issues or RAD scar tissue, and the stress over these assignments magnifies. My take on this is very different from many who believe such assignments should be banned from school curriculums altogether. To me such topics are just a part of life. Facing these issues and dealing with them as they occur can help a child to process their adoption related issues.

In the early elementary years parents definitely should step in when difficult assignments crop up. Even better is to take a proactive approach and meet with the teacher prior to the start of the school year and present some adoption-friendly information on typical school assignments. Teachers certainly do not intend to create an awkward situation for children and usually have just not given adoption issues a thought. As children get older, however, I feel it is important that we arm them with the ability to address these issues themselves. Of course parents need to take into account the personality of their child. Some children will need strong parental advocacy through the high school years, while others can be taught to self-advocate at a younger age.

For some kids these assignments may actually be beneficial, as they bring to the surface issues that our children might otherwise keep repressed. I do feel, however, that these assignments should be presented in a manner friendlier to diverse families. This is not an adoption issue. This is an issue of respecting the diversity of families in modern society. I also feel that while it may help a child to address some of the issues these assignments bring up, the classroom is no place for a public display of these struggles. Certainly if a child truly cannot cope with an assignment it is appropriate for a parent to intervene and request an alternate assignment. Some parents have found it necessary to go to the principal for support when teachers fail to see the validity of their concerns.

My son generally weathers these types of assignments well, although twice in his more vulnerable fall period Dima struggled with adoption unfriendly assignments. In the fall of seventh grade Dima was asked to make a family tree and explore why his ancestors came to America. And yes, for three weeks my son refused to do anything about the project and detested the teacher for assigning it. Once I found out and we talked, Dima seemed happy to know he had options. He could pick someone else to interview and do the assignment on his family. He could do a family tree on just his family by adoption (not a preferred choice for me because it denies the existence of his birth parents); or he could combine his family by birth and adoption, which is the option Dima chose. Once my son had made peace with that decision, he worked very hard on the assignment. Dima would not, of course, include himself in the paper he wrote about immigration. But we still discussed what we imagined were the immigration issues of his birth family and the fact that he was indeed an immigrant.

What is interesting is that later that winter Dima had a journaling assignment from his English teacher. They were to address what it might feel like if you went to a new land where you didn't speak the language. This caused no angst at all in my son. Dima chose to use a personal angle on that story and wrote about how he felt when coming here at four years of age. This teacher has a very different personality from the social studies teacher. So perhaps my son felt safer with him, or perhaps it was simply a time when he was more psychiatrically stable.

At the start of eighth grade, my son had a reading assignment about a child in an orphanage and his fantasy wish to have contact with his biological mother. The child is befriended by a writer who then graphically shares her emotions regarding parents who abandon their children. Again my son initially shut down and refused to do the assignment and again we discussed his options. I read the story, gave him the CliffsNotes version and then let it go for a few days. Dima was then willing to put some surface effort into the assignment, which gave him a grade much better than the "zero" he was initially willing to accept.

Over the years I have found that for Dima the shock of initially facing an insensitive assignment is worse than the actual assignment itself. I feel that if my son is emotionally prepared for these challenging tasks, then he is better able to face them. I have requested that teachers give me at least two or three days notice on any assignments that might be difficult for a child from his background. I can then discuss the assignment with him and help Dima process his feelings toward it, as well as discuss his options.

ADULTHOOD: WHAT DOES THE FUTURE HOLD FOR OUR KIDS

For the past few years I have chatted with Dima about some of the rules and unwritten aspects of driving (like not braking hard in the snow). Learning to drive is likely to be a challenge for Dima given his sensory processing difficulties. Already having a good handle on the smarts behind driving will leave him with more concentration to direct toward the mechanics of driving. Dima is already helping at home with things like cooking, laundry, shopping, and housework. He has written out his own bank deposit slips and helped me balance the checkbook—all with an eye toward increasing his independence as an adult.

Starting in the teen years, I feel it is important to have our children start reaching outside the home for some of their support. This is of course assuming their attachment to you is now well-solidified. I have linked up Dima with a good guidance counselor at school. They meet weekly, and Dima can turn to this man for academic needs rather than always depending on Mom. Sure, I am still involved, but am trying to expand his support system beyond me. I have encouraged Dima to someday consider sharing with his closest friend that he has Bipolar Disorder. While he is not ready for this at fourteen, someday it may be critical. If a good friend knows the warning signs of mania or depression, he can push Dima toward support when he needs it (which is essential as an acutely manic person is not likely to recognize his own need for help). Dima chose to share this diagnosis with the adults who lead a teen group he is involved in, an excellent choice on his part. This is the first time Dima has felt safe enough to share this information outside our home, and I am proud of him for having taken this step.

Dima has been provided with access to the tools and resources necessary for him to succeed. And with the RAD resolved, he's much better able to use those supports. Life may always be more of a struggle for Dima than for his peers from more typical childhoods. But for Dima, I have a feeling that having overcome so much adversity is going to make for some great character strengths. Dima is already demonstrating more caring and concern toward others than is typically seen in the teenage years. Our children are so lucky to have been born in a time when the understanding and treatment of traumatized and neglected children is on the rise. And with time, more research, and better acceptance of this field, more children will be freed from the legacy of their neglectful start in life.

13

Resources and Approaches for Parents

Robert Spottswood

This chapter details healing ways parents/caretakers of wounded children can steer toward emotional connection. You'll find brief examples for responding to difficult behaviors including both intuitive and counter-intuitive attention to emotional states. Recommendations for books, articles, and websites offer additional resources.

DYADIC DEVELOPMENTAL PSYCHOTHERAPY

I was thinking on the way over here, What are the hard times I can bring up in session this week? There aren't many. There are no more out-of-control times. She's like a regular bratty kid now. I'm not afraid of what might happen anymore—not one little bit. My heart understands her heart. Do you have any more books I can read?

—therapeutic adoptive parent wanting more

The other night she [ten-year-old adopted survivor] clung to my arm when she was afraid. That's the first time I've seen her be real. Well . . . I guess the other times she was being real in disguise.

—insightful pre-adoptive foster parent

Dyadic Developmental Psychotherapy supports parents especially with setting priorities that make connection. "It's about connections not compliance" (Becker-Weidman, pers. comm.). The first priority is safety, next is

227

regulating emotions, and finally, creating new meanings. It's very easy for parents to begin with creating new meanings by asking, "Why did you DO that!?" before it feels safe for the child to be aware of why. ("Why? Well I was driven by immense feelings of deep shame about myself growing up under horrific neglect, and it is so terrifying to remember, that I just act out the shame without much self-awareness or analysis. Why do you ask?") Most often children, and even many adults, don't know "why" they did "that." Another reason not to ask "why" is that often why is perceived as a critical question. How often has your boss asked you, "Why did you do such a good job?" Usually when someone asks us why we did something, we sense that somehow we are in trouble. So, asking a child why may actually make the child more anxious and prone to act out.

Dyadic Developmental Psychotherapy also suggests a therapeutic attitude called PLACE to help frustrated parents and children in despair of finding emotional connection.

> It really makes the difference! It's really the difference! I think she loves me now. I really do—even when she's mad at me! And I'm loving her with everything I've got!
>
> —mother of angry wounded teen, after finding connection with PLACE

Our Therapeutic Priorities

> I would simply say that we *help the child to feel safe* enough to access memories of past events that were full of shame and terror, *regulate the affect* associated with the process, and then help the child to *re-create new meanings* of the event. All of this occurs within the present.
>
> —Dan Hughes (pers. comm., May 26, 2006)

The order in which we interact is important. Attachment theory describes the natural development of trust between a child and parent. First we help the child feel safe, then we help regulate feelings and emotions, then we help create new meanings.

Help the Child Feel Safe

After a resulting session took us through songs, lap time, hand claps, headstands (therapist, too!), jokes, loving eyes, and a quick game of cards, the child, age nine, caught on that her parent and I were deeply accepting of her and everything about her. A total turnaround from the week's rejections and shame. They left smiling together.

Helping a child feel safe results from a deeply accepting attitude expressed to the child through therapeutic interactions that mean "You are okay, every part of you."

> She asked me, "Momma, why my eyes wet?" I told her, "You are feeling sad, you are crying." She asked, "Is it okay to cry?"
>
> —mother of a seven-year-old girl, adopted at age six from an overseas orphanage where she had stopped crying, because it brought scorn or punishment

Regulate the Affect

Affect means emotions and feelings,

> emphasis on maintaining an affectively attuned relationship with the child, a deep acceptance of the child's affect and experience, and greater emphasis on experience and process rather than on verbalization and content.
>
> —Arthur Becker-Weidman (pers. comm.)

Dr. Becker-Weidman is describing how to relate to children so that the emotional connection is central and shared. As with preverbal infants, wounded children listen to your tone of voice, your eyes, your body language, and your patterns. The infant learns: I can see and manage my big feelings because I can see them being felt and reflected by you in a safe way.

It almost matters less what you say than how you say it.

After a violent outburst, a developmentally delayed ten-year-old slid a note under the door of her adoptive mother's room. She had printed in large, emotion-filled letters: "I am sad that I did not see my reel mom I am very sad you can cry to with me mom I am reel sad."

Re-create New Meanings

Wounded children often blame themselves for the failures of their (previously) maltreating caregivers. The child's interpretation of loss, abuse, and neglect is viewed by the child as representative of deep flaws best kept hidden. We try to help children understand how their current behaviors express past hurts they were not responsible for creating.

> Many wounded children had to become independent before they could be dependent. They believe, "I must take care of myself even if I'm only

ten" or four, or one. But the steps they may skip in childhood become triggers as adults—feeling close, feeling dependent, feeling cared for. No matter how old or competent we appear we must learn how to be dependent and nurtured before we can have healthy interdependent relationships as adults.

—Leslie Fisher-Katz (pers. comm.)

OUR THERAPEUTIC ATTITUDE:
CREATING A HEALING PLACE

To help a child feel safe and emotionally regulated, and eventually see things from a better perspective—what approach helps the most? Many parents are most successful when they create a healing PLACE. PLACE is the Dyadic Developmental Psychotherapy therapeutic attitude of being: Playful, Loving, Accepting, Curious, and Empathic. PLACE is created with a complete absence of sarcasm, cynicism, competition, or "gotcha" messages. The goal is to make all interactions with your child feel safe and connected.

The model rests on the attitude we naturally use with helpless infants, so full of feelings and just beginning their development. Don't be afraid to try that compassionate parental attitude, even if no one did it for you. Especially if no one did it for you. We want to give the next generation a new world, "a new way of thinking," as Albert Einstein once put it, "to survive." It is about connection not compliance. The messages are primarily emotional and experiential.

P Is for Playful

Message to your child: You are delightful, special, and important to me. You are in my thoughts. I think about you. I pay attention to you. I care about you. I don't miss small chances to connect with you. I like to leave you a sticker or a jelly bean or a note. (Note: If a child is upset, save playful for another time. Empathic will serve better to soothe.)

L Is for Loving

Message to your child: When you drive me crazy with totally impossible behavior and I'm losing my mind, and it makes sense to everybody else to give up on you . . . that is not even on the radar screen for me. Never. Ever. Why? No reason except that you are my kid and I love you to pieces and I'll hang in there and protect you and put your developmental needs before my needs. Forever.

A Is for Accepting

Message to your child: All your thoughts and feelings are totally 100 percent accepted. I will set limits on behavior because you need that to learn how to do it for yourself, but thoughts and feelings will always be accepted without judgment. When children are expressing internalized shame, rage, fear, and rejection, you can "consequence" the unacceptable behavior *later*, after the feelings have been identified and accepted ("You're mad at me! That's hard, but it's okay.") Accepting "I hate you!"—your child's projected fear of being abandoned—sounds like, "It's okay to hate me. I won't kick you out." Some children feel such overwhelming shame that they can only try to convince everybody, everywhere, every day that they are worthless and rotten, then refuse forever to talk about their behavior, or their past, or anything. For them acceptance can be tolerated only indirectly. A squeeze on your way out, a quick wink in passing, a special treat on their plate, a note, a casual song when they are near. . . . Let them reject it, then accept the rejection. As Canadians say, "A steady rain soaks."

C Is for Curious

Message to your child: Everything about you and your inner life (thoughts, feelings) is fascinating to me. I really can't learn enough. "Wow, what did that feel like?" "Huh, what do you think that's about?" "How do you know?" (Stress "know," not "you.") "Hm, I wonder why . . ." Let your child reject your curiosity at first. When your child answers, keep listening.

E Is for Empathic

Message to your child: This is hard for you and I'm sorry; thank you for helping me understand how hard it is. (Accurate empathy acts as an emotional painkiller for hurt feelings.) Empathy involves sharing the feeling which your child is feeling, without trying to change the child or tell the child it doesn't make sense to feel that way or it doesn't matter, or to try to forget about it. It is feeling with and feeling for or about; shared emotions.

> To do this you almost have to slow down a little so you don't trip. You have to stop and think about what you're doing.
>
> —single father, turning his parenting around after prison

Any time you create a healing PLACE, it helps children who learned to mistrust adult motives.

P.L.A.C.E. . . . . I realize that's how I am now.

—adoptive parent after hard-won success

Below are some examples of common situations and parental responses, followed by a therapeutic response that demonstrates the effective use of PLACE.

A twelve-year-old adoptee with an extensive history of severe abuse tells his new parents, "Nobody would want a stupid kid like me."

A parent's first reaction might be:

- "WE do! WE want you!" (Quick reassurance unfortunately races past all those sad, scared feelings the child just tossed onto the table.)
- "YOU'RE not stupid!" (Quick reassurance, version two.)
- "Thanks a lot! After all we've done for you, that's all you think of yourself?!" (Resentment overflow—time for parent support.)
- "Let's look at whether the facts support your statement. For one thing, your grades tell us . . ." (Lecture alert: What feelings?)

A more therapeutic response from parents (responding to inner thoughts and feelings, rather than arguing, lecturing, correcting, or even reassuring) would be: (*Acceptance*) "Those are some of the hardest feelings anybody can have in the whole world: not feeling lovable, not feeling wanted." (*Love*) "I bet feeling unwanted makes it even harder to believe our love will still be there later." (*Curiosity*) "What was it like back when you weren't wanted?" (*Empathy*) "I'm glad you let me know you have those feelings—it's so hard for you!"

An eleven-year-old foster child who grew up as his first family's scapegoat (scapegoats receive shunning, persecution, and exclusion; from repeated emotional abandonment they learn fear and they conclude they are all alone) explains how he sleeps in his new foster home:

> After I lock all the windows and check them three times, I sleep straight like this, without rolling either direction, so I can watch four points—the door, the two windows, and the closet. Sometimes I turn my legs one way, like this, but I keep my shoulders and chest straight so I can watch all four points.

A parent's first reaction might be:

- "What are you, nuts?"
- "It's clear you had reasons in the past to have these fears, but that was then and this is now." (Your feelings aren't logical. You should stop having them.)

- "My great uncle did the same thing! He lived in Chicago, and . . ." (Other people do that, so it's normal, so don't worry about it.)

In this situation, it may not be helpful to react playfully, however a therapeutic response from parents could be: (*Acceptance*) "That makes a lot of sense. You used to never know when you were safe, so now you take extra care because nobody helped you feel safe." (*Empathic*) "I'm glad you helped me understand—and I'm sorry you have to work so hard." (*Curious*) "Are there other ways you've found to feel safe in your new home?" (*Loving, Empathic*) "Let's think about what I can do to help you, for however long it takes in the whole world until you feel safe again."

Another challenging situation might be when the child tells one of the parents, either Mom or Dad, "My dad (or mom) hates me!"

A parent's first reaction might be to say:

- "You KNOW that's not true!" (Feelings ignored, child silenced.)
- "Yeah, he hates me, too." (Joining against the other parent. Poor choice.)
- "Hm. Say, where did you put the remote?" (Parent not listening. No remote.)

In this situation, exploring what lies hidden under the child's words may lead to increased understanding as new meanings are created. Here's an example: (Empathy, Acceptance, Curiosity delivered in order) "I'm sorry (eye contact). That's so hard, to feel hated by a parent. (Genuinely sad face as you imagine being there) What's it like for you?"

The child goes on to explain that mom told him, "No cookies before supper." The child wanted to jiggle some sympathy out of the other parent, and maybe start an argument in case he got bored. Or, the child may have mistaken the parental limit as meaning the parent doesn't like the child. Using empathy, acceptance, and curiosity provides appropriate sympathy while focusing on the child's feelings. If the issue is serious, however, adults can give empathy to the child and then consult with other supportive adults regarding staying regulated when the child expresses negative interpretations of either parent's parenting.

> If we act different, she acts different. After I left in anger I had to diagram the words in my head to remember them, and then picture her as a little wild wolf. Then I went back in the room and talked to her that way. "Oh," I said, "I walked away and didn't tell you where I was going, did I? I feel so bad that I didn't tell you first!" She totally responded.
>
> —adoptive parent of a child who survived abandonment

Example of PLACE with a Younger Child

Following the first Dyadic Developmental Psychotherapy session with her eight-year-old adopted daughter, the child's mother reported a rage that had happened at home. This parent was sensitive to her daughter having experienced two rage-filled failed placements before coming to live with her.

> Instead of agonizing over the rage I accepted it and tried empathy and curiosity. I said to her, "This must be so hard for you, I'm sorry. What's it like?" Out of the blue she said, "I hate it when they fight!! I hate it when they fight!! It makes me so mad!!" Now, I'm a single mom. So I said, "Are you talking about the last people you lived with?" She said, "Yes, and I hate it when they fight!" Carrying on with this, I used curiosity about her feelings. "How did you feel when they would fight?" She said, "Mad! Scared. I hated it." And in five minutes she was calm for the rest of the day.
>
> Next day she told me, "You love the [newly adopted] baby more than you love me. You're never nice to me—you hate me!" Guessing her feeling, I said, "Are you worried that you're not as special to me since Baby came to live with us?" (Curiosity, Acceptance) "Yes, and I HATE Baby." She gasped and covered her own mouth, suddenly terrified of being evicted. She said, "I LOVE Baby!!!" And I told her that her feelings were okay and she can feel both ways. It was a new experience for her. (Acceptance)
>
> Finally, the next time she started hitting me I told her, "You can have all of your feelings, but this behavior has to stop!" (Acceptance of feelings) She looked at me at first with an evil grin. Then she thought about it, and then she stopped. I notice since I use this counterintuitive approach that she's handling other things better. She doesn't need to be first any more, and she can wait patiently while I finish with the baby.

This mother built an emotionally secure base which this child never had when she was flailing and failing her way through foster homes. Suddenly Mother sees and accepts all of the child's thoughts and feelings, yet still cares enough to set limits and guide her behavior! Is this, like, heaven?

Example of PLACE with a Wounded Teen (the Canoe Analogy)

Angry, wounded teens can be reached with PLACE, but be patient. I sometimes make the analogy of using a beautifully handcrafted canoe to rescue an emotionally troubled teen stuck in the mud on the other side of a river. After paddling over to the teen's swampy side and helping him or her (cold and covered with muck) into the canoe, you give the teen a paddle and off you go, heading back to the comfortable side. (Reminder: the props here are not real. They help display emotions. Damage is symbolic and does not require consequences.)

But soon you notice a paddle floating by. The teen's paddle. He or she has thrown it in the river and is refusing to help. As you reach for the paddle you see another paddle soaring overhead, far out of reach. Your paddle. And when you look at the teen he or she is sitting with arms folded, refusing to talk.

You are perfectly justified in wondering why in the world you even bothered to help. (Later you can take that question to another supportive adult.) Right now your goal is helping the teen find emotional safety. How to connect by using PLACE? With practice you can come up with dozens of lines. Here are some possibilities to use when paddles go overboard:

- P—PLAYFUL "Wow, good arm!" (no sarcasm)
- L—LOVING "I'm afraid you're thinking nobody could love you right now."
- A—ACCEPTING "No need to talk; you can stay safe as long as you need to."
- C—CURIOUS "What's this like for you? Let's figure it out."
- E—EMPATHIC "Looks like this is really hard for you, and I feel bad about that."

Scene two: The teen reaches into his/her coat pocket and pulls out (remember cartoon physics?) a big drill and starts drilling holes in the bottom of the boat, such that the river begins to make itself at home. You are totally within your rights to wonder, "Why me?" (Later you can talk to a religious leader about that.) Right now how do you stay emotionally connected to the teen, using PLACE? Here are some ideas to try when holes are made:

- P—PLAYFUL "No fair, can I have a turn?"
- L—LOVING "Looks like you are trying hard to tell me something. I want so much to hear you!"
- A—ACCEPTING "Thank you for wanting to take charge right now."
- C—CURIOUS "I wonder what makes this so frightening for you?"
- E—EMPATHIC "I'm sorry this is scary for you. That's really hard."

Your vulnerable caring attitude by now touches the shame hidden in the teen's heart. Shame often reacts with the rage of abandonment (stored in the heart from the past). In our story the teen now blows up in a raging rejection of you and everybody who looks like you. The heat of screaming fear, shame, and self-hatred sets the canoe on fire—at least the edge that is still above water. So you are sitting in your burning, sinking canoe with a fearful, hostile, rageful teen. At this point you are absolutely justified in wishing you were a shepherd on a distant mountain and the teen was a passive sheep. (Later you can ask a therapist for help with that.) Right now how do you respond with PLACE when shame ignites rage? (Remember consequences rarely work with shame.)

- P—PLAYFUL (When kids are upset avoid Playful; use Empathy)
- L—LOVING "You have all my attention. I'll stay and help as long as it takes."
- A—ACCEPTING "It's okay to hate me. I won't leave you."
- C—CURIOUS "Does *any*body know what you've been through?"
- E—EMPATHIC "I'm sorry it's so hard to have these feelings. I totally wish I knew an easier way to help!"

Finally, after you have hung in there way longer than you thought you could stand it, after all the teen's emotional defenses have been tried, after they all have been accepted and empathized with, the teen sits back, defenses exhausted. He may look at you or look away. He may lean passively against the charred remains of the canoe's bow. The teen's hand may dangle in the water, fingers leaving little trails in the current. For a brief moment the door to the teen's heart is open—maybe for ten minutes, maybe ten seconds. In that moment of open attunement you can deliver all the safety and connection you have saved in your bruised heart for this child. Because this is what caretakers do for wounded young people. When inner life opens, even briefly, pour in PLACE. Give eye contact. Give patterns and connection.

- P—PLAYFUL (at this moment use Empathy instead of Playful)
- L—LOVING "My heart is so grateful to you for letting me be close."
- A—ACCEPTING "Thank you for keeping yourself safe. You work so hard at that, work so hard at letting people know when you feel tender and need protection. You work so hard at feeling safe and then suddenly it's safe—this is how it should feel. Thank you so much."
- C—CURIOUS "I wonder and wonder how to make this easier for you, make it less painful to have your feelings, to feel safe . . ."
- E—EMPATHIC "I am so grateful for your finding a way to stay here, and so sorry I didn't know how to make it easier for you. It seems really hard and I feel very sad . . ." (While you feel this sadness consider letting it show. Gently.)

It is normal for teens to reject you. Hang in there. It is within the normal range of teen development to process whatever adults say by:

- Rejecting it.
- Then denying it.
- Then rejecting and denying the adult.
- Then leaving.
- Finally—in total privacy—they think it over.

The take-home message for caretakers: Don't be too hurt, nor too discouraged. And don't be afraid to have hope. Teens are often learning when they least act like it.

Here are some examples of ways different aspects of PLACE can help parents in various situations.

Playful

An adoptive mother finally gave up trying to always remain calm, logical, and fair with her two wild girls from different continents. She invented a snuggling game with them both on her lap, using loud exaggerated voices and over-the-top playfulness.

I remarked to this formerly controlled mom, "You're playful!"

Mother: I feel freed up. It doesn't always work. And I'm inconsistent. But I have no self-censorship—I'm trying it all!

Father: She's "losing it" a lot less with the kids. Previously she would have felt personally hurt when they misbehaved.

Here is an example of playful by a single parent of an adopted teen when she returned from a weekend away and found the kitchen a huge mess. She went ballistic. She yelled again when it had not been cleaned up the next day. In counseling we talked about it.

Teen: But the second day it was A LOT better than when you first saw it.

Parent: (Turns to me) How can he SAY that?!! Well . . . actually . . . the second day I have to admit—[no sarcastic tone] the breadboards WERE off the floor . . .

We all laughed heartily as we imagined the breadboards, and it was clear that she felt better. Through a little playfulness she was able to interrupt her own hurt and anger. If this severely neglected young person could articulate his inner life, it might sound like:

I'm sorry I still need help taking care of a house by myself. I can talk like an adult, but my self-organization is still really little. Please, if you want a weekend away, help me organize things! Being left alone triggers me to feel helpless until a parent returns. Then I'm so embarrassed, I act nasty to cover.

Loving

This is sometimes the hardest to express, and often sounds the most irrational.

> My girlfriend finally told me, "Your teenager has made it abundantly clear that he hates me. I can't live with him any longer. You need to choose who moves out—him or me." I had to tell her, "He's been through hell and he needs me. I love you and really hope we can stay in love and stick together until he's eighteen, and then he can move out.'"
>
> —committed father of wounded teen

Loving means commitment to helping a teen love himself or herself, by seeing it through with a teen who struggles with emotions, misinterprets and misunderstands other's motives, and needs your help to feel safe enough to expose vulnerabilities, accept nurturance, support, empathy, and love.

Accepting

"What has changed the most?" I asked the parents of an adopted teen after they appeared more relaxed. Father said, "We're more accepting of who he is." Mother said, "I used to just be so frustrated with him all the time. My problem—I'm a type-A—everything had to be just so. Now I just accept that he is who he is."

The parent of a developmentally delayed adopted daughter describes her experience with acceptance:

> This time before all my biological grandkids came over, I told her that she's special to me and I'd like her special help taking care of all the younger ones when they are here. She was great—for the first time she seemed secure and wasn't consumed by jealousy.

The single father of an exceptionally bright ten-year-old describes how he learned to accept that an extended-family trauma had left his daughter wounded and emotionally young. Now he could see her conduct as a cry for help, instead of a threat.

> I'm not as bad a parent as I thought. But I have to deal with more than ordinary parents do. I don't know why sometimes I have more authority than other times . . . Last night I took the PlayStation out of her bedroom and said it wasn't going back until the homework was finally done. At first she said she'd stick a knife in my heart if I didn't put it back. Then she threatened suicide. Then she tried to beat me up and pull my hair. Finally she broke down and sobbed and asked me to get her up early. I left the PlayStation out of her room and we both got up early to help her catch up her homework. It only took twenty minutes—she amazed me!

Sometimes *acceptance* is best given indirectly. In that situation the daughter needed her father to set limits she couldn't set for herself. Her reaction indicated other unresolved issues were surfacing. Her father recognized his daughter's need for acceptance, not anger or fear of her threats. Maybe she feared parental control (yet needed it, too), due to past trauma.

Some children are so down on themselves they even dislike compliments—compliments do not fit with their core shame. And compliments are also judgments. These children may allow you to accept them quietly by including them to help shop, play games, or help you figure something out. Does such indirect acceptance feel safer to them? Go with that.

Curiosity

Listening to your child, wondering with him about how it must feel to experience what he perceives, can result in really feeling connected to who your child is now and who he is becoming.

> When I stopped rushing to solve the problem and just listened and asked, "What's that like?" and "What's up with that?" I found out a lot about Eddie this week. When I was simply interested, he really wanted to talk.
>
> —parent of teen

Empathy

Letting go of judgments, teaching, or preaching can free you to give empathic responses to your child's emotional expression.

> We've had the very first pleasant family vacation we've ever had! When I learned to give empathy instead of lectures, she was able to let me rock her in my arms again.
>
> —mother of girl, age eight, adopted years ago

Sometimes wounded children hear even your soft voice as trying to humiliate them. Their inner shame from the past cannot trust adult motives in the present. Distortion happens. When you shed a tear in *empathy* for their hard life they may turn on you like an angry hornet:

> "WHERE did you learn to fake cry!" remarked a cynical eleven-year-old with four failed placements behind her.

Her new parent, imagining the terror of being betrayed once again, keeps showing his tears and giving back PLACE:

> It makes sense from what you've been through that you can't believe someone would cry for you. (Acceptance) I'm so sorry it was awful. (Empathy) How did you deal being faked out and abandoned by grown-ups over and over?

What did you do? (Curiosity) You don't have to believe I'll never leave you (Love)—you can know it now and believe it later.

With practice the emotional connection from using PLACE will begin to replace the power and control of endless punishment.

> This is so hard for me, Robert. For years [in our fundamentalist church] it was "Sin, sin, sin" and "Drive sin out of the child." When we adopted him we threw a huge open house to celebrate. Many church members came. He was raging a lot in those days [pre-therapy]. All the church members told me, "Wait 'til you see the difference now that he's adopted and you can spank him!"
>
> —adoptive parent

> Most of our upbringing (in Sweden, 1920s) was based on such concepts as sin, confession, punishment, forgiveness and grace, concrete factors in relationships between children and parents and God. There was an innate logic in all this which we accepted and thought we understood. This fact may well have contributed to our astonishing acceptance of Nazism. . . . In a hierarchical system, all doors are closed.
>
> —film director Ingmar Bergman, in his autobiography
> *The Magic Lantern* (2007, pp. 7–8)

RENEWAL AND SUPPORT FOR PARENTS/CAREGIVERS

What to do when you feel like your best is not good enough? Here are some protective factors for parents, similar to "burnout prevention" for therapists.

Life Outside of Parenting

Many relaxation lists mention "hobbies" and "bubble baths," but how about leafleting neighbors for a first annual neighborhood picnic or block party? (Some neighbors will show up.) Or a monthly potluck with friends? A late night weekly video date with your partner? Doing something regularly for peace and climate stabilization? A few of these things children can participate in, yet the motive remains: emotional renewal for tired and hungry caretakers.

Contact with Supportive People

When in doubt, consult. Ask a favorite pediatric or counseling professional. Call or meet monthly with one or two or three others who respect and listen to each other's lives. Bring snacks. This parenting is hard work, and you deserve the support! If you join ATTACh.org you can participate in the parents' list serve, where questions and answers can be shared as you feel comfortable. (ATTACh also maintains an active list serve for therapists doing this work.)

> I don't think it will ever be easy. But everyone notices the early change in him [age ten]. Not so cold. Not so flippant.
>
> —adoptive mother

Therapy for Self

Therapy is considered a support, and you deserve support. Ask friends whom they would recommend/use, then shop around to find a therapist you feel safe with.

Courses, Talks, and Trainings for Parenting Wounded Children

A conference or two each year can feed your hungry mind and provide support for your therapeutic efforts and interests. Scholarships are usually available if requested. A new book (ask the library to please find a copy) on a favorite topic can provide healthy balance. Remember to take time to hear a favorite speaker or author or a videotape of a talk. How about books-on-tape for the car? (When I am trying to learn a new therapeutic idea, I read it onto tape myself to play on the way to the office. We learn what we practice.)

Hanging in There, or Why Does This Take So Long?

> He hates Mother's Day, and I don't look forward to it. That's something you don't expect when you adopt a wounded little boy. Put that in your book someday.
>
> —discouraged mother of a twelve-year-old boy,
> pulled from his brutal first home at age four

Clinical consultant Leslie Fisher-Katz points out, "It can be very hard for caretakers to hang in there with the day-to-day 'uck' when a struggling child regresses, or is shut down 90 percent of the time." She suggests that it can feel validating for parents to be reminded that notable improvement may be hard to highlight. Improvement may be measured in terms of *fewer* instances of serious problems, with perhaps a doubling of the still-rare occurrences of appropriateness.

From an emotional perspective, the child may always remain a special-needs child. It's helpful for caretakers/parents to be reminded that learning how to care for their child has been a process that may have put everyone through very difficult times. And they, the caretaker/parents, are amazing. It's a challenge to have one's defenses "on" most of the time; telling oneself to "think first before reacting," to "be appropriate," to "stay positive"—this can be really hard to do! Keeping in mind that hurt children may "stir things up" to distract from their inner pain, or attempt to re-create negative interactions that validate the child's poor sense of self-worth, can result in parents feeling trapped or manipulated. Knowing that a caregiver/parent's anxiety comes from caring deeply, while at the same time feeling helpless to fix the child's hurt, can help you to accept your own ambivalence as part of the parenting process.

Here is an excerpt from a 2006 consultation with an adoptive mother:

> I've always believed parents are in the best position to heal these issues. I also feel strongly that they need a lot of support to be able to consistently give the right messages to their kids. That's probably the most important role that therapy has played in our lives

PATTERNS AND ROUTINES TO PREVENT BURNOUT FOR EVERYONE

Burnout happens to anyone when we don't feel effective. The mother of a very difficult adopted child found relief after two sessions—simply when things *stopped* going backwards. "We're treading water! I don't feel like I'm sinking!"

Humans are born "pattern-dependent" organisms. We are born looking for patterns which help us organize ourselves, our world, and how we fit in. What patterns do we make for children?

"The payoff comes from keeping her life in a routine," explain the adoptive parents of a cheerful fifteen-year-old with a history of severe early maltreatment. "If there's no routine, she'll act out, or get sneaky. Then we have to keep a tighter ship and increase the rules and structure for awhile."

Another parent reports, "Finally this holiday I realized he needs it simple, quiet, and peaceful. We had the relatives over for only three hours. It was lovely. All-day anything is too much for him."

The need for external structure and boundaries normally decreases as we mature and "self-regulate." With developmental delays this process can be a long time coming. The mother of an emotionally delayed adopted child realized one day, "She lives 100 percent in the present. There is no time for her. There is only 'now,' and 'not-now.' She's a Zen-master."

Structure to children feels like attention. Age appropriate structure helps them feel secure at home or at school. When routines are disrupted, "abandonment" alarms go off.

Sound familiar? This parent describes what happened following several sudden interruptions to the family's routine.

> After we celebrated her adoption anniversary, the ice storm hit. The storm knocked out our town's electricity and school was called off. She [six-year-old Romanian orphanage survivor] was a big help through it all, but the next day she was stubborn, angry, and she tried to hit me.

A common trigger for regression is sensing that the adult is not in charge. Or is ill. Or injured. Tired. Confused. Intimidated. Or any other condition which the child associates with emotional unavailability (feels like abandonment.)

> Kayla [age six, newly from a Russian orphanage] rode her first sled down the hill. It looked too fast, so my wife stepped out to slow her down—I don't know how she planned to do that. Anyway Kayla's sled knocked my wife over and in the morning her neck hurt. Well, next thing you know, Kayla tells her, "You not a good mom. I fly back to Russia!"
>   What did you want to tell her? I asked.
>   What the hell are you talking to your new mother like that for?!

I suggested to the adoptive parents that the child was overwhelmed with the belief that (1) she had injured her new mom, and (2) new mom and dad would blame her and throw her out, (3) after they beat her first, like in the orphanage. So she projected her unlovable worthlessness onto the mother, thereby rejecting Mom before Mom could reject her. By volunteering to leave immediately, she hoped to escape the imagined beating.

Short Story of Success

One adoptive mom of a developmentally delayed girl, age ten, tried standard therapy for a year until she heard, "Your daughter refuses to talk to me so there's no point continuing. Because her violent rages won't stop, I'm afraid she will need long-term residential care."

Hearing these words spoken from a professional resulted in heartbreak. But then, this determined mother held out for one more option: she sought out emotion-focused attachment therapy. After driving two hours each way for the initial appointment she admitted later that she did not intend to come back . . . but then she had a cell phone experience:

> After I heard all this new stuff I thought, "I'm not driving all this way again!" But on the way home I called my daughter on the cell phone. And when she

blew up I had a chance to try out the *empathy* response. And it worked! From a car! Over a cell phone! So I kept using it, and later that week she suddenly told me, "You're the nicest person I ever met!"

And the next week she asked me, "Why are you doing everything I need?" And when she got anxious about her awful past she started bringing bottles for me to feed her.

When I met the daughter I made a guess that this outwardly angry child was consumed by fear that this mom might cancel the adoption, even though it was finalized years ago. After all, she had been rejected by a previous home where they had promised to adopt her.

So after we had talked a bit awkwardly about her life I tried a little mind-reading, sitting near, talking slowly, and looking wide-eyed.

I have a hunch that when this mom tells you *No* about something, you remember when Linda said *No*, and how bad that felt, and how later on Linda kicked you out of her home. And maybe the feeling is the same, and that's *so* scary!

This girl did not nod her head, but she stared at me steadily—a shift from her anxious hyperactivity. I sensed I had connected, so I moved on, ready to back off any second and apologize if I was wrong.

What would this mom say if you told her, "Mom when you say *No* I get the same scared feeling that I had when Linda used to say *No*. The feeling tells me that you might want to get rid of me too."

She turned and looked at her Mom and then leaned into her, relaxed, and sighed. In four years she had never been so vulnerable. That was the cue this mother needed to return the following week with several break-throughs to report, opening with, "I'm just so grateful," though it was she (mom) who kept creating emotional safety during the week.

Eventually this mother, an educator, went back to college for her own counseling degree. "There's nobody in our area who does this work!" she said.

RESPONDING COUNTERINTUITIVELY

During a therapists' training at Colby College, Daniel Hughes answered a trainee's question:

Trainee: What would you do if a child kicked you during a session? (I assume he was asking from sad experience.)

Dan Hughes: I'd probably apologize to the child.

Group gasp: Why?

Dan Hughes: Because whatever I was doing at that moment was overwhelming the child's ability to regulate his own emotions, and I didn't realize that. And I'm the grown-up who's supposed to help!

This view of the adult-child relationship is fundamentally different from what is commonly thought of as the norm (e.g., retaliation, anger at the child, punishment). The difference comes from interpreting the child's behavior as anxiety/fear driven and therefore requires a supportive response. It's the adult's responsibility to respond appropriately to the underlying emotion that drives the child's reaction, delivered without denial, distortion, sarcasm, or defense.

Dan Hughes continued:

And then I might thank him for letting me know in the only way he knew in that moment, that whatever I was doing was overwhelming him, that perhaps he was being flooded with shame and he didn't know how to stop it or how to ask me for help with it—maybe his life experience taught him that help was impossible.

An adoptive father, a race-car driver, thought of an analogy to describe how he learned to respond to his child's underlying emotion before addressing behavior, "Yeah—it's like thinking backwards. And then it works!"

Let's explore some situations that can help you sharpen your counter-intuitive thinking/reacting skills.

Let's imagine that your child is caught red-handed and to your amazement says: "You don't TRUST me!"

Here are some typical responses a parent might have:

- "Let's look at whether you deserve to be trusted. In the past week how many times have you . . ." (The lecture response . . . after the third word no one is listening so, good luck.)
- "I DO trust you! Here, take the car keys, take my credit card—come home when you decide it's appropriate." (I can't tolerate hearing criticism! Obviously this response isn't going to create trust where there isn't any and may result in negative outcome.)
- "I'll NEVER trust you again, you little sneak!!" (When I feel disappointed by you, I get to dysregulate.)
- "I ALWAYS trust you! It's just this one thing that needs explaining . . ." (Double message)

A more therapeutic response that speaks to the underlying emotions and feelings driving the child's negative deed would be to say: "I love you and am sorry I haven't shown you that in a way you can feel. . . . You're trying really hard to get my attention now and you've got it; let's get a snack and chat."

The counterintuitive part of this response is that you are responding first to the real issue, that your child doubts, on a very deep level, the constancy of your commitment and love for him. By letting the child know you understand and accept these feelings, your child is likely to feel more validation, less isolation, and eventually, reduce the negative behaviors. If you offer the child attention and a snack and your child refuses or is oppositional, you are still helping the child to understand that your motives are to support his feelings, and that your child's feelings are okay. It's a good transition statement to say out loud. You can postpone consequences and talk again later when everyone is calmer.

Other trying behaviors include: hiding, lying, stealing, sneaking, shoplifting, cheating, and so on. If your child's wounded heart could speak, this might be helpful to hear:

> These behaviors come from feeling shame about myself, deep in my inner thoughts and feelings. If I am really so worthless, then it makes sense to try to hide it. But I'll still act out from where it is hidden deep inside.
>
> I am unacceptable. I don't deserve to be cared for. When adults finally realize what a crummy kid I am, they won't care about me or take care of me anymore. So I have to go underground to get what I need. As soon as they see me for who I am, I'll be on my own, so I need to practice being sneaky to survive.

Another version:

> Since I feel worthless, I am certain no one cares about me. Since no one cares, no one will notice what I do. If they DO notice, they won't care. And if they DO care, all I have to do is say "I didn't do it" and they will stop caring and say, "Oh, okay." If they forget to say, "Oh, okay," I'll keep saying, "I didn't do it" until they remember, or until they give up and tell me what a disgusting liar I am. That proves I am worthless . . . (begin again).

Another version:

> Help! Even though I do it over and over and I laugh when I am caught, it scares and saddens me to be able to trick grown-ups. How can I trust an adult to take care of me if they can be tricked by a kid? Criminy! Help! What does a kid have to do around here to get more attention, more caring, more eyes-on supervision . . . anybody!? I feel emotionally little, and I'm scared. Need more Mama! Need more Papa! Help, help!

Try to resist these responses to hiding, lying, stealing, sneaking, shoplifting, cheating, and so on:

- "Nice day out. Want pancakes for breakfast?" (Don't ask. Don't tell. Don't care.)
- "Explain yourself." (Talk to the hand . . . of the robot.)
- "Lying/stealing isn't NICE. YOU know that." (Smiley Face speaks! He shames!)
- "WHY did you LIE?! TELL me!!!" (In other words, when you disappoint me, I get to act out my grief, fear, and despair at you.)

Now let's try a more therapeutic response that sounds something like this: "Huh. Sounds like you're having a hard time feeling lovable or worthwhile. What's that about? Is it from something recent or way back? Let's figure it out. Any guesses? (curiosity) No? Can I share a thought? No? Well, I will anyway."

You can pull this off because your tone and presence are soft and safe. You could continue with, "Maybe you're afraid you're not okay and we parents won't love you anymore? (love, acceptance) If that's so, then I'm sorry, 'cause I'll be sad if you have that lonely feeling. (empathy) Want a hug right now and we can figure out a repair for this and move on? (love)"

If your child says, "No!" you can say, "Okay, when you're ready let me know." Then stick around. (acceptance) You can add, "If it happens again I'll ask sooner what feels so bad and we'll take more time to help you feel better and do a really big repair. You can also ask for some loving-up first, before you miss our attention" (love, acceptance of feelings).

With a slow compassionate tone, you offer safety. If it isn't resolved now, there is plenty of time and opportunity ahead. Keep trying when things are calm. It will wait.

Another situation that frequently occurs with insecure children is relentless questioning: "Are you going to die? Is my sister? Am I? . . ." (etc., etc., fifty times).

A first reaction might be to say things like: (Hint: dying sounds to kids like abandonment):

- "Well, yes, every living thing eventually comes to the end of its life, but don't worry—I probably won't die until you are grown up. (Child's note to self—"Never Grow Up!") Um . . . unless I die in a plane crash or something. Not likely, but I'm not going to lie to you . . . hey what are you crying for?!"
- "Got yer nose!! Now let's see a SMILE!" (Avoidance training)
- "Not this crap again! Same question, every night. Jeez!!" (I'm scared, too.)

Keeping in mind that worries about dying are usually abandonment fears, a more therapeutic response would be to say, "Are you worried about us ever being apart! Thank you for reminding me how HUGELY scary that is! To think about being apart from you makes ME want to yell 'NO! I DON'T EVER WANT TO EVER BE APART FROM DOREEN—EVER!' like that, so everybody can hear. Do you worry when you're at school and we're apart? That's so hard. I hate having that kind of worry. Thanks so much for helping me understand! Do you want a hug?"

Suggestions for Intuitive Dads Seeking Counterintuitive Ideas

"What were your thoughts after our first session?" I asked adoptive parents who drive ninety minutes each way. Father said, "Enlightenment! We've been searching so long for answers. Wow, now it makes sense!" Mother said, "Angry. We've struggled with her for so long—why didn't somebody tell us this before?!"

Sometimes dads wonder how to be with kids and what to say to them. I think this is such a mystery because many of our own dads had either disappeared, were gone a lot for financial reasons, or were emotionally gone—distracted by spoken or unspoken conflict—or they were needy, overwhelmed themselves, or overwhelming others. It was often hard to learn from dads how to be present, safe, connected, and helpful to kids.

> My philosophy is, whatever happens to you in life, you brought it on yourself.
>
> —father of very depressed boy, age nine

Tips? The short version, from the Circle of Security project (Cooper, Hoffman, Powell & Marvin, 2005):

> Always: be Bigger, Stronger, Wiser, and Kind. Whenever possible: follow your child's need. Whenever necessary: take charge.

Here are some suggestions for dads: First, be safe. Children's top need is a sense of security, which means reducing sarcasm and put-downs. And here's the counterintuitive part: if you need something back, need to be liked, have to be obeyed, must be their friend, or they have to show you their love on demand, then there is no safety. Because when they want to stay up late, eat junk food, watch violence, steer the car, or ride without seat belts, you might become a pushover, hoping for that smile you want so much from them. When it comes to paying attention to safety and boundaries, you always need confidence to say, "No, sorry," the way you would tell a tiny child who didn't want to go to bed. If a child can manipulate a parent to change the rules for the child's reasons, the child can't trust that parent for care-taking.

Second suggestion: if the child feels safe with you, stick around. A parent's presence and attention is the gold standard for kids. Next suggestion: back up the other parent every time you can. Perhaps most confusing for boys are fathers who overtly or covertly undermine the other caretaker, usually out of hurt feelings. For example, "Your mom doesn't want you on the riding mower. But I'm in charge and so we can do what we want!" is much more helpful to the child when it becomes, "Your mom doesn't want you on the riding mower. And I support your mom, especially when she's not here. We're your parents together!" Next suggestion: pay attention using PLACE. Show that you're thinking about kids and care what they do. Organize them in healthy ways. You can limit TV, video games, and violent behavior. "It's time to turn that off." No response. "Do you need some help turning it off?" Grunt. "I'll help you." Now, you turn it off and be ready without sarcasm to hear feelings. You might respond to the feelings by saying, "No, but thanks for asking." Or, "No, sorry. You can be mad at me. I'm sorry it's hard." Have some listening lines ready. "Really?" "Wow." "How come?" "How do you know?" (emphasize "know," not "you.") Say everything without sarcasm, put-downs or resentment. If you slip, you can repair it later when all is calm. "I'm sorry I was sarcastic to you. I like you and it makes me feel apart from your heart when I hurt your feelings. I apologize." Bigger, stronger, wiser, kind. Safe dad.

Next suggestion: give it a rest. When an infant has had enough fun and play, she turns her head and looks away—her signal for a break. When an older child falls apart, allow him some space and don't leave. Closeness does not come from winning, forcing, or dominating. Closeness comes from feeling understood. Feeling dad's listening presence.

Final suggestion: while setting limits as parents should, replace lectures and judgments with gentle interest in the child and his or her thoughts and feelings. Keep listening and asking friendly questions about what he or she says. "Really?" "Wow." "How come?" "How did you find out?" Hint: this is the opposite of competition, winning, or dominance. You might be thinking, "What's the point?" The point is that your child's isolation and resistance to connection becomes less when your child is free to explore his inner life of feelings and thoughts with you. The child can experience self-competence (expressing thoughts, feelings, beliefs) and emotional closeness to you at the same time. Your reflection on your child's life helps the child practice expressing his or her own reflections; by sharing their own thoughts and feelings about their own experiences with a dad who is deeply interested in their inner life, your child's safety and security slowly grow. Good dad. Listening dad.

At first kids may expect you to return to before—distant, aggressive, avoidant, whatever. When a parent/caretaker improves, the child's only safe assumption may be, "This is nice but it's way too good to last." Kids can't afford to believe too soon and then find out it wasn't true. You can reflect on that as well—"You thought I was still only interested in you when we wrestle, but I'm different now. What do you think about that?" The child might not be so sure. "That's okay, you can think about it and tell me later how I'm doing and how it feels. I like to hear your thoughts and feelings."

> *Mother:* He turned off the TV when I asked, but he refused to come upstairs. So I went to his dad and said, "Your turn."

> *Father:* I went down there and just sat with him for a while. I ended up cradling him like a baby, telling him he must have been such a beautiful baby and it's so sad his first parents didn't tell him that. He kept his eyes closed and lay there for some time, then he climbed out of my arms. But he kept nudging me with his foot. I ended up patting his foot and talking to him.

PITFALLS

Love Is All We Need?

Sometimes the hardest part of parenting an emotionally hurt child is *not* rushing in to reassure, but staying with PLACE. Here is an example of a common situation:

> *Seymour* (young, newly adopted child): I hate you!

> *Adoptive parents:* We love you, Seymour.

> *Seymour:* I hate you!

> *Adoptive parents:* We love you.

> *Seymour:* I hate you!

> *Adoptive parents:* We love you.

Seymour rages on, wondering, "Who is listening to my terror of being unlovable? These people are in total denial! They need counseling!"

While "We love you," is easy to remember and soothing to say, what helps more than these broken-record contests is Acceptance of the child's feeling, Curiosity about what it's like for him, and Empathy for his early life which makes it so hard for him to accept love and parenting. A more therapeutic response might be:

> *Seymour:* I hate you!

> *Adoptive parents:* You can hate us. (Acceptance) We won't kick you out. (Seymour's biggest fear) Are you afraid we'll think you're a bad kid and not want you here? (Curiosity) Thinking that makes sense after what you lived through at your first home. (Acceptance) I'm really sorry it's so hard. (Empathy)

You might want to try reading this passage out loud to screen for defenses, especially sarcasm.

Taking It Personally

When parents long for something back from a wounded child, I try to help them grieve for their dream that the child would be grateful by now, or have social skills by now, or that things would be easier, take less work, less time. These dreams are so natural they can sneak up on any of us. There is no fault here. Remember, "This may take longer than any of us wants."

According to therapist Betty Dixon, it is helpful to expect teenagers to settle down about six months after you can't stand it anymore. In my work I find it can be three months if all the stars are aligned.

> When she said "I want to go home!" the most therapeutic response we used was, "That makes sense. Sometimes this doesn't feel like home. Home was a place where people were mean to each other."
>
> —parents of adopted daughter, age thirteen, survivor of trauma

Ignoring Structure and Routine

Kids need caretakers and they need the caretakers to be in charge. That is the only way kids will feel safe and be okay—for adults to pay attention and care. Structure is a form of attention, and lack of structure can feel like a form of abandonment. A poignant example occurred after the first full day of an "almost-no-rules vacation" ("Yippee!"), when a wounded twelve-year-old adopted child complained, "Shouldn't we keep the rule about making my bed?"

Early Success

Whether it is the honeymoon phase or genuine progress, the early success experience is a bit unfair to the long-haul heavy lifting which parent/caretakers must do. The early good feelings are still valid. But it can make us want to avoid returning to day-to-day dealing with the child's long-term pain.

I once e-mailed a pre-adoptive parent who noticed that her foster child was worse after therapy sessions

> If I am doing my job of making sure she is really better, I will be scraping a little to help her integrate her past. Things will feel bad from time to time. The trajectory usually resembles the slow progress of the tide coming in—four forward, three back, four forward, three back—and the regressions become

shorter and less intense. It helps our patience to envision the speed of corn growing.

Trying to Be "Completely Honest" with Children

While the motive is good (not lying to children) there are several problems with insisting on "being completely honest" with a child (different from not lying). These problems have to do with "parent-child boundaries," necessary because children cannot raise themselves or take care of parents. They need caretakers and they need the caretakers to be in charge. Think of the difference between not lying and being completely honest if a child asks you about your sex life.

Not lying: "You want to know something about me that is usually private for grown-ups. I'm glad you have curiosity, and I'm not going to talk about my private life to kids. And I'm still glad you're our kid and that you ask me interesting stuff."

Being completely honest: "Um, I guess because you asked, my rule is I have to tell you . . . so, um, well . . . the first time I had sex, um . . ." Time for boundaries!

The other trouble with parents insisting on "being completely honest" is that it is a subtle way to avoid the child's needs. "Look at this, see? I handle my crummy feelings with alcohol, porn, pills, affairs, cheating, gambling, and untreated depression—you see why you shouldn't expect better parenting from me? See how hopeless it is? Now go play."

"What It Is"

What it is, is that I miss their lovely smells, smiles,
voices, thoughts, feelings that I had in my midst for
nearly thirty years.
I'd go back to having my babies all over again,
in a heartbeat if I could. There is absolutely nothing like it in this world.
I remember each of them, in so many ways, and I
cherish them now out in the world, living each day,
each year, and I miss them.
When they're with me, I'm present, and when they're gone,
so quickly, I feel my empty arms, the silence, the traces of them.
It's life, it's death, it's a circle. I know we'll part
one day, through death, and it will be an ending that
I dread, although I know it's also right.
My tears flow because our hearts ache for each other,
I know the love between my children and me and my spouse is a
pull, always, even though we need to be apart and do
our life's work.
Sometimes I want to make time stop.

Living hurts, sometimes.
That's what I wanted to say,
That's all.

—Deborah Shell, describing her attached
feelings after a holiday visit from her adult children

A Few Thoughts on Children's Movies

One of my own early movie memories was of our family walking innocently into Disney's new movie, *Bambi*. There I watched in horror as Bambi's mother was eliminated. Because I was inconsolable, we left early. What followed for me was a lifelong curiosity about the roots of Disney's choice of movie plots. As an adult therapist, I finally turned up Dorfman and Mattelart's 1972 primer, *How to Read Donald Duck*:

> There is one basic product which is never stocked in the Disney store: parents. Disney's is a universe of uncles and grand-uncles, nephews and cousins; the male-female relationship is that of eternal fiancés. Scrooge McDuck is Donald's uncle, Grandma Duck is Donald's aunt (but not Scrooge's wife), and Donald is the uncle of Huey, Dewey, and Louie. (33)

Dorfman and Mattelart suggested that Walt Disney's elimination of parents, especially mothers, is tied to his own family history:

> His father was also in the habit of giving him, for no good reason, beatings with a leather strap, to which Walt submitted "to humor him and keep him happy." Walt's mother, meanwhile, is conspicuously absent from his memories, as is his younger sister. All his three elder brothers ran away from home, and it is a remarkable fact that after he became famous, Walt Disney had nothing to do with either of his parents. . . . The elimination of true parents, especially the mother, from the comics, and the incidence in the films of mothers dead at the start, or dying in the course of events, or cast as wicked stepmothers (*Bambi, Snow White,* and especially *Dumbo*), must have held great personal meaning for Disney. (22)

> The world of Disney, inside and outside the comics, is a male one. The Disney organization excludes women from positions of importance. Disney freely admitted "Girls bored me. They still do." (22)

Unless I am mistaken, creating Disney themes without mothers is paralleled in other media creations for kids. Many children's films bring in violence and sadism like a Trojan horse. The first Batman film should have been adventurous fun, but seemed to want to make certain that we knew Jack Nicholson's character was the absolute bottom of the evil barrel. What is the message intended by such graphic, narcissistic sadism? What is the message received about men? Women? Hopelessness if we don't happen to have a superhero handy?

RESOURCES FOR CHILDREN

Appelt, K. 2000. *Oh my baby, little one.* San Diego, CA: Harcourt, Inc.

Barrett, J. D. 1989. *Willie's not the hugging kind.* New York: HarperCollins.

———. 2001. *Things that are most in the world.* New York: Scholastic, Inc.

Bashista, A. E., and C. Sykes. 2004. *When I met you: A story of Russian adoption.* Pittsboro, NC: DRT Press. A story of the adoption of an older child from a Russian orphanage. "From scenes in the orphanage to the child's Russian birthmother, this is one of the first children's picture books to chronicle the special background of children adopted from Russia" (quoted from the DRT Press website).

Brown, L. K., and M. Brown. 1986. *Dinosaurs divorce: A guide for changing families.* Boston, MA: Little Brown & Company. Colorful, kind, positive, well-researched (interviewed lots of real children), and includes a page kids love on how *kids* can feel when parents break up. Goes on to show healthy examples (using the dinosaur family) of how kids can handle parents' dating, new stepsiblings, and refusing to be in the middle of parents' arguments.

Brown, M. W., and C. Hurd. 1972. *The runaway bunny.* New York: HarperCollins.

Bush, J., and R. Spottswood. 2005. *The bean seed.* Hartland, VT: Adoption Conversations. A short, colorful picture book for learning to trust again after maltreatment. Younger survivors finally with safe parents have been known to respond, "That's like me!" Story has a positive ending and is not re-traumatizing.

Crooke, T. 1994. *So much.* Cambridge, MA: Candlewick Press.

Curtis, J. L. 1998. *Today I feel silly & other moods that make up my day.* New York: HarperCollins.

Girard, W. L. 1984. *My body is private.* Morton Grove, IL: Albert Whitman & Company

———. 1986. *Adoption is for always.* Morton Grove, IL: Albert Whitman & Company.

———. 1989. *We adopted you, Benjamin Koo.* Morton Grove, IL: Albert Whitman & Co.

Gleeson, K., and C. Kennemuth. 1993. *Kate Gleeson's wonderful you.* Racine, WI: Western Publication Company.

Harris, R. 1996. *It's perfectly normal: Changing bodies, growing up, sex and sexual health.* Cambridge, MA: Candlewick Press. This cartoon-illustrated walk through puberty is inclusive of race, sexual orientation, handicap, gender, and body-type. It talks about the importance of feelings when getting close to other people. Parents can check it out, then leave it lying around if they approve.

Hazen, B. S. 1992. *Even if I did something awful.* New York: Aladdin Library.

Hoban, R. 2002. *The little brute family.* 1st ed. Elgin, IL: Sunburst. Newer story from Russell Hoban, of *Bread and jam for Francis* fame.

hooks, b. 1999. *Happy to be nappy.* New York: Hyperion Books for Children. bell hooks turns to children's books. This book helps African American children with self-esteem.

Jarrell, R. 1996. *The animal family.* 1st ed. New York: HarperCollins. For bedtime chapter reading, it's hard to beat Randall Jarrell's classy, old, simple, calm, quirky story of an orphaned hunter hermit who finds one after another fantastic members with which to form a family. From magical to practical, the unspoken theme is about connection and relationship and making room for a range of feelings as each imperfect new member is accepted. A kind story, sparingly illustrated by Maurice Sendak.

Joosse, B. 1991. *Mama do you love me?* San Francisco: Chronicle Books LLC.

Koehler, P. 1990. *The day we met you.* New York: Bradbury Press. Talks about what the parents did to prepare for their child coming home. It's a book designed for parents to embellish and tell their child's story throughout the book.

Kuchler, B. L. 2001. *Just moms: A mother by any other squawk, cheep, yip, or mew is still as sweet.* Minocqua, WI: Willow Creek Press.

Lacher, D. B., T. Nichols, and J. C. May. 2005. *Connecting with kids through stories: Using narratives to facilitate attachment in adopted children.* London: Jessica Kingsley Publishers. I heard Todd Nichols and Joanne May in Albuquerque in 2005, and I bought five copies. It will put your thoughtful creativity to work making up four kinds of therapeutic stories, depending on what your child needs at the time.

Lite, L. 2005. *Indigo teen dreams: Guided meditation/relaxation techniques designed to decrease stress, anger, and anxiety while increasing self-esteem and self-awareness.* (Audio CD). Medicine Hat, Alberta, Canada: LiteBooks.net. Has four fifteen-minute tracks for relaxation: affirmations, breathing, visualizations, and muscle relaxation.

Long, S. 1997. *Hush, little baby.* San Francisco: Chronicle Books LLC.

Marshall, J. *George and Martha* series for children. NY: Houghton Mifflin Books for Children; collectors edition. While some of James Marshall's books are stereotyping and excluding (*The Stupids* series does little for children or parents with cognitive delays or mental illness), George and Martha exemplify over and over how a good friendship can always repair things after the inevitable mistakes and breakdown. We (like George and Martha) can do this by directly expressing our feelings, saying what we want or don't like . . . then moving on. This is how real friendships repair real issues! When a problem happens between friends, be direct to the friend, speak for yourself ("I don't like it when I see . . ."), and be done.

McBratney, S., and A. Jeram. 1995. *Guess how much I love you.* Cambridge, MA: Candlewick Press. We have the set of bunnies that go with this book. My son loved playing with them while we read the story. While the gender of the bunnies is not specified, my son always saw this as a story about a father and son.

McCourt, L. 1997. *I love you stinky face.* New York: Troll Communications LLC.

McMullan, K. 1996. *If you were my bunny.* New York: Scholastic Press.

Menzel, P. 1994. *Material world: A global family portrait.* San Francisco: Sierra Club Books. Depicts thirty families from as many countries, outside their homes with all of their belongings. Everywhere, humans live in cooperative family groups, some with a lot of stuff to make life softer, others with only each other's softness.

Minarik, E. H. 1979. *Little bear's visit.* New York: Harper Trophy.

———. 1992. *Little bear.* New York: HarperCollins Juvenile Books.

Modesitt, J. 1996. *I love you the purplest.* San Francisco: Chronicle Books.

———. 1999. *Mama, if you had a wish.* New York: Simon & Schuster Books for Young Readers.

Numeroff, L. 1998a. *What daddies do best.* New York: Simon & Schuster Books for Young Readers.

———. 1998b. *What mommies do best.* New York: Simon & Schuster Books for Young Readers.

Penn, A. 2006. *The kissing hand.* Haute, IN: Tanglewood Press, Inc. Helps with separation anxiety. Take my kiss with you on your hand all day.

Pringle, L. 1993. *Octopus hug.* Honesdale, PA: Boyds Mills Press.

Rice, D. L. 1999. *Because Brian hugged his mother.* Nevada City, CA: Dawn Publications.

Rohde, S. 1999. *Adoption is okay.* Martinsville, IN: Airleaf Publishing. This is a Russian story about adoption of an older child from an orphanage. It's neat because it's both in English and Russian.

Ross, D. 2000. *A book of hugs.* New York: HarperCollins.

Schlein, M. 2000. *The way mothers are.* Morton Grove, IL: Albert Whitman & Co.

Scott, A. H. 1972. *On mother's lap.* New York: Clarion Books.

Tafuri, N. 1998. *I love you, little one.* New York: Scholastic Press.

Taylor, A. 1999. *Baby dance.* New York: Harper Festival.

Teen Voices magazine [hardcopy and website]. A healthy teen girl magazine, without advertising. It's by teen girls for teen girls and is solid on health, diversity, politics, issues, and activism. (For preteen girls, try New Moon magazine, also noncommercial). New online feature is Guidance for Grown-ups, which supports active discussion around issues facing teens. Recent excellent article in Volume 15:2—"Teacher or Abuser? Dealing with Sexual Harassment in School." www.teenvoices.com.

Treays, R. 1996. *Understanding your brain.* London: Usborne Pub. Good book for kids with neurological impairment.

Wood, A. 1990. *Weird parents.* New York: Puffin Books. A boy is embarrassed by his parents' nonconformist behavior before realizing that their love is what is most exceptional about them.

Wyeth, S. D. 1998. *Something beautiful.* Prince Frederick, MD: Doubleday Books for Young Readers.

RESOURCES FOR PARENTS/CARETAKERS

Archer, C., and C. Gordon. 2006. *New families, old scripts: A guide to the language of trauma and attachment in adoptive families.* London: Jessica Kingsley Publishers.

ATTACh. 2008. *Therapeutic parenting manual.* Lake Villa, IL: Association for the Treatment and Training in the Attachment of Children.

———. 2009. *Professional practice manual.* Lake Villa, IL: Association for the Treatment and Training in the Attachment of Children.

Becker-Weidman, A., 2007. *Principles of attachment parenting.* Three DVD set.

Becker-Weidman, A., and D. Shell, eds. 2005; reprinted 2008. *Creating capacity for attachment: Dyadic developmental psychotherapy in the treatment of trauma-attachment disorders.* Oklahoma City: Wood 'N' Barnes Publishing & Distribution. A fair amount of theory and technique for DDP therapists, and some solid writing by and for parents. Several chapters by parents about their experiences and material for parents about parenting.

Berger, J. 1972. *Ways of seeing*. New York: Viking Press. Perhaps we all collect those tools which most help us make meaning of the patterns of our experiences. Empathic affect-focused therapy helped me understand how to help angry wounded kids. The writing of John Berger (perhaps England's most famous art historian) does the same for my understanding of how feelings interact with how society is organized. After a good day working with children's (and parents') big feelings, I find Berger's meanings about the individual in society, while not compulsively positive, are refreshing to my adult brain. An "aha!" experience comes with nearly every page, and I think, Why can't I write like that?

Bergman, I. 1994. *The magic lantern: An autobiography*. New York: Penguin Books. I may never get to thank this groundbreaking Swedish film director for his terrific autobiography, especially the quote used here.

Best, M. H. 1998. *Toddler adoption: The weaver's craft*. Indianapolis, IN: Perspectives Press. This is a great book for understanding kids who are toddlers, or functionally toddlers upon adoption.

Briggs, D. C. 1970. *Your child's self-esteem*. New York: Doubleday. Dorothy Briggs' early classic on giving children the emotionally secure base they need.

Brown, N. W. 2001. *Children of the self-absorbed: A grown-ups guide to getting over narcissistic parents*. Oakland, CA: New Harbinger Publications, Inc. Not the easiest read, and Brown is somewhat harsh. See Eleanor Payson's book below, which does a better job for adults who survived growing up under their parents for whom it was "all about me."

Clarke, J. I. 1999. *Time-in: When time-out doesn't work*. Seattle, WA: Parenting Press. When children are acting out and dysregulating, they usually need more of our organizing, strength, and wisdom—not more isolation. Consider a time-in policy.

Dacey, J., L. B. Fiore, and G. T. Ladd. 2002. *Your anxious child: How parents and teachers can relieve anxiety in children*. San Francisco, CA: Jossey-Bass. The book has a wide variety of activities to try with kids, so that even my teen who thinks stress management stuff is "boring" will likely find something that appeals to him.

Dozier, M., K. C. Stovall, K. E. Albus, and B. Bates. 2001. Attachment for infants in foster care: the role of caregiver state of mind. *Child Development* 70:1467–1477. For those wanting more on the technical side, Mary Dozier's research into the importance of a loving attitude toward babies is widely cited in the field.

Eldridge, S. 1999. *Twenty things adopted kids wish their adoptive parents knew*. New York: Dell Publishers. While the twenty ideas presented could be described on a one- or two-page handout, the concept is excellent.

Faber, A., and E. Mazlish. 2002. *How to talk so kids will listen and listen so kids will talk*. New York: HarperCollins. Written by two moms. I often recommend this old standby. It pays attention to feelings and includes examples of how to be mad in ways kids can hear. Nice bits on how to give empathy instead of trying to solve the problem for kids. (Look up pages under "empathy.") And they do their own cartoon illustrations! Very fine book.

Fahlberg, V. I. 1996. *A child's journey through placement*. Indianapolis, IN: Perspectives Press. For kids who have had a lot of placements, I think this is an excellent read. This book helps to get a feel for what the experience is like for the kids themselves. It's a book that I wish all CPS (Child Protective Services) caseworkers were made to read and reread.

Ginott, H. G., A. Ginott, and H. W. Goddard, eds. 1969. *Between parent and child: The bestselling classic that revolutionized parent-child communication.* New York: Three Rivers Press.

Herman, J. 1997. *Trauma and recovery.* New York: Basic Books. The best book I have found on this topic. Judith Herman, MD, gives full historical treatment to how PTSD (Post-Traumatic Stress Disorder) came to be recognized, including the political history of when we did recognize it (soldiers at various times) and when we didn't (rape and incest survivors). You can skip the clinical discussions. Herman does a good job taking us into the subject without re-traumatizing us.

Hughes, D. A. 2006. *Building the bonds of attachment: Awakening love in deeply troubled children.* 2nd ed. Lanham, MD: Jason Aronson. Consistently recommended by caretakers of struggling adoptees. Most parents find something personally enriching in this composite story of a child going through maltreatment, failed placements, and finally empathic attachment therapy and adoption. You can skip the initial maltreatment story if you prefer. This latest edition pays increased attention to the experiences and needs of the parents.

———. 2007. *Attachment-focused family therapy.* New York: Norton. This is the latest book by Dan Hughes, PhD, expanding the emotionally focused therapy directly to family relations.

Jernberg, A. M., and P. B. Booth. 1998. *Theraplay: Helping parents and children build better relationships through attachment-based play.* San Francisco: Jossey-Bass. Theraplay helps parents connect with isolating or rejecting children, using comfortable structured playfulness, acceptance, and empathy. In progressive doses it helps searching parents find and practice their healthy role as parents who both love and guide young children.

Keck, G., R. M. Kupecky, and L. G. Mansfield. 2002. *Parenting the hurt child: Helping adoptive families heal and grow.* Colorado Springs, CO: Pinon Press.

Koehler, P. 1990. *The day we met you.* New York: Bradbury Press. Talks about what the parents did to prepare for their child coming home. It's a book designed for parents to embellish and tell their child's story throughout the book.

Kranowicz, C. S. 1998. *The out of synch child: Recognizing and coping with sensory integration dysfunction.* New York: The Berkley Publishing Group.

———. 2003. *The out of synch child has fun: Activities for kids with sensory integration dysfunction.* New York: The Berkley Publishing Group.

Lacher, D. B., T. Nichols, and J. C. May. 2005. *Connecting with kids through stories: Using narratives to facilitate attachment in adopted children.* London: Jessica Kingsley Publishers. I heard Todd Nichols and Joanne May in Albuquerque in 2005, and I bought five copies. This book will put your thoughtful creativity to work for your child, making up four kinds of therapeutic stories, depending on what they need at the time.

Lakoff, G. 2004. *Don't think of an elephant: Know your values and frame the debate.* White River Junction, VT: Chelsea Green Publishing. The relevance of this little white book struck me when I first read it. A cognitive psychologist shows how to respond honestly and calmly to aggression, distortion, and regression in political arguments—very much like talking to angry teens. This book can provide parents of teens support and renewal at the cognitive level of thought and conversation.

Lite, L. 2005. *Indigo teen dreams: Guided meditation/relaxation techniques designed to decrease stress, anger, and anxiety while increasing self-esteem and self-awareness.* Audio CD. Medicine Hat, Alberta, Canada: LiteBooks.net.

McCreight, B. 2002. *Parenting your adopted older child: How to overcome the unique challenges and raise a happy and healthy child.* Oakland, CA: New Harbinger Publications.

Menzel, P. 1994. *Material world: A global family portrait.* San Francisco: Sierra Club Books. Depicts thirty families from as many countries, outside their homes with all of their belongings. Everywhere, humans live in cooperative family groups, some with a lot of stuff to make life softer, others with only each other's softness.

Miller, L. J. 2006. *Sensational kids: Hope and help for children with sensory processing disorder (SPD).* New York: Penguin Group. This is a book I read in just a few days. Easy to read and yet full of great information.

Payne, R. 2003. *A framework for understanding poverty.* Highlands, TX: aha! Process, Inc. Ruby Payne's book on understanding poverty is the best I've found to help us grasp the culture gap at work for some survivors. Her simple chart—comparing the values supported by life as wealthy, versus middle class, versus poor—is itself worth the small price of the book. Middle-class parents might not have expected a foster child's way of using language for survival, seeing people as property, or expecting entertainment in personal relationships.

  Payne introduces us to the differences in values around various issues. Food: in poverty we ask, Did you have enough? Middle class will ask, Did you like it? Wealth asks, Was it presented well? Social emphasis: in poverty we include people we like; middle class values people for self-sufficiency and self-governance; wealth does not necessarily value people, but emphasizes social exclusion. Get this book.

Payson, E. 2002. *The Wizard of Oz and other narcissists: Coping with the one-way relationship in work, love, and family.* Royal Oak, MI: Julian Day Publications. Clinical narcissism includes a number of possible features such as grandiosity, entitlement, envy, arrogance, lack of empathy for others, exploitation, and so on. People who struggle to reflect and grow may project their discomfort onto others. This book is for those who deal with them on a regular basis.

Pinkley, S. L. 2002. *Shades of black: A celebration of our children.* New York: Scholastic Inc.

Reynolds, J. 1996. *Mother and child: Visions of parenting from indigenous cultures.* Rochester, VT: Inner Traditions Intl Ltd.

Siegel, D. J. 2007. *The mindful brain: Reflection and attunement in the cultivation of wellbeing.* New York: W. W. Norton & Company. Dr. Dan Siegel's latest enlightening book on the brain. "We each have a brain" so let's learn about how it works in us and within our close relationships. This book fit well for me with Sunderland's text on parenting (below), in which brain research is applied directly to parenting advice.

Siegel, D. J., and M. Hartzel. 2003. *Parenting from the inside out: How a deeper self-understanding can help you raise children who thrive.* New York: J. P. Tarcher.

Sunderland, M. 2006. *The science of parenting: Practical guidance on sleep, crying, play, and building emotional well-being for life.* New York: Dorling Kindersley.

Tatum, B. D. 2003. *"Why are all the black kids sitting together in the cafeteria?" And other conversations about race.* New York: Basic Books. The articulate author is president of Spelman College. Get this book.

Walker, B., N. J. Goodwin, and R. C. Warren. 1992. Violence: A challenge to the public health community. *Journal National Medical Association* 84:490–496. An important part of the medical community recognizes that domestic violence, gun violence, and child abuse are extremely expensive public health problems.

Wesselmann, D. 1998. *The whole parent: How to become a terrific parent even if you didn't have one.* New York: Plenum Publishing Corp.

For Up Through Age Eleven

Wolf, A. 1996. *It's not fair, Jeremy Spencer's parents let him stay out all night! A guide to the tougher parts of parenting.* New York: Farrar, Straus & Giroux.

———. 2000. *The secret of parenting: How to be in charge of today's kids—from toddlers to preteens—without threats or punishment.* New York: Farrar, Straus & Giroux.

For Over Age Eleven

Wolf, A. 1991. *Get out of my life, but first could you drive me & Cheryl to the mall: A parent's guide to the new teenager, revised and updated.* New York: Farrar, Straus & Giroux.

For Parents Divorcing

Wolf, A. 1998. *Why did you have to get a divorce? And when can I get a hamster? A guide to parenting through a divorce.* New York: Farrar, Straus & Giroux.

For Parents of Siblings

Wolf, A. 2003. *Mom, Jason's breathing on me: The solution to sibling bickering.* New York: Ballantine Books.

14

End Notes

Arthur Becker-Weidman and Deborah Shell

By now you probably have a pretty good idea of various things you can to do promote a healthy attachment between you and your child. The importance of PLACE and the use of a variety of supportive modalities such as art therapy, Theraplay, narrative, and other approaches should be clearer to you. In addition, we hope that you now have a better understanding of the effects of chronic early maltreatment on your child's psychology, relationships, emotional development, and patterns of attachment. It probably seems clearer that so many of your child's "symptoms" are "driven" by a deep underlying fear. Early chronic maltreatment has deeply scarred your child and distorted the "lenses through which he filters" current experiences and interactions with you. Developmentally you can see that your child may be years younger than your child's chronological age. Treating your child based on developmental age is much more likely to result in a satisfying and healthy outcome.

One final point that we would like to directly address is that it should be very clear that coercive and intrusive approaches have no place in creating a healing PLACE. Interactions that are shaming or coercive are not helpful and can actually create more damage. This book, our recommendations, and Dyadic Developmental Psychotherapy do not endorse or condone coercive, shaming, or intrusive parenting methods. Coercion has no place in helping a child heal. As we have discussed, shame has no place in parenting a child with Complex Post-Traumatic Stress Disorder and attachment problems. Frequently that child experiences overwhelming shame so that shaming interventions only add to the child's sense of being unloved, unlovable, not valued, and as intrinsically bad. Our approach is consistent with the standards set by the American Academy of Child and Adolescent Psychiatry's "Practice Parameter for the Assessment and Treatment of Children and Adolescents with Reactive Attachment Disorder of Infancy and Early Childhood" (2005). Find the full article, "Practice Parameter for the Assessment of Children and Adolescent with Reactive Attachment Disorder of Infancy and Early Childhood" in the *Journal of the American Academy of Child and Adolescent Psychiatry* 44 (November 2005) (www.aacap.org/galleries/Practice Parameters/rad.pdf). Their first recommendation is clear on this point: "Interventions designed to enhance attachment that involve non-contingent physical restraint or coercion . . . are not endorsed." Recommendation five states, "The most important intervention for young children diagnosed with reactive attachment disorder and who lack an attachment to a discriminated caregiver is for the clinician to advocate for providing the child with an emotionally available attachment figure." We have discussed the vital importance of your being attuned and emotionally available to your child, despite his "attempts" to push you away, which are clearly driven by a deep and abiding fear of intimacy. This fear has a firm basis in the early chronic history of maltreatment. Recommendation six states, "Although the diagnosis of reactive attachment disorder is based on symptoms displayed by the child, assessing the caregiver's attitudes toward and perceptions about the child is important for treatment." We have discussed how mindfulness and use of self are important. As one parent said to one of us, "Mariah really knows how to push my buttons. She can sure get me going and get me cranked up. But, you know, I keep reminding myself that these are my buttons, and it is my job as her Dad to figure out how to disconnect 'em so that when she pushes them, nothing bad happens." We are not saying that this is your fault. We are saying that you are responsible for figuring out how to help your child and that often means looking at your own past and how you react to develop more effective and productive approaches to having a healing relationship with your child. Recommendation seven reinforces the previous point: "After ensuring that the child is in a safe and stable placement, effective attachment treatment must focus on creating positive interactions with caregivers."

The Report of the APSAC Task Force on Attachment Therapy, Reactive Attachment Disorder, and Attachment Problems (*Child Maltreatment*, 11 [1] 2006: 76–89) is another document that we support and with which this book is consistent and in accord.

The report recommends the following regarding treatment and interventions (pp. 86–87):

a. Treatment techniques or attachment parenting techniques involving physical coercion, psychologically or physically enforced holding, physical restraint, physical domination, provoked catharsis, ventilation of rage, age regression, humiliation, withholding or forcing food or water intake, prolonged social isolation, or assuming exaggerated levels of control and domination over a child are contraindicated because of risk of harm and absence of proven benefit and should not be used.

(1) This recommendation should not be interpreted as pertaining to common and widely accepted treatment or behavior management approaches used within reason, such as time-out, reward and punishment contingencies, occasional seclusion or physical restraint as necessary for physical safety, restriction of privileges, "grounding," offering physical comfort to a child, and so on.

b. Prognostications that certain children are destined to become psychopaths or predators should never be made based on early childhood behavior. These beliefs create an atmosphere conducive to overreaction and harsh or abusive treatment. Professionals should speak out against these and similar unfounded conceptualizations of children who are maltreated.

c. Intervention models that portray young children in negative ways, including describing certain groups of young children as pervasively manipulative, cunning, or deceitful, are not conducive to good treatment and may promote abusive practices. In general, child maltreatment professionals should be skeptical of treatments that describe children in pejorative terms or that advocate aggressive techniques for breaking down children's defenses.

d. Children's expressions of distress during therapy always should be taken seriously. Some valid psychological treatments may involve transitory and controlled emotional distress. However, deliberately seeking to provoke intense emotional distress or dismissing children's protests of distress is contraindicated and should not be done.

e. State-of-the-art, goal-directed, evidence-based approaches that fit the main presenting problem should be considered when selecting a first-line treatment. Where no evidence-based option exists or where evidence-based treatment options have been exhausted, alternative treatments with sound theory foundations and broad clinical acceptance are appropriate. Before attempting novel or highly unconventional treatments with untested benefits, the potential for psychological or physical harm should be carefully weighed.

f. First-line services for children described as having attachment problems should be founded on the core principles suggested by attachment theory, including caregiver and environmental stability, child safety, patience, sensitivity, consistency, and nurturance. Shorter term, goal-directed, focused, behavioral interventions targeted at increasing parent sensitivity should be considered as a first-line treatment.

g. Treatment should involve parents and caregivers, including biological parents if reunification is an option. Fathers, and mothers, should be included if possible. Parents of children described as having attachment problems may benefit from ongoing support and education. Parents should not be instructed to engage in psychologically or physically coercive techniques for therapeutic purposes, including those associated with any of the known child deaths.

Each of these recommendations is consistent with the approaches and suggestions we have offered you. Finally, we offer for your review the Association for the Treatment and Training's White Paper on Coercion (2006). This document, much more so that the previous two documents, provides clear and specific principles and guidance for parents.

WHITE PAPER ON COERCION IN TREATMENT

The purpose of this document is to set guidelines and standards for ethically and clinically appropriate treatment for children with attachment problems. This document is intended to provide guidance to parents and therapists so that they avoid the use of coercive techniques. ATTACh believes a central focus of treatment[1] for children with attachment problems is to create an environment in which the individual can safely work to integrate previously unmanageable information and emotions related to early traumatic experiences with caregivers. Those post-traumatic emotional reactions interfere with the development of healthy relationships and may have serious negative effects on a child's overall development.

All forms of attachment therapy have been construed by some as using coercive techniques. *Merriam-Webster's Dictionary* defines coercion as "the use of express or implied threats of violence or reprisal . . . or other intimidating behavior that puts a person in immediate fear of the consequences in order to compel that person to act against his or her will" (coercion, n.d.). ATTACh believes an approach that relies on a base of coercion (as so defined) is contraindicated in working to create a secure parent-child relationship characterized by safety, reciprocal love, trust, and perceived security.

However, we recognize that children who have had early experiences of trauma may be predisposed to misperceive threat in benign and even positive interactions. Consequently, their real experiences of trauma, coupled with often distorted perceptions of threat, call for a treatment approach

---

1. In this document, the term "treatment" refers to both psychotherapy and parenting.

that is sensitive to the critical need for safety, and provides real assistance with emotional regulation, making meaning of experiences, and enhanced social connections (Cook, Blaustein, Spinazzola, & van der Kolk, 2003). The problems of these children may interfere with their relationships, particularly with parents or other primary caregivers. The need for treatment and the challenges in providing it are very real.

It is important at the outset to clarify that a coercive treatment approach is separate and distinct from the occasional and judicious use of strategies such as logical and reasonable consequences, safety interventions, enforcement of limits and other legitimate interventions in the socialization of and provision of safety for children. Though these can be defined as "coercive," they are not typically accompanied by fear and are a legitimate part of a parenting toolbox for parents of all children. When used in the context of a loving parent child relationship, the occasional and judicious use of such techniques is a constructive intervention of parenting.

Harmful and threatening forms of coercion have previously been used in treatment with children. Some of these practices were done in the name of attachment therapy. Examples include wrapping children in blankets and not allowing them to leave; poking children during therapy and strongly encouraging (even demanding) them to express anger at previous abusers; adults lying on children; and therapists forcing a child to carry out explicit instructions for behavior (e.g., sitting in a specific manner) as dictated by the therapist or risk serious consequences. These practices, and similar ones, fall in an area that is clearly coercive. We believe that the use of this type of coercion is not appropriate in treatment for children.

In recent years, several organizations have issued statements regarding treatment for children with attachment disorders. ATTACh concurs with the American Psychiatric Association's 2002 Position Statement on Reactive Attachment Disorder that "there is a strong clinical consensus that coercive therapies are contraindicated in this disorder" (American Psychiatric Association, 2002). ATTACh also concurs with the American Academy of Child and Adolescent Psychiatry, "Practice Parameter for the Assessment and Treatment of Children and Adolescents with Reactive Attachment Disorder of Infancy and Early Childhood" (American Academy of Child and Adolescent Psychiatry, 2003). In addition, ATTACh supports recommendations in the 2006 Report of the APSAC Task Force on Attachment Therapy, Reactive Attachment Disorder, and Attachment Problems. (Chaffin et al., 2006) Specifically, we agree with following recommendation:

> techniques involving physical coercion, psychologically or physically enforced holding, physical restraint, physical domination, provoked catharsis, ventilation of rage, age regression, humiliation, withholding or forcing food or water intake, prolonged social isolation, or assuming exaggerated levels of control and domination over a child are contraindicated (Chaffin et al., 2006, p. 86)

Each of these statements condemns the use of coercion in treatment. However, none gives guidance about what distinguishes coercive interventions from acceptable authoritative practices. It is easy to distinguish between the extremes. However, a wide continuum exists between the endpoints. This is the area in which parents and therapists have struggled to find interventions that effectively address the population of children who have experienced early life maltreatment and their current challenging behaviors. ATTACh believes it is important to give usable guidance to those courageous enough to work with these children, even if giving such guidance is fraught with difficulties.

The therapeutic use of confrontation and directive therapeutic techniques is widely viewed as appropriate and beneficial when appropriately applied (Hammond, Hepworth, & Smith, 2002). The phrase "confrontation" is used in therapeutic literature as a technique to help the clients resolve maladaptive defenses. **ATTACh believes the proper use of therapeutic confrontation and other directive techniques may be beneficial but must be done in a manner that promotes attunement, sensitivity, and developmental appropriateness.** A primary purpose of this paper is to describe critical issues related to providing treatment to children with early life maltreatment or adverse childhood experiences and to give guidance about appropriate therapeutic confrontation versus inappropriate coercion when working with this population.

Background

ATTACh's historical roots contribute to the continued perception that the organization supports coercive interventions. ATTACh founders organized around therapeutic work with a group of children with histories of maltreatment and loss who had been found to be highly resistant to treatment. These practitioners primarily practiced a form of treatment that included catharsis, provocation of rage, and intense confrontation, among other overtly coercive techniques. Such treatment was originally called Rage Reduction Therapy (Zaslow & Menta, 1975). To the credit of these practitioners, they were among the few who sought to develop outpatient treatments for this underserved population (O'Connor & Zeanah, 2003). Current attachment therapy as supported by ATTACh has evolved significantly away from these early roots. The fundamental shift has been away from viewing these children as driven by a conscious need for control toward an understanding that their often controlling and aggressive behaviors are automatic, learned defensive responses to profoundly overwhelming experiences of fear and terror. **Due to ATTACh's earlier association with Rage Reduction Therapy, we believe it is important that we now unequivocally state our opposition to the use of coercive practices in therapy and parenting.**

Just as medicine has moved from highly intrusive interventions to less intrusive yet more effective ones, so has the field of attachment therapy evolved. Over time, findings in the fields of trauma, neuroscience and attachment discredited the more coercive approaches (Kelly, 2003). In recent years, the use of coercive techniques among ATTACh's membership has declined for two primary reasons. First, a number of practitioners who worked with the same population of children but employing other techniques joined ATTACh after its formation. These clinicians practiced therapy with a primary emphasis on sensitivity and attunement. Their techniques included narrative therapy, some types of play therapies, corrective emotional experiences, and other methodologies focused on increased emotional regulation and trauma processing. Second, many of the practitioners who employed the more coercive techniques began to move away from these approaches in response to research findings in many fields including trauma, attachment, and neuroscience. Movement away from the use of coercive techniques was also partially in response to adverse events involving such techniques, including the tragedy of one child's death.

As the organization's leadership and membership moved away from coercive therapies, ATTACh adopted its first position paper, *ATTACh Position Statement on Coercive Therapy*, in 2003 (Association for Treatment and Training in the Attachment of Children, 2003). This position paper was intended to be a strong statement in opposition to the use of coercion in treatment. ATTACh hoped that this statement would serve a two-fold purpose of (1) signaling to those outside ATTACh that the organization was separating from its historical roots and (2) signaling to those who still practiced coercive therapy and parenting that they would no longer have the support of the organization in such practices. ATTACh updated this statement in 2006 to reflect continued advances in neurology, trauma treatment, and related fields (Association for Treatment and Training in the Attachment of Children, 2006).

ATTACh remains committed to educating the professional and general public about state-of-the-art treatment in work with children who have experienced attachment disruptions and trauma. Moreover, we believe the field of child therapy needs an organization focused on serving this important population. These children present with emotional, behavioral, and developmental difficulties that can be very challenging to any who would attempt to help them. Too often in the past they were simply deemed untreatable or in need of institutional care. Today we know that there is reason for hope given promising approaches that help resolve traumatic reactions, promote greater security in attachment, and facilitate more appropriate development. However, this hope is tempered with very real challenges.

These children do not seek nor easily accept treatment. Indeed, their fundamental difficulties in establishing a trusting, reciprocal relationship often cause them to actively push away offers of assistance. For some, a child's failure to consent to treatment implies that the child is being coerced into treatment. Many children with histories of maltreatment who are brought by parents or professionals for treatment exhibit oppositional behavior and have high control needs (van der Kolk, 2005). If given complete choice, a large number would refuse to participate in therapy. Some would argue that no child should be made to participate in therapy if he or she does not want to do so. We disagree. Experienced, well-trained therapists and attuned, sensitive parents can better make the decision regarding a child's need for therapy than can the child. Even if the child does agree to participate, he or she may wish not to face difficult issues. Children may not be able to see the link between early maltreatment experiences and current life problems (Perry, 1995). However, their caregivers and/or professionals do see these links and see the need for appropriate treatment when their functioning and development have been adversely affected by trauma or loss. In the most extreme cases, the severity of these children's emotional and behavioral difficulties compromises their functioning and development across domains. They are often at risk of more restrictive placements (e.g., hospitalization, residential treatment, placement disruption) or increased chemical restraint through medication. The severity of this risk may indicate a more directive approach, but one that is still grounded in an understanding of the need for sensitivity and regulation.

Decision Making Process: Is It Coercive?

Where does appropriate therapeutic confrontation end and coercion begin? In beginning to answer this question, we believe that lists of do's and don'ts, while useful, are inadequate. Too many unique situations are encountered in a therapeutic setting, and no list can ever be complete. Rather, we think it useful to provide therapists and caretakers with principles and guidelines to employ.

> A child with a serious infection may need an injection to promote healing. Young children react to shots with predictable resistance and/or emotional distress. Nonetheless, parents persist due to the overriding concern for the child's long-term health. Nurturing parents use this as an opportunity to provide comfort and to make meaning of the experience.

ATTACh believes that the field of child therapy in general, and practitioners of attachment therapy specifically, would benefit from a greater understanding of what interventions and techniques constitute coercion and how this differs from the use of appropriate therapeutic confrontation. It is one thing to oppose the use of coercion in treatment; it is quite another to more specifically articulate a definition of what constitutes coercion in treatment.

In many situations (such as the examples of coercion cited previously in this document), the line between appropriate therapeutic confrontation and coercion is clear. One can also draw clear guidance from legal standards that define child abuse and neglect or ethical standards that seek to ensure the safety of the client.

Where such "bright line distinctions" end, one enters the gray area of potential harm where there are no clear guides for actions. In these cases, a framework for ethical decision making should be the guide. Without clear standards of appropriate behavior or intervention, one must look to how research or other accepted standards can be applied to the situation. There are three important guidelines to consider:

1. Is the approach principled; is it grounded in ethical values?
2. Is the approach reasoned; is it based on valid rationales?
3. Is the approach generalizable; can it be applied to other situations (instead of being immediately expedient for this individual circumstance)?

These principles need to guide the consideration of what is and is not coercion in any situation that falls into a gray area. Ethical decision making in gray areas is an ongoing process of thoughtful consideration, development of a plan, and continuing review and modification of the plan as needed.

For example, some have suggested that touch has no place in therapy, but we believe that affectionate, voluntary touch can offer support, encouragement, and safety for a child. To determine the appropriate parameters for the use of touch we would consider whether:

1. It is grounded in ethical values and carried out in a way that is respectful of the child's development and history.
2. It is grounded in valid rationales in that there is significant research indicating the value of nurturing touch in physiological regulation and neurological development (Hofer, 1984; Field, Healy, & Goldstein, 1990; Schore, 2001).
3. It is a practice widely used by adults with children.

In contrast, we do not feel it is appropriate for parents or therapists to hold a child forcibly, while insisting on emotional engagement on the adult's terms. For example, forcibly holding the child and demanding eye contact or emotional sharing is premised on the adult's expectations and is not responsive to the child's state (e.g., shame, terror, etc.). This technique is not supported as:

1. It is a violation of the child's dignity and autonomy.
2. It is not supported by current research as it intentionally causes dysregulation and may re-traumatize the child.
3. It is not a practice generally used with children.

In such complex situations it is helpful to consider the interaction of other principles that may guide decision making. These would include the consideration of the interplay among the parent's or therapist's behavior and intentions; the child's perceptions and experience; power differentials in the relationship; and the nature and quality of the relationship between the persons involved. This approach leads to a focus on the *effects* of the parent's or therapist's actions on the child.

Critical Concepts

Decision making in complex treatment situations with the population of children damaged by early-life maltreatment involves the consideration of a number of critical concepts and how the concepts apply to specific individuals and situations. Practitioners and parents would do well to have a working knowledge of these critical concepts. These concepts are described in this section.

Regulation and Dysregulation

One such critically important concept in this process is regulation versus dysregulation of emotions, impulses, and physical states. Security provides children with opportunities to develop the capacity for regulation. Lack of sustained regulation puts the child at risk of inadequate development of the capacity to regulate physical and emotional states (Cook, Blaustein, Spinazzola, & van der Kolk, 2003). Research has shown that children learn best during times they are regulated (e.g., when the child is in a calm, receptive state) (Schore, 2001). It is important to support and promote children's regulation during interventions. If a child becomes dysregulated, attempts should be made to restore regulation as soon as possible (e.g., a parent might actively assist the child in regaining a calm, receptive state by soothing the child and making sense of the experience).

Dysregulation occurs when the developing child's capacities for managing physiological, emotional, behavioral, and/or interpersonal functioning are overwhelmed by distress to the extent that the child is unable to regain equilibrium independently. Dysregulation should never be a goal of an intervention; indeed, it may undermine other progress by unintentionally reinforcing the child's distorted beliefs that others are hurtful, untrustworthy, and neglectful. Sometimes children with attachment disorders who become dysregulated respond with angry or aggressive behaviors that require safety interventions that are perceived as more forceful than empathic. In situations where safety is threatened and less intrusive interventions have been tried and failed, it may become necessary to use restraint including physical holding to maintain safety. In these special situations, the use of force should be terminated as soon as possible, and efforts made to repair the break in relationship that results from its use. Restraint in these situations is not seen as part of treatment but solely as a necessary intervention to maintain safety. Given that children with histories of trauma may misperceive the actions of others as intentionally hurtful, it is critically important that the adults help the child make meaning of such experiences (e.g., "We are keeping you safe when you feel out of control" to counter the child's likely perception of "They will hurt me and/or I am bad").

When dysregulation does occur during treatment, interventions must be incorporated that will assist the child in regaining regulation and managing the distress. This concept is also called "interactive repair" (Tronick & Gianino, 1986). When the child responds with discomfort and distress, the therapist or parent uses empathy and emotional support to help regulate the child's affect so that the child does not move into dysregulation. While experiencing discomfort and distress, the child maintains regulation of affect, cognition, and behavior. However, when a child shows terror, rage, or dissociative features, indicating movement into dysregulation, the child requires help to regain a calm receptive state. So, for example, in a therapeutic situation a child may willingly discuss an event that is upsetting and increases the child's discomfort and distress. However, if the child then indicates a desire to stop, yet this signal is ignored by the therapist or parent, so that the child is forced to continue, this is coercive. This does not mean that the therapist and/or parent join with the child in avoidance of this painful material. Instead it means that they stay attuned to the child's needs and work to "dose" the exposure to this material in a way that supports the child's ability to process and integrate the information. This gradual consolidation of the material within the context of a helpful, sensitive relationship promotes a greater sense of security in the child which in turn facilitates greater security in attachment. This is very different from earlier approaches in which continued confrontation and exposure to painful material was maintained or increased until the child was exhausted or had a "break through." Such an approach is coercive and indeed countertherapeutic due to the risk of re-traumatizing the child. For children with histories of attachment-related traumas this may unintentionally reinforce negative beliefs about others as harmful, coercive, and controlling, which may impede, if not prevent, the formation of truly secure attachment. In addition, it is coercive treatment if a child becomes dysregulated, even through an unintended triggered reaction, and the therapist or parent does not act to attempt to decrease the child's dysregulation and repair the relationship break. Power struggles and control battles may only serve to increase the dysregulation and are not recommended unless there is a clear and imminent need to establish safety.

Helping the client to explore traumatic memories or conditioned emotional reactions in order to promote integration is an appropriate goal of treatment. It is the process of exploration and how it must be handled that is the focus of this paper. Some degree of dysregulation may occur along with the processing.

Research on maltreated children has shown that a significant percentage experience chronic dysregulation (Teicher, 2002). Extreme cases may result in chronic defensive manifestations (e.g., hypervigilance, compulsive self-reliance, dissociation). These children may be highly reactive and very difficult to assist in re-regulation. Their defensive reactions are rooted in anxiety and profound fear from their traumatic experiences. It is important to recognize that even gentle and sensitive interventions may be perceived by these children in a threatening way, and may push them into a dysregulated state. The therapist or parent may still provide such interventions even knowing that the child may be triggered into a dysregulated state, but must take care to appropriately "dose" the intervention so that the child is not overwhelmed and is still able to perceive the adult as actively working to assist the child in handling any difficult emotions that arise. The intention is to provide the corrective emotional experiences of attunement that help the child resolve these maladaptive reactions with the assistance of an empathically connected adult.

Therapeutic Window

The concept of a "therapeutic window" is related to the concept of dysregulation and is vital to understanding effective treatment for victims of childhood maltreatment (Briere, 2002). A therapeutic window is the psychological space in which a client is able to learn and change because it is neither overwhelming to the individual's defenses nor does it allow the client to move to the relatively easy (and often preferred) avoidance of the traumatic material. The challenge is to activate conditioned emotional reactions (i.e., triggers) to access avoided emotional content, but to do so ONLY in a way that does not overwhelm the individual's coping resources. If such

In *The Developing Mind,* Dan Siegel (1999) describes dysregulation. "Each of us has a 'window of tolerance' in which various intensities of emotional arousal can be processed without disrupting the functioning of the system. . . . One's thinking or behavior can become disrupted as arousal moves beyond the boundaries of the window of tolerance. . . . The width of the window of tolerance within a given individual may vary, depending upon the state of mind at a given time, the particular emotional valence, and the social context in which the emotion is being generated. For example, we may be more able to tolerate stressful situations when surrounded by loved ones with whom we feel secure and understood. Within the boundaries of the window, the mind continues to function well. Outside these boundaries, function becomes impaired . . . under these conditions, the 'higher' cognitive functions of abstract thinking and self-reflection are shut down. . . . The mind has entered a suboptimal organizational flow that may reinforce its own maladaptive pattern. This is now a state of emotion dysregulation" (pp. 253–55).

coping resources are overwhelmed, then the individual may be flooded by intrusive stimuli and re-traumatized.[2]

Informed Consent

Another issue is the child's informed consent. Psychotherapy with children involves special considerations. Children generally do not present themselves for therapy; their parent, or caretaker, does. Children cannot fully comprehend and assent to treatment in the way an adult can. Children's reactions range from cooperation to acquiescence to resistance.

---

2. Briere's Self-Trauma Model suggests that early and severe child maltreatment is associated with significant deficits in what he calls self-capacities (most importantly, affect regulation). The deficits in affect regulation place the individual at risk of becoming overwhelmed by the emotional distress associated with reminders/triggers of earlier trauma. Due to limited affect regulation skills, the traumatized individual resorts in greater and greater degrees to avoidance strategies as a form of self-protection against such overwhelming experiences. Therapy that fails to provide adequate safety may result in an unintended reinforcement of avoidant strategies and maneuvers by the client. For therapy to be effective, it must take place in what Briere calls the "therapeutic window." This is the psychological location between overwhelming exposure on one hand and excessive avoidance on the other. If the therapist pushes the client to move outside that window the result is that the client may use heightened strategies of avoidance to manage the overwhelming affect. This may be seen as "resistance" by the therapist, but may more accurately reflect limited, but appropriate protective responses by the client. Effective trauma therapy therefore seeks to provide sufficient safety and containment, recognizing the likely deficits in the client's affect regulation capacity. The therapist seeks to carefully measure therapeutic exposure so that such activation does not exceed the internal coping resources of the client. This allows the client to begin to explore difficult content without the risk of being re-traumatized.

One important instance that highlights issues regarding coercion is when the child's reactions move toward resistance. A potential danger occurs when parents and/or therapists perceive the child's severely disruptive behaviors as requiring an escalating response to confront and control the behavior without a simultaneous focus on the distorted perceptions and beliefs that may be driving these behaviors. One technique would be to avoid control battles in which the child is given only one option of responding. Choices that are within the adult's accepted limits of safety and appropriateness may help the child feel less controlled and therefore less threatened. Assuredly, many children who come for therapy have high control needs. However, **ATTACh believes that addressing the internal beliefs that drive these needs is the proper stance for an attachment-focused therapist. Engaging in power struggles may be contraindicated.**

The autonomy of the child is an important consideration, but again one that must be considered within the overall context of the child's development and functioning. In the course of healthy development, autonomy is granted as a result of proven competence. For example the 12 year old with years of proven responsibility may be allowed to go to the mall with friends where a 16 year old with an attachment disorder and years of dangerous behaviors and poor choices may not be allowed to go to the mall except with an adult chaperone. Similarly, the parent of a child with only mild social anxiety may deem that the child's negative feelings toward therapy might outweigh any skill training to be learned and decide not to push the child. Yet a parent of a child with a much more disabling attachment disorder might well perceive that any negative feelings engendered in the short run are well worth the long-term benefits of improved family functioning and supported developmental functioning. These negative feelings may increase the child's dysregulation. However, the parent and therapist realize this negative reaction must still be handled sensitively and with constructive assistance to help move the child toward greater regulation within the context of the therapy. This is done by helping the child make meaning of the situation so as to begin to perceive the positive intentions of the adult while receiving active assistance to manage and cope with the feelings engendered. These efforts help the child stay within the "therapeutic window" and maximize the chance for successful resolution of the posttraumatic responses. Similarly, there are times during normal discipline when parents will knowingly increase dysregulation by normal disciplinary practices such as saying no or enforcing limits (for example, enforcing a reasonable bedtime). At these times, children need to be assisted to regain regulation without the parent giving up on the reasonable disciplinary point.

Shame

The role of shame is also important to take into consideration in this context. Children who have been abused or neglected or have had other adverse childhood experiences have experienced pervasive shame without interactive repair as a normal state of being. They bring this shame into new relationships and tend not to trust when a parent or therapist attempts to provide interactive repair. As a result, parents and therapists have a particular obligation to avoid any intervention that might increase the child's shame. Moreover, if a child is seen as experiencing shame as the result of an adult's behavior, the adult should immediately reach out to the child in interactive repair. Similarly, helping the child understand that the adults do not see the child as "bad" even when they discuss the child's inappropriate behaviors is a primary goal of treatment. Without it the child will not be able to learn to trust and work cooperatively.

Developmental Level of Functioning

Another critical issue to consider is the child's developmental functioning. Trauma tends to distort emotional and social development and the level of functioning may also fluctuate dramatically from one time to another depending on the degree to which traumatic triggers are affecting the child (van der Kolk, 2005). One generally accepted psychometric instrument for assessing the level of developmental functioning is the Vineland Scales of Adaptive Behavior II (Sparrow, Balla, & Cicchetti, 1984). Proper assessment of social and emotional functioning can help guide selection of developmentally appropriate interventions. Activities that appear regressive given the child's chronological age may be considered by some to be coercive; however, we believe that when an intervention is developmentally appropriate and provided in a sensitive and attuned way it is not coercive.

For example, a twelve-year-old child whose social and emotional functioning is at the four- or five-year-old level may benefit from regressive

Giving a child a choice to play "momma-bird/baby-bird" and feeding the child by hand may be a delightful and relationship-enhancing experience for parent and child.

Telling a thirteen-year-old that she cannot go to the mall unsupervised or with peers because of her socially indiscriminate behavior is not coercive because the child lacks the ability to do what age peers do. Indeed she would be at risk in that situation.

activities if they are conducted in a voluntary and well-attuned manner. Such activities are not inappropriately regressive but are *developmentally* appropriate and provide an emotional experience of attunement the child missed in early development.

Continuing this example, if the parent and child are involved in a nurturing activity and the parent is comfortable with offering a sippy cup or bottle and the child willingly accepts it and does not become dysregulated it is not coercive. If the activity comforts the child, then the activity would not be coercive. On the other hand, if the child has a tantrum like a two-year-old, and the parent or therapist forces the child to drink from the sippy cup because he is "acting like a two-year-old" this would be coercive because it would intentionally increase the child's shame, leading to dysregulation.

It is important that the parent and therapist are acutely sensitive to the child's experience of such an activity. The power differential in the therapist (or parent)-child relationship makes it critical that the adults ensure that such an activity is truly voluntary on the part of the child. Due to the power differential the child may comply with such a request, and this might be interpreted as voluntary. Such compliance may be internally dysregulating to the child, and the intervention would be counter-therapeutic. It may be difficult for the child to freely disagree to engage in the activity. Therefore the therapist and parent must pay careful ongoing attention to the child's cues both verbal and nonverbal.

Meaning of Behavior

A final consideration in determining whether an intervention is coercive is to focus on the deeper rather than the surface meaning of behavior. In considering this issue, it is important to consider **intention, effect, and process**; and to focus on the effects of the behavior on the client. If one must force the child to engage in the activity despite the child's protests, then the action is coercive.

Is asking a child to sit and think for a few minutes coercive and abusive or therapeutic? It is not the action that determines whether this request is coercive or supportive, but it is the **intention, effect, and process**. How the child is asked to sit quietly for a few minutes to contemplate some interaction, exchange, or choice is one factor. Is the action implemented to punish or dominate and is the action intended to enforce compliance for the sake of compliance? These would be factors that make the action coercive and not therapeutic. If the action is implemented to provide the child with a brief time-in or time-out to gather thoughts and the child is capable of self-regulating, then this action is therapeutic. Demanding rigid compliance and turning the interaction into a power struggle which must be "won" by the parent or therapist by having the child sit exactly as instructed turns a potentially therapeutic activity into a coercive power battle for compliance by domination. It is not appropriate to demand that a child sit "your way" as long as the child is sitting quietly. Similarly, forcing engagement on the adult's terms is counter-therapeutic. Of course, at times appropriate limits need to be set and enforced in the course of normal parenting (e.g., brushing teeth, going to bed, table manners) or in any situation where safety concerns exist.

For any activity to be therapeutic it must be implemented in a developmentally appropriate manner, based on the child's level of developmental functioning (Perry et al., 1995). For example, while it may be appropriate to ask a twelve-year-old child to sit and take a break in order to regulate behavior, it would not be appropriate to expect a child who is developmentally functioning as a five-year-old to sit quietly for twenty minutes.

Summary

In summary, ATTACh recognizes that children with attachment disorders present with very challenging behaviors that are defensive reactions to profound fear and shame. It is the position of ATTACh that there is never a basis for the use of the described coercive interventions in parenting or psychotherapy. Instead these children need corrective experiences of attunement, security, and regulation to heal their posttraumatic reactions. ATTACh believes that addressing the internal beliefs that drive these behaviors is the proper stance for attachment-focused treatment. Engaging in power struggles is, in most situations, contraindicated. The concept of a therapeutic window is vital to understanding effective therapy for victims of childhood maltreatment. The challenge is to activate conditioned emotional reactions (triggers) to access avoided emotional content, but to do so ONLY in a way that does not overwhelm the individual's coping resources and promotes a sense that the adult is an active source of support and assistance. In addition, all interventions should take into account the child's social and emotional level of functioning so that the approach is congruent with the child's developmental needs and provides corrective emotional experiences for reparation of the early experiences of maltreatment, insecurity, mistrust, and fear.

ATTACh also recognizes that ongoing research in the fields of trauma, attachment, and neuroscience will and should continue to inform the practices of attachment-focused therapy. Best practice should always be dictated by state-of-the-art knowledge. Given the many challenges of attachment therapy and the relative newness of the field, therapists who practice attachment therapy have a special duty to stay current with developments that affect the evolution of this field.

Therefore . . .

As a matter of policy and practice, ATTACh does not support and indeed actively discourages the use of coercion in treatment. ATTACh does not condone its members, registered clinicians, registered agencies, or presenters using coercive therapies or parenting techniques.

ACCEPTED BY ATTACh BOARD OF DIRECTORS: APRIL 21, 2007

REFERENCES

American Academy of Child and Adolescent Psychiatry. (2003). Policy statement: Coercive interventions for reactive attachment disorder. Washington, DC: Author.

American Psychiatric Association. (2002). Reactive attachment disorder: Position statement. Washington, DC: Author.

Association for Treatment and Training in the Attachment of Children. (2003). ATTACh position statement on coercive therapy. Downloaded April 19, 2007, from http://www.attach.org/position.htm.

Association for Treatment and Training in the Attachment of Children. (2006). ATTACh policy statement regarding coercive treatment. Downloaded April 19, 2007, from http://www.attach.org/position.htm.

Briere, J. (2002). Treating adult survivors of severe childhood abuse and neglect: Further development of an integrated model. In J. E. B Myers, L. Berliner, J. Briere, T. Reid, and C. Jenny (Eds.). *The APSAC handbook of child maltreatment* (2nd ed.). Newbury Park, CA: Sage.

Chaffin, M., Hanson, R., Saunders, B. E., Nichols, T., Barnett, D., Zeanah, C., et al. (2006). Report of the APSAC Task Force on Attachment Therapy, Reactive Attachment Disorder, and Attachment Problems. *Child Maltreatment*, 11, 76–89.

Cook, A., Blaustein, M., Spinazzola, J., & van der Kolk, B. (Eds.). (2003). *Complex trauma in children and adolescents: White paper from the National Child Traumatic Stress Network Complex Trauma Task Force.* National Child Traumatic Stress Network: Los Angeles.

Field, T., Healy, B. T., & Goldstein, S. (1990). Behavior-state matching and synchrony in mother-infant interactions in non-depressed dyads. *Developmental Psychology*, 26, 7–14.

Hammond, D. C., Hepworth, D. H., & Smith, V. G. (2002). *Improving therapeutic communication: A guide for developing effective techniques.* San Francisco: Jossey-Bass.

Hofer, M. A. (1984). Relationships as regulators: a psychobiologic perspective on bereavement. *Psychosomatic Medicine, 46(3)*, 183–197.

Kelly, V. (2003). Theoretical rationale for the treatment of disorders of attachment. Downloaded April 19, 2007, from http://www.attach.org/theorational.htm.

Marvin, R., Cooper, G., Hoffman, K., & Powell, B. (2002). The Circle of Security Project: Attachment-based interventions with caregiver-pre-school child dyads. *Attachment and Human Behavior, 4*, 107–124.

O'Connor, T. G., & Zeanah, C. H. (2003). Attachment disorders: Assessment strategies and treatment approaches. *Attachment & Human Development, 5,* 223–244.

Perry, B. D., et al. (1995). Childhood trauma, the neurobiology of adaptation, and use-dependent development of the brain: How states become traits. *Infant Journal of Mental Health, 16(4),* 271–291.

Schore, A. (2001). The effects of secure attachment relationship on right brain development, affect regulation, and infant mental health. *Infant Journal of Mental Health, 22,* 7–66.

Siegel, D. (1999). *The developing mind: Toward a Neurobiology of Interpersonal experience.* New York: Guilford.

Sparrow, S. S., Balla, D. A., & Cicchetti, D. V. (1984). *Vineland adaptive behavior scales.* Circle Pines, MN: American Guidance Service, Inc.

Teicher, M. H. (2002). Scars that won't heal: The neurobiology of child maltreatment. *Scientific American, 286(3),* 68–75.

Tronick, E. Z., Gianino, A. (1986). Interaction and repair: Challenge to the coping infant. *Zero to Three Bulletin of the National Child and Infant Program, 5,* 1–6. Washington, DC: Zero to Three.

van der Kolk, B. A. (2005). Developmental trauma disorder. *Psychiatric Annals,* 401–408.

Zaslow, R. W., & Menta, M. (1975). *The psychology of the Z process: Attachment and activity.* San Jose, CA: San Jose State University Press.

References

Abidin, A. *Parenting Stress Index*. 3rd ed. Professional Manual. Lutz, FL: Psychological Assessment Resources, 1995.

Ackenbach, T. M. *Manual for the Child Behavior Checklist 4–18 and 1991 Profile*. Burlington, VT: University of Vermont Department of Psychiatry, 1991.

Ainsworth, M., M. Blehar, E. Waters, and S. Wall. *Patterns of Attachment*. Hillsdale, NJ: Lawrence Erlbaum, 1978.

Alborough, J. *Hug*. Sommerville, MA: Candlewick Press, 2000.

Alexander, R., C. Levitt, and W. Smith. "Abusive Head Trauma." In *Child Abuse: Medical Diagnosis and Management*, 2nd ed., edited by R. M. Reece and S. Ludwig, 47–80. Philadelphia: Lippincott, Williams & Wilkins, 2001.

Allan, J. *Traumatic Relationships and Serious Mental Disorders*. New York: Wiley, 2001.

American Academy of Clinical Neuropsychology. *American Academy of Clinical Neuropsychology (AACN) Practice Guidelines for Neuropsychological Assessment and Consultation*. 2006.

American Academy of Pediatrics. *Shaken Baby Syndrome: Rotational Cranial Injuries*. 2001. A technical report.

American Psychiatric Association. *Diagnostic and Statistical Manual of Mental Disorders*. 4th ed. Washington, DC: American Psychiatric Association, 1994.

American Psychological Association, Division 40. "Definition of a Clinical Neuropsychologist." *The Clinical Neuropsychologist* 3, no. 22 (1989).

Ames, E. W. "Spitz Revisited: A Trip to Romanian Orphanages." *Canadian Psychological Association Developmental Psychology Newsletter* 9, no. 2 (1990): 8–11.

———. *The Development of Romanian Orphanage Children Adopted to Canada*. Ottawa: National Welfare Grants, 1997.

Andrews, B., C. R. Varewin, S. Rose, and M. Kirk. "Predicting PTSD Symptoms in Victims of Violent Crime." *Journal of Abnormal Psychology* 109 (2000): 69–73.

Anderson, F. E. *Art for All the Children: Approaches to Art Therapy for Children with Disabilities*. Springfield, IL: Charles C. Thomas, 1992.

Arrington, D., and P. Yorgin. "Art Therapy as a Cross-Cultural Means to Assess Psychological Health in Homeless and Orphaned Children in Kiev." *Art Therapy: Journal of the American Art Therapy Association* 18, no. 2 (2001): 80–88.

Astley, S. J. "Comparison of the 4-Digit Diagnostic Code and the Hoyme Diagnostic Guidelines for Fetal Alcohol Spectrum Disorders." *Pediatrics* 118 (2006): 1532–45.

ATTACh. "White Paper on Coercion in Treatment." Website of the Association for Treatment and Training in the Attachment of Children (ATTACh). www.attach .org. 2006.

———. *Therapeutic Parenting: A Handbook for Parents of Children Who Have Disorders of Attachment*. ATTACh, 2008. www.attach.org.

———. *Attachment-Focused Therapy: A Professional Practice Guide*. ATTACh, 2009. www .attach.org.

Ayers, A. J. *Sensory Integration and the Child*. Los Angeles: Western Psychological Services, 1979.

———. *Sensory Integration and Praxis Test Manual*. Los Angeles: Western Psychological Services, 1989, 1991.

Bailey, B. A. *I Love You Rituals*. New York: Quill, 2000.

Bannister, A. *Creative Therapies with Traumatized Children*. London and Philadelphia: Jessica Kingsley Publishers, 2003.

Baron, I. S. *Neuropsychological Evaluation of the Child*. New York: Oxford, 2004.

Betts, D., ed. *Creative Arts Therapies Approaches in Adoption and Foster Care: Contemporary Strategies for Working With Individuals and Families*. Springfield, IL: Charles C. Thomas, 2003.

Becker-Weidman, A. "Treatment for Children with Trauma-Attachment Disorders: Dyadic Developmental Psychotherapy." *Child and Adolescent Social Work Journal* 23, no. 2 (2006a): 147–71.

———. "Dyadic Developmental Psychotherapy: A Multi-Year Follow-Up." In *New Developments in Child Abuse Research*, edited by S. M. Sturt, 43–60. New York: Nova Science Publishers, 2006b.

———. *Principles of Attachment Parenting*. 3-DVD set. Williamsville, NY: Center for Family Development, 2006c.

———. *Assessing Children with Complex Trauma and Disorders of Attachment*. 2-DVD set. Williamsville, NY: Center for Family Development, 2007.

———. "Sensory-Integration Screener." Center for Family Development. http://www .center4familydevelop.com/sensorychecklist.htm (accessed August 24, 2009). 2008.

———. "Effects of Early Maltreatment on Development: A Descriptive Study Using the Vineland." *Child Welfare* 88, no. 2 (2009): 137–61.

Becker-Weidman, A., and D. Hughes. "Dyadic Developmental Psychotherapy: An Evidence-Based Treatment for Children with Complex Trauma and Disorders of Attachment." *Child & Family Social Work* 13 (2008): 329–37.

Becker-Weidman, A., and Deborah Shell. *Creating Capacity for Attachment*. Oklahoma City: Wood 'N' Barnes, 2005. Second printing in 2009.

Bergman, I. *The Magic Lantern*. Chicago: University of Chicago Press, 2007.

Bernstein, J. H. "Developmental Neuropsychological Assessment." In *Pediatric Neuropsychology: Research, Theory and Practice*, edited by K. O. Yeates, M. D. Ris, and H. G. Taylor, 405–38. New York: Guilford Press, 2000.

Bowlby, J. *Attachment, Separation, and Loss*. New York: Basic Books, 1980.

———. *A Secure Base*. New York: Basic Books, 1988.

Bretherton, I., D. Ridgeway, and J. Cassidy. "Assessing Internal Working Models of the Attachment Relationship: An Attachment Story Completion Task for 3-Year-Olds." In *Attachment in the Preschool Years: Theory, Research, and Intervention*, edited by M. Greenberg, D. Cicchetti, and E. Cummings. Chicago: University of Chicago Press, 1990.

Briere, J. "Treating Adult Survivors of Severe Childhood Abuse and Neglect: Further Development of an Integrative Model." In *The APSAC Handbook on Child Maltreatment*, 2nd ed., edited by J. E. B. Meyers, L. Berliner, J. Briere, C. T. Hendrix, T. Reid, and C. Jenny. Newbury Park, CA: Sage Publications, 2002.

Bruce, D. A., and R. A. Zimmerman. "Shaken Impact Syndrome." *Pediatric Annals* 18 (1989): 482–94.

Buck, J., and W. Warren. *House-Tree-Person Projective Drawing Technique: Manual and Interpretive Guide*. Los Angeles: Western Psychological Services, 1992.

Carlson, V., D. Cicchetti, D. Barnett, and K. Braunwald. "Finding Order in Disorganization: Lessons from Research on Maltreated Infants' Attachments to their Caregivers." In *Child Maltreatment: Theory and Research on the Causes and Consequences of Child Abuse and Neglect*, edited by D. Cicchetti and V. Carlson, 135–57. New York: Cambridge University Press, 1995.

Casler, L. "The Effects of Extra Tactile Stimulation on a Group of Institutionalized Infants." *Genetic Psychology Monographs*, 1965.

Chapman, L., D. Morabito, C. Ladakakos, H. Schreier, and M. Knudson. "The Effectiveness of Art Therapy Interventions in Reducing Post Traumatic Stress Disorder (PTSD) Symptoms in Pediatric Trauma Patients." *Journal of the American Art Therapy Association* 18, no. 2 (2001): 100–104.

Chisholm, K. "A Three-Year Follow-Up of Attachment and Indiscriminate Friendliness in Children Adopted from Romanian Orphanages." *Child Development* 69, no. 4 (1998): 1090–1104.

Cicchetti, D., E. M. Cummings, M. T. Greenberg, and R. S. Marvin. "An Organizational Perspective on Attachment Beyond Infancy." In *Attachment in the Preschool Years*, edited by M. Greenberg, D. Cicchetti, and M. Cummings, 3–50. Chicago: University of Chicago Press, 1990.

Cook, A., M. Blaustein, J. Spinazzola, and B. van der Kolk. "Complex Trauma in Children and Adolescents." White paper from the National Child Traumatic Stress Network Complex Trauma Task Force, National Center for Child Traumatic Stress, Los Angeles, 2003.

Cook, A., J. Spinazzola, J. Ford, C. Lanktree, M. Blaustein, M. Cloitre, et al. "Complex Trauma in Children and Adolescents." *Psychiatric Annals* 35 (2005): 390–98.

Cooper, G., K. Hoffman, B. Powell, and R. Marvin. "The Circle of Security Intervention." In *Enhancing Early Attachments: Theory, Research, Intervention, and Policy*, edited by L. J. Berlin, Y. Ziv, L. M. Amaya-Jackson, and M. T. Greenberg. New York: Guilford Press, 2005.

Courtois, C., and J. Ford, eds. *Treating Complex Traumatic Stress Disorder*. New York: Guilford Press, 2009.

Cozolino, L. *The Neuroscience of Human Relationships: Attachment and the Developing Social Brain*. New York: Norton, 2006.

DeBellis, M. D. "The Psychobiology of Neglect." *Child Maltreatment* 10 (2005): 150–72.

DeBellis, M. D., and L. A. Thomas. "Biologic Findings of Post-Traumatic Stress Disorder and Child Maltreatment." *Current Psychiatry Reports* 5 (2003): 108–17.

DeBellis, M. D., and T. Van Dillen. "Childhood Post-Traumatic Stress Disorder: An Overview." *Child and Adolescent Psychiatric Clinics of North America* 4 (2005): 745–72.

Deitrich, P. "Environmental Neurotoxicants and Psychological Development." In *Pediatric Neuropsychology: Research, Theory and Practice*, edited by K. O. Yeates, M. D. Ris, and H. G. Taylor, 206–36. New York: Guilford, 2000.

Dozier, M., K. C. Stovall, and K. Albus. "Attachment and Psychopathology in Adulthood." In *Handbook of Attachment*, 2nd ed., edited by J. Cassidy and P. Shaver, 718–45. New York: Guilford Press, 2008.

Dozier, M., K. C. Stovall, K. E. Albus, and B. Bates. "Attachment for Infants in Foster Care: The Role of Caregiver State of Mind." *Child Development* 70 (2001): 1467–77.

Dunn, W. *Sensory Profile*. San Antonio, TX: The Psychological Corporation, 1999.

Emde, R. "Early Narratives: A Window to the Child's Inner World." In *Revealing the Inner Worlds of Young Children*, edited by R. Emde, D. Wolf, and D. Oppenheim, 3. New York: Oxford University Press, 2003.

Emde, R., D. Wolf, and D. Oppenheim. *Revealing the Inner Worlds of Young Children*. New York: Oxford University Press, 2003.

Farmer, J. E., J. Dondres, and S. Warschausky, eds. *Treating Neurodevelopmental Disabilities*. New York: Guilford, 2007.

Feldman, C. *The Buddhist Path to Simplicity*. London: Thorssons, 2001.

Finzi, R., O. Cohen, Y. Sapir, and A. Weizman. "Attachment Styles in Maltreated Children: A Comparative Study." *Child Development and Human Development* 31 (2000): 113–28.

Fisher, A. G., E. A. Murray, and A. C. Bundy. *Sensory Integration Theory and Practice*. Philadelphia: F. A. Davis Company, 1991.

Fivush, R. "Constructing Narrative, Emotion, and Self in Parent-Child Conversations about the Past." In *The Remembering Self: Construction and Accuracy in the Self-Narrative*, edited by U. Neisser, 136–57. New York: Cambridge University Press, 1994.

Fletcher, J. M., G. R. Lyon, L. S. Fuchs, and M. A. Barnes. *Learning Disabilities: From Identification to Intervention*. New York: Guilford, 2007.

Frick, S., R. Frick, P. Oetter, and E. Richter. *Out of the Mouths of Babes: Discovering the Developmental Significance of the Mouth*. Hugo, MN: PDP Press Inc., 1996.

Germer, C., R. Siegel, and P. Fulton, eds. *Mindfulness and Psychotherapy*. New York: Guilford Press, 2005.

Gioia, G., P. Isquith, S. Guy, and L. Kenworthy. *Behavior Rating Inventory of Executive Function: Professional Manual*. Lutz, FL: Psychological Assessment Resources, Inc., 2000.

Gonick, R., and M. Gold. "Fragile Attachments: Expressive Arts Therapy with Children in Foster Care." *The Arts in Psychotherapy* 18 (1992): 433–40.

Groze, V., and D. Ileana. "A Follow-Up Study of Adopted Children from Romania." *Child & Adolescent Social Work Journal* 13, no. 6 (1996): 541–65.

Hanh, Thich Nhat. *The Miracle of Mindfulness*. Boston, MA: Beacon Press, 1975.

Hannay, H. J., L. A. Bieliauskas, B. A. Crosson, and T. A. Hammeke, et al. "Proceedings of the Houston Conference on Specialty Education and Training in Clinical Neuropsychology." *Archives of Clinical Neuropsychology* 13 (1998): 157–58.

Harvey, S. "Dynamic Play Therapy with Adoptive Families." In *Creative Arts Therapies Approaches in Adoption and Foster Care: Contemporary Strategies for Working With Individuals and Families*, edited by Donna J. Betts, 77–96. Springfield, IL: Charles C. Thomas, 2003.

Harvey, S., and K. E. Connor. "Evaluation of the Quality of Parent-Child Relationships: A Longitudinal Study." *The Arts in Psychotherapy* 20 (1993): 387–95.

Hass-Cohen, N. *Art Therapy: When Words Are Not Enough*. London: Jessica Kingsley Publishers, 1999.

Henley, D. "Attachment Disorders in Post-Institutionalized Adopted Children: Art Therapy Approaches to Reactivity and Detachment." *The Arts in Psychotherapy* 32 (2005): 29–46.

Hesse, E. "The Adult Attachment Interview." In *Handbook of Attachment*, edited by J. Cassidy and P. Shaver, 552–99. New York: Guilford Press, 2009.

Horovitz, Ellen G. "Art Therapy in Arrested Development of a Pre-Schooler." *The Arts in Psychotherapy* 8 (1981): 119–25.

Hughes, D. "An Attachment-Based Treatment of Maltreated Children and Young People." *Attachment and Human Development* 6 (2004): 263–78.

———. "The Development of Dyadic Developmental Psychotherapy." In *Creating Capacity for Attachment*, edited by A. Becker-Weidman and D. Shell, vii–xvii. Oklahoma City, OK: Wood 'N' Barnes, 2005. Second printing 2009.

———. *Building the Bonds of Attachment*. 2nd ed. Lanham, MD: Jason Aronson, 2006.

———. *Attachment-Focused Family Therapy*. New York: W. W. Norton, 2007.

Hurwitz, A. "Nina and the Bad Animals Who Bite: The Use of Art Therapy with Children in Foster Care." In *Creative Arts Therapies Approaches in Adoption and Foster Care: Contemporary Strategies for Working With Individuals and Families*, edited by Donna J. Betts, 68–90. Springfield, IL: Charles C. Thomas, 2003.

Individuals with Disabilities Education Act (IDEA). U.S. Department of Education, Office of Special Education Programs, 2004. http://idea.ed.gov/ (accessed March 29, 2010).

Kabat-Zinn, M., and J. Kabat-Zinn. *Everyday Blessings: The Inner Work of Mindful Parenting*. New York: Hyperion, 1998.

Klorer, P. G. "Expressive Therapy with Severely Maltreated Children: Neuroscience Contributions." *Art Therapy: Journal of the American Art Therapy Association* 22, no. 4 (2005): 213–20.

Koren-Karie, N., D. Oppenheim, Z. Haimwoich, and A. Etzion-Carasso. "Dialogues of 7-Year Olds with Their Mothers about Emotional Events." *In Revealing the Inner Worlds of Young Children*, edited by R. Emde, D. Wolf, and D. Oppenheim, 338–47. New York: Oxford University Press, 2003.

Kramer, E. *Art as Therapy with Children.* Chicago: Magnolia Street Publishers, 1993.

Kranowitz, C. S. *The Out-of-Sync Child: Recognizing and Coping with Sensory Integration Dysfunction.* New York: Perigee, 1998.

Lacher, D., T. Nichols, and J. May. "Claiming Narratives." Chap. 4 in *Connecting with Kids through Stories: Using Narratives to Facilitate Attachment in Adopted Children.* London: Jessica Kingsley Publishers, 2005.

Landgarten, H. B. *Clinical Art Therapy: A Comprehensive Guide.* New York: Brunner/Mazel, 1981.

Levine, S. "Stimulation in Infancy." *Scientific American,* May 1960.

MacMillian, H. L. "Childhood Abuse and Lifetime Psychopathology in a Community Sample." *American Journal of Psychiatry* 158 (2001): 1878–83.

Main, M. "Cross-Cultural Studies of Attachment Organization: Recent Studies, Changing Methodologies, and the Concept of Conditional Strategies." *Human Development* 33 (1990): 48–61.

———. "Metacognitive Knowledge, Metacognitive Monitoring, and Singular (Coherent) vs. Multiple (Incoherent) Models of Attachment." In *Attachment Across the Life Cycle,* edited by C. M. Parkes, J. Stevenson-Hinde, and P. Marris. London: Routledge, 1991.

Main, M., and J. Cassidy. "Categories of Response with the Parent at Age Six." *Developmental Psychology* 24 (1988): 415–26.

Main, M., and E. Hesse. "Parents' Unresolved Traumatic Experiences are Related to Infant Disorganized Attachment Status." In *Attachment in the Preschool Years,* edited by M. T. Greenbert, D. Cicchetti, and E. M. Cummings. Chicago: University of Chicago Press, 1990.

Malchiodi, C. A. *Handbook of Art Therapy.* New York and London: Guilford Press, 2003.

McEwen, B. "Development of the Cerebral Cortex XIII: Stress and Brain Development–II." *Journal of the American Academy of Child and Adolescent Psychiatry* 38 (1999): 101–3.

Murray-Slutsky, C. and B. A. Paris. *Is It Sensory or Is It Behavior?* San Antonio, TX: PsychCorp, a division of Harcourt Assessment, Inc., 2005.

Napthali, S. *Buddhism for Mothers: A Calm Approach to Caring for Yourself and Your Children.* Crows Nest, Australia: Allen and Unwin, 2003.

Nelson C. A., III, C. H. Zeanah, N. A. Fox, P. J. Marshall, A. T. Smyke, and D. Guthrie. "Cognitive Recovery in Socially Deprived Young Children: The Bucharest Early Intervention Project." *Science* 318 (December 21, 2007): 1937–40.

O'Connor, T., and C. Zeanah. "Attachment Disorders: Assessment Strategies and Treatment Approaches." *Attachment & Human Development* 5 (2003): 223–45.

Olson, H. C., and D. M. Burgess. "Early Interventions for Children Prenatally Exposed to Alcohol and Other Drugs." In *The Effectiveness of Early Intervention,* edited by M. J. Guralnick, 109–45. Baltimore: Brookes Publishing Company, 1997.

O'Malley, R. D., and L. Storz. "Fetal Alcohol Spectrum Disorder and ADHD: Diagnostic Implications and Therapeutic Consequences." *Expert Review Newsletter 3* (2003): 477–89.

Oppenheim, D., and H. S. Waters. "Narrative Processes and Attachment Representations: Issues of Development and Assessment." In *Caregiving, Culture, and Cognitive Perspectives on Secure Base Behavior and Working Models: New Growing Points of*

Attachment Theory and Research, edited by W. Waters, B. Vaughn, G. Posadda, and K. Kondo-Ikermura. *Monographs of the Society for Research in Child Development* 60 (1995): 197–215.

Perry, B. D., R. Pollard, T. Blakely, W. Baker, and D. Vigilante. "Childhood Trauma: The Neurobiology of Adaptation and 'Use-Dependent' Development of the Brain; How 'States' Become 'Traits.'" *Infant Mental Health J* 16, no. 4 (1995): 271–91.

Phillips, J. "The Use of Art Therapy in Impacting Individual and Systemic Issues in Foster Care." In *Creative Arts Therapies Approaches in Adoption and Foster Care: Contemporary Strategies for Working With Individuals and Families,* edited by Donna J. Betts, 143–51. Springfield, IL: Charles C. Thomas, 2003.

Picard, E. M., J. E. Del Dott, and N. Breslau. "Prematurity and Low Birthweight." In *Pediatric Neuropsychology: Research, Theory and Practice,* edited by K. O. Yeates, M. D. Ris, and H. G. Taylor, 237–51. New York: Guilford, 2003.

Prino, C. T., and M. Peyrot. "The Effect of Child Physical Abuse and Neglect on Aggressive, Withdrawn, and Prosocial Behavior." *Child Abuse and Neglect* 18 (1994): 871–84.

Proulx, L. *Strengthening Emotional Ties through Parent-Child-Dyad Art Therapy.* London and Philadelphia: Jessica Kingsley Publishers, 2003.

Reese, E., and R. Fivush. "Parental Styles of Talking about the Past." *Developmental Psychology* 29 (1993): 596–606.

"Reports of the INS-Division 40 Task Force on Education, Accreditation, and Credentialing." *The Clinical Neuropsychologist* 1, no. 1 (1987): 29–34.

Robb, M. "Beyond the Orphanages: Art Therapy with Russian Children." *Art Therapy: Journal of the American Art Therapy Association* 19 (2002): 146–50.

Robbins, A. "An Object Relations Approach to Art Therapy." In *Approaches to Art Therapy: Theory and Technique,* edited by J. Rubin, 63–74. New York: Brunner/Mazel, 1987.

Robins, L. N. "Longitudinal Studies: Sturdy Childhood Predictors of Adult Antisocial Behavior." *Psychological Medicine* 8 (1978): 611–22.

Rubin, J. A. *Child Art Therapy.* New York: Van Nostrand Reinhold, 1978.

Schore, A. N. "The Effects of Early Relational Trauma on Right Brain Development, Affect Regulation, and Infant Mental Health." *Infant Mental Health Journal* 22 (2001): 201–69.

———. *Affect Dysregulation and Disorders of the Self.* New York: Norton, 2003.

Schreiber, R., and W. J. Lyddon. "Parental Bonding and Current Psychological Functioning among Childhood Sexual Abuse Survivors." *Journal of Counseling Psychology* 45 (1998): 358–62.

Serafetinides, E. A., J. T. Shurley, R. Brooks, and W. P. Gideon. "Electrophysiological Changes in Humans During Sensory Isolation." *Aerospace Medicine,* 1971.

Siegel, D. J. *The Developing Mind.* New York: Guilford Press, 1999.

———. "Toward an Interpersonal Neurobiology of the Developing Mind: Attachment Relationships, 'Mindsight,' and Neural Integration." *Infant Mental Health Journal* 22 (2001): 67–95.

Siegel, D., and M. Hartzell. *Parenting from the Inside Out.* New York: Jeremy P. Tracher/Penguin, 2003.

Sparrow, S., D. Cicchetti, and D. Balla. *Vineland Adaptive Behavior Scales (Survey Forms Manual).* 2nd ed. Circle Pines, MN: AGS Publishing, 2005.

Steele, H., and M. Steele, eds. *Clinical Applications of the Adult Attachment Interview.* New York: Guilford Press, 2008.

Steig, W. *Pete's a Pizza.* New York: HarperCollins, 1998.

Steinberg, E., ed. *Your Children Will Raise You.* Boston, MA: Trumpeter Books, 2005.

Streissguth, A. P, H. M. Barr, J. Kogan, and F. L. Brookstein. *Understanding the Occurrence of Secondary Disabilities in Clients with Fetal Alcohol Syndrome (FAS) and Fetal Alcohol Effects (FAE).* Centers for Disease Control and Prevention, Final Report, August 1996.

Streissguth, A. P., and K. O'Malley. "Neuropsychiatric Implications and Long-Term Consequences of Fetal Alcohol Spectrum Disorders." *Seminars in Clinical Neuropsychiatry* 5 (2000): 177–90.

Sunderland, M. *The Science of Parenting.* New York: Dorling Kindersley, 2006.

Teeter, P. A., and M. Semrud-Clikeman. *Child Neuropsychology: Assessment and Interventions for Neurodevelopmental Disorders.* Boston: Allyn & Bacon, 1997.

Teicher, M. "Scars That Won't Heal: The Neurobiology of Child Abuse." *Scientific American,* March 2002, 68–75.

Teicher, M., Y. Ito, and C. A. Glod. "Neurophysiological Mechanisms of Stress Response in Children." In *Severe Stress and Mental Disturbances in Children,* edited by C. R. Pfeffer, 59–84. Washington, DC: American Psychiatric Press, 1996.

Teicher, M., A. Tomoda, and S. L. Anderson. "Neurobiological Consequences of Early Stress and Childhood Maltreatment: Are Results from Human and Animal Studies Comparable." *Annual of the New York Academy of Sciences* 1071 (2006): 313–23.

Thompson, W. R., and R. Melzack. "Early Environment." *Scientific American,* 1956.

Tizard, B. *Adoption: A Second Chance.* London: Open Books, 1977.

Tyrell, C., M. Dozier, G. B. Teague, and R. Fallot. " Effective Treatment Relationships for Persons with Serious Psychiatric Disorders: The Importance of Attachment States of Mind." *Journal of Consulting and Clinical Psychology* 67 (1999): 725–33.

Ulman, E., and P. Dachinger. *Art Therapy in Theory and Practice.* Chicago: Magnolia Street Publishers, 1996.

Van de Kolk, B., and D. Fisler. "Dissociation and the Fragmentary Nature of Traumatic Memories: Overview." *British Journal of Psychotherapy* 12 (1996): 352–61.

Vick, R. "A Brief History of Art Therapy." *In Handbook of Art Therapy,* edited by C. A. Malchiodi, 5–15. New York and London: The Guilford Press, 2003.

Wilbarger, P., and J. L. Wilbarger. *Sensory Defensiveness in Children Ages 2–12: An Intervention Guide for Parents and Other Caretakers.* Santa Barbara, CA: Avanti Educational Programs, 1991.

Williams, V. *"More More More" Said the Baby: 3 Love Stories.* New York: Greenwillow Books, 1990.

Wolkind, S., F. Hall, and S. Pawlby. "Individual Differences in Mothering Behaviour." In *Epidemiological Approaches in Child Psychiatry,* edited by P. Grahm, 107–23. New York: Academic Press, 1977.

Yeates, K. O. "Closed-Head Injury." In *Pediatric Neuropsychology: Research, Theory and Practice,* edited by K. O. Yeates, M. D. Ris, and H. G. Taylor, 92–116. New York: Guilford, 2000.

Yeates, K. O., and L. A. Bieliauskas. "The American Board of Clinical Neuropsychology and American Academy of Clinical Neuropsychology: Milestones Past and Present." *The Clinical Neuropsychologist* 18 (2004): 489–93.

Index

American Professional Society on the
Abuse of Children (APSAC): report,
262–64
APSAC. *See* American Professional
Society on the Abuse of Children
art: activities, 142–43, 155–56;
developmental stages, *146*;
examples, *147–50*; supplies, 63, 155
assessment. *See* evaluation
Association for the Treatment and
Training in the Attachment of
Children: White Paper on coercion,
264–78
ATTACh. *See* Association for the
Treatment and Training in the
Attachment of Children
attachment: attachment theory, 1;
development of, 3–6; neurobiology
of, 11–14, 32, 108–10; patterns
of attachment, 2–3; styles, 39–41.
See also disorders of attachment;
neurobiology
Attention Deficit Hyperactivity Disorder
(ADHD), 10, 110, 113, 121
attunement, 3, 15, 18, 33–35, 55

autobiographical narrative, coherent,
12, 15, 38, 162; parents and, 32–35.
See also narrative

Complex Trauma, ix, 10, 23, 61;
developmental age and, 51
consequences, 9, 38; discipline, 78;
natural, 51, 57–60, 154

developmental age, 51–53, 59, 61, 66,
261
disorders of attachment, 6–7; Reactive
Attachment Disorder, ix, 7, 23, 45;
symptoms, 7–9
Dyadic Developmental Psychotherapy:
described, 15–16, 28–28; evaluation
session, 26; evidence-based, vii,
18–19; model, *36*
dysregulation, 14, 30, 40; ATTACh
White Paper and, 270–74

engagement, 25, 33–34; Theraplay and,
96–99
evaluation, 22–26; child session,
25–26; differential diagnosis,

About the Contributors

Arthur Becker-Weidman, PhD, directs the Center for Family Development providing evaluations and treatment for families of children with complex trauma and disorders of attachment, consulting with departments of social services, school districts, residential treatment centers, and mental health clinics, as well as providing training for therapists and governments across the United States, Canada, Australia, Finland, Singapore, and the Czech Republic. He is coeditor of *Creating Capacity for Attachment* and author of four DVDs: *Principles of Attachment Parenting; Assessing Children with Complex Trauma & Attachment Disorders; Assessing Caregiver Reflective Capacity, Commitment, Insightfulness, and Sensitivity;* and *An Introduction to Dyadic Developmental Psychotherapy.* Dr. Becker-Weidman has published many articles in professional peer reviewed publications and is a frequent presenter at various international, national, and regional professional conferences. Dr. Becker-Weidman is a certified therapist, consultant, and trainer with the Dyadic Developmental Psychotherapy Institute where he is the president of the board. Dr. Becker-Weidman is a registered clinician with the Association for the Treatment and Training in the Attachment of Children (ATTACh) and is vice president for clinical matters and chairs the clinical registration committee for ATTACh. E-mail: AWeidman@Concentric .net. Website: www.Center4FamilyDevelop.com.

Deborah Shell, MA, LCMHC, provides therapy for children and families, individuals and couples, in a private practice setting in northern Vermont. She specializes in attachment and trauma issues impacting relationships. Although her formal training spans four decades, from Livingston College, NJ, to the California College of Arts and Crafts to Johnson State College, VT, her interest in attachment-style parenting began more than thirty years ago and has led to extensive work with La Leche League International and later as developer of a resource center for homeschoolers.

She has trained with Daniel Hughes, PhD, developer of Dyadic Developmental Psychotherapy, and is a certified DDP therapist, consultant, and trainer. She is a registered ATTACh clinician. She provides trainings for professionals and parents and teaches family counseling in the graduate program at Johnson State College, VT. She resides in a handmade house with her husband and beloved shih tzus, and looks forward to her children returning home for their family reunion held each summer on Lake Champlain.

CONTRIBUTORS

Daniel Hughes, PhD, a clinical psychologist, has specialized—for many years—in the clinical application of research in attachment and intersubjectivity. He is the author of many books and articles on this treatment model and he is very active in training other therapists in his clinical model throughout the United States and internationally. He is chairperson of the Board of Directors of the Dyadic Developmental Psychotherapy Institute.

Karen A. Hunt, MSW, has more than twenty-five years' experience working with individuals who have disabilities and fourteen years of personal experience parenting a child significantly impacted by his early childhood trauma. Dima has responded well to treatment and is presently a regular education eleventh grader with IEP supports.

Ash Lednur, RN, grew up on Long Island, NY, where she worked as a psychiatric registered nurse. She currently resides in the New England area with her spouse of twenty years and their two children.

Audrey Mattson, PhD, ABPP, received her doctorate in clinical neuropsychology from the University of Houston in 1991 and is board certified in clinical neuropsychology through the American Board of Professional Psychology (ABPP). Over the years Dr. Mattson has provided services to children and adults in a variety of medical and psychiatric settings. She currently has a private practice in southwest Montana and is the neuropsychologist for a nonprofit agency that operates therapeutic group homes throughout the state for youth with severe emotional and behavior disorders.

Kristen Mayrose, OTR/L, is a pediatric occupational therapist specializing in sensory integration since 1990. She focuses her work on the education of therapists, teachers, parents, and other professionals in the areas of sensory integration and how it relates to our children regarding difficulties in behavior and learning.

Miranda Ring Phelps, PsyD, is a child and family clinical psychologist who works at the Edmund Ervin Pediatric Center of the Maine General Medical Center in Waterville, ME. She is a clinical supervisor and chairs a team in education and training at the Pediatric Center.

Phyllis B. Rubin, CCC-SLP, PsyD, is a licensed clinical psychologist, speech and language pathologist, and a certified Theraplay® therapist and trainer with a private practice in Oak Park, IL. Her specialty is working with foster and adoptive families on attachment and trauma issues.

Robert Spottswood, MA, LCMHC, is director of North Star Counseling Services in Springfield, VT, where he sees children, teens, parents, couples, and families. He also provides regular phone consultations on emotion-focused approaches to difficult cases, and is coauthor of *The Bean Seed*, a short picture book for children who are learning to trust again after maltreatment. He is a certified Dyadic Developmental Psychotherapy therapist and consultant.

Julie Szarowski-Cox, LCAT, ATR-BC, is a licensed, board-certified art therapist living in Buffalo, NY. She received her master's degree in art therapy from Nazareth College in Rochester and since 2004, has been working with children diagnosed with attachment issues.